中国思想文化术语多语种对外翻译
标准化建设项目成果
CHINESE THINKING AND CULTURE
MULTILINGUAL TERMINOLOGY DATABASE

中华源·河南故事
CHINESE CIVILIZATION
Stories from Henan

少林功夫
SHAOLIN KUNGFU

主编 万正峰
EDITOR-IN-CHIEF: WAN ZHENGFENG

河南大学出版社
HENAN UNIVERSITY PRESS
·郑州·

图书在版编目（CIP）数据

中华源·河南故事．少林功夫 / 万正峰主编． —郑州：河南大学出版社，2019.3（2020.7 重印）

ISBN 978-7-5649-2663-2

Ⅰ．①中… Ⅱ．①万… Ⅲ．①地方文化－河南－通俗读物 ②少林武术－通俗读物 Ⅳ．① G127.61-49 ② G852-49

中国版本图书馆 CIP 数据核字（2019）第 047023 号

责任编辑	马元珍
责任校对	时　娇
封面设计	翟淼淼
出版发行	河南大学出版社
	地址：郑州市郑东新区商务外环中华大厦2401号　邮编：450046
	电话：0371-86059701（营销部）　0371-86059753（大众读物分公司）
	网址：hupress.henu.edu.cn
排　　版	河南博雅彩印有限公司
印　　刷	河南博雅彩印有限公司
版　　次	2019年12月第1版　　印　次　2020年7月第2次印刷
开　　本	710 mm×1010 mm　1/16　印　张　12.75
字　　数	183千字　　　　　　　　定　价　63.00元

版权所有　侵权必究

本书如有印装质量问题，请与河南大学出版社营销部联系调换

"中华源·河南故事"系列丛书编委会

顾　　问　黄友义　杨　平　范大祺
名誉主任　穆为民　何金平
主　　任　付　静
副 主 任　陈志伟　刁玉华　李向前　李　镇　梁留科　刘金锋
　　　　　孔留安　史永庆　许二平　万正峰　杨建伟　杨玮斌
　　　　　王建修　王自文　张改平　张松文　赵卫东

主　　编　付　静
执行主编　杨玮斌
编　　委　陈　玮　丁　锐　高　阳　徐恒振

中华源·河南故事·少林功夫

主　　编　万正峰
副 主 编　康红阳　吕宏军　刘国仕（英文）
中文撰稿　吕宏军　吕道玉
英文译者　焦　丹　刘红强　张　翼　李世锋
英文审校　〔美〕Donald Richard Weck
摄　　影　和来贵　刘彦辉

The Editorial Committee
Chinese Civilization
Stories from Henan

Consultants	Huang Youyi Yang Ping Fan Daqi
Honorary Directors	Mu Weimin He Jinping
Director	Fu Jing
Deputy Directors	Chen Zhiwei Diao Yuhua Li Xiangqian Li Zhen
	Liang Liuke Liu Jinfeng Kong Liu'an Shi Yongqing
	Xu Erping Wan Zhengfeng Yang Jianwei
	Yang Weibin Wang Jianxiu Wang Ziwen
	Zhang Gaiping Zhang Songwen Zhao Weidong

Chief Editor	Fu Jing
Executive Chief Editor	Yang Weibin
Editors	Chen Wei Ding Rui Gao Yang Xu Hengzhen

Chinese Civilization
Stories from Henan
Shaolin Kungfu

Editor-in-Chief	Wan Zhengfeng
Associate Editors-in-Chief	Kang Hongyang Lyu Hongjun
	Liu Guoshi (English Text)
Writers	Lyu Hongjun Lyu Daoyu
Translators	Jiao Dan Liu Hongqiang Zhang Yi
	Li Shifeng
Translation Proofreader	Donald Richard Weck (U.S.)
Photographers	He Laigui Liu Yanhui

总 序

中国是世界四大文明古国之一,也是世界上唯一的古代文明传统未曾中断的国家。河南省地处中国中东部,是中华文明和中华民族的重要发祥地,在中国五千年的文明史上,河南作为国家政治、经济、文化的中心就长达三千多年。从某种意义上讲,一部河南史就是半部中国史。这里是中华人文始祖黄帝的故乡,是古丝绸之路的东方起点,是少林功夫和陈氏太极的发源地,这里创建了中国历史上最早的都城,镌刻了中国最古老的文字,诞生了中国最初的商业文明。

伴随着新时代的荣光,河南经济社会发展迅速,人民生活水平显著提升,这是自力更生、艰苦奋斗的历史结果,也是对外开放带来的益处。河南经济社会的发展、人民生活方式的改变都植根于深层次的文化积淀。为了让世界更多地了解河南,让河南更好地走向世界,2018年以来,河南省外事办认真研析了这片古老土地上的历史文化资源和时代风貌,组织各领域权威专家学者,编译了"中华源·河南故事"中外文系列丛书,选取少林功夫、太极拳、中医、汉字、文物、焦裕禄、红旗渠、丝绸之路、古都、农业、手工艺等多个主题,力图以故事的方式向世界展现一个立体、全面、真实的河南。

当今世界,人类文明无论在物质还是精神方面都取得了巨大进步,特别是物质的极大丰富是古代世界完全不能想象的。同时,当代人类也面临着许多突出的难题,比如,贫富差距持续扩大,物欲追求奢华无度,个人主义恶性膨胀,社会诚信不断消减,伦理道德每况愈下,人与自然关系日趋紧张,等等。要解决这些难题,不仅需要运用人类今天发现和发展的智慧和力量，而且需要运用人类历史上积累和储存的智慧和力量。河南历史文化底蕴深厚、包容性强，在今天仍极具现实意义。中原文化蕴含的思想智慧有助于修身养性，推动人类社会进步发展，焦裕禄精神、红旗渠精神所体现的为民爱民、艰苦奋斗的价值取向是构建人类命运共同体的力量源泉。我们期待与读者们一起从河南故事中汲取更多的智慧和力量，共同创造更加美好的未来。

Series Foreword

China is one of the four ancient civilizations in the world, and is also the only country in the world where the ancient civilization has not been interrupted. Located in east-central China, Henan province is an important cradle for the Chinese nation and the Chinese civilization. In the course of the five thousand years of Chinese history, for more than three thousand years it served as the political, economic and cultural center of the country and therefore, as generally accepted, represents half of the history of China. Henan is the native place of Yellow Emperor, the cradle of Chinese culture, the starting point of the ancient Silk Road in the east, and the birthplace of Shaolin Kungfu and Chen-style Taijiquan—typical examples of the world-renowned Chinese martial arts. It was here that the earliest capital city in China was founded, the oldest Chinese characters engraved, and the earliest commerce took shape.

In the new era, Henan has witnessed rapid growth in its economy and remarkable improvement of people's living conditions, owing to the national reform and opening-up policy and unremitting endeavoring of the people. Modern economic achievements and social development as well as the changes of way of life could be traced back to its traditional values and cultural heritages. To enable people from other countries to understand Henan, and let the province integrate more efficiently into the world development, the Foreign Affairs Office of the People's Government of Henan province, has organized teams of authoritative experts and scholars in relevant fields to compile this *Chinese Civilization: Stories from Henan* in Chinese and other foreign languages since 2018, by crystallizing the excellence of traditions and outstanding features of modern development. The book series include *Shaolin Kungfu, Taijiquan, Traditional Chinese Medicine, Chinese Characters, Cultural Heritage, A Model Official — Jiao Yulu, Man-made River — Hongqiqu Canal, the Silk*

Road, *Ancient Chinese Capitals*, *Handicraft* and *Feeding the People — Agriculture*, etc, attempting to present a panoramic picture of the province.

In today's world, human civilization has made great progress in both material accumulation and cultural and ethical advancement, and the great abundance of materials today, especially, is beyond the imagination of the ancient people. At the same time, however, modern people are also confronted with a lot of problems, such as the widening gap between the rich and the poor, the indulgence in pursuit of luxury and extravagance, the undesirable extension of individualism, the decline of social integrity, and the increasing tension between man and nature. To solve these problems, we need to draw on the wisdom and powers developed today as well as those accumulated in the past. Henan is endowed with a rich historical and cultural heritage characterized by its inclusiveness, and such a heritage remains significant today. The intelligence and wisdom in Henan culture are conducive to self-cultivation and to the promotion of social development. The spirit of serving the people and relentless struggle, as embodied in *Jiao Yulu* and *Hongqiqu Canal*, provides source of strength for building a community with a shared future for mankind. It is our hope that, wisdom and strength from Henan stories, could lead us to a shared brilliant future.

前 言

少林功夫是中国宝贵的文化遗产，是中华传统武术的杰出代表。少林功夫内容广博、种类繁多、技法精湛、变化无穷。演练少林功夫不仅可以锻炼筋骨、祛病延年，还可以磨炼意志、陶冶情操。少林功夫龙腾虎跃、优美动人，演练起来会给人以美的艺术享受。少林功夫作为中国流传最广、影响最大的武术流派，不仅在中国久负盛名，而且也是世界上最具影响力的中国功夫。

少林功夫因发源于嵩山少林寺而得名。千百年来经历代少林功夫家的综合、演练和提高，少林功夫已成为一个门类齐全、体系完备的武术流派。少林功夫自明代起，广泛传入登封民间，使登封成为传习少林功夫的中心。目前，登封有少林武术学校46所，有来自全国各地及世界上十多个国家的学员10万余人。同时，少林功夫在世界上流传之后，也成为世界上传习最广的功夫。

本书力求通过准确、系统、简明、通俗的方法，向国内外读者介绍源远流长的少林功夫的起源和发展、少林功夫博大精深的基本内容、少林功夫独具的风格和特点以及少林功夫丰厚的文化内涵，并希望通过这些介绍，为人们了解少林功夫、认识少林功夫提供一个窗口。

Preface

Shaolin Kungfu, as one of China's most precious cultural heritages, is an outstanding representative of Chinese traditional martial arts. It is extensive in contents, rich in varieties, superb in techniques, and changeful in movements. Practicing Shaolin Kungfu can not only exercise the muscles and bones, dispel diseases and prolong life, but also temper the willpower and cultivate the sentiment. The Kungfu performance shows vitality, strength and grace, which gives people artistic enjoyment. As the most popular and influential school of the Chinese martial arts, Shaolin Kungfu is not only well-known in China but also the most influential throughout the world.

Shaolin Kungfu is named after the Shaolin Temple in which it originates. Through thousands of years of integrations, practices and improvements by martial masters, the techniques, Shaolin Kungfu has shaped into a Wushu school with a complete range of categories and a self-contained system. Since the Ming Dynasty, Shaolin Kungfu has widely been spread among the folks of Dengfeng county, making the country a Wushu practicing and teaching center of the world. At present, there are 46 Shaolin Wushu schools in Dengfeng county with over 100 thousand practisers from all over the world. What's more, with the wide spread of it around the globe, Shaolin Kungfu has become the most popularly practiced martial arts in the world.

In an accurate, systematic, concise, and popular way, what this book tries to introduce to the readers at home and abroad is: the long history of Shaolin Kungfu, its profound basic content, unique style and features, and rich cultural connotations. We hope that this introduction serves as a window through which the readers could get to know and understand this Chinese Kungfu.

目录　　　　　　　　　　　　　　　　Contents

第一章　源远流长的少林功夫　　　　　　001
　　一、初创　　　　　　　　　　　　　002
　　二、形成　　　　　　　　　　　　　016
　　三、发展　　　　　　　　　　　　　026
　　四、现代少林功夫　　　　　　　　　056
　　五、海外的少林功夫　　　　　　　　066

Chapter I　The Developing History of Shaolin Kungfu　　001
　　I. Origins　　　　　　　　　　　　003
　　II. Taking Shape　　　　　　　　　017
　　III. Development　　　　　　　　　027
　　IV. Modern Shaolin Kungfu　　　　　059
　　V. Overseas Shaolin Kungfu　　　　067

第二章　博大精深的少林功夫　　　　　　075
　　一、拳术　　　　　　　　　　　　　076
　　二、棍术　　　　　　　　　　　　　078
　　三、刀术　　　　　　　　　　　　　082
　　四、剑术　　　　　　　　　　　　　084
　　五、其他兵器　　　　　　　　　　　086
　　六、其他功法　　　　　　　　　　　086

Chapter II　The Profound Shaolin Kungfu　　075
　　I. Fist and Palm Techniques　　　　077
　　II. Staff Techniques　　　　　　　079
　　III. Broadsword Techniques　　　　083
　　IV. Sword Techniques　　　　　　　085

Ⅴ. Other Weapons	085
Ⅵ. Other Kungfu Forms	087

第三章　独具特色的少林功夫　089
　　一、影响深远的功夫　090
　　二、特点鲜明的功夫　096

Chapter III　The Unique Style of Shaolin Kungfu　089
　　Ⅰ. Kungfu with Profound Influence　091
　　Ⅱ. Kungfu with Distinctive Features　097

第四章　内涵丰厚的少林功夫　115
　　一、兼容并蓄的少林功夫　116
　　二、少林禅武医的完美结合　124
　　三、少林功夫与军事　132
　　四、少林功夫与艺术　148
　　五、少林功夫与文学　170

Chapter Ⅳ　The Rich Connotation of Shaolin Kungfu　115
　　Ⅰ. Inclusive Shaolin Kungfu　117
　　Ⅱ. Combination of Shaolin Chan, Kungfu and Medicine　125
　　Ⅲ. Shaolin Kungfu and Military　133
　　Ⅳ. Shaolin Kungfu and Arts　153
　　Ⅴ. Shaolin Kungfu and Literature　169

附录　中国历史年代简表　188
Appendix　A Brief Chronology of Chinese History　188

第一章

源远流长的少林功夫

Chapter I

The Developing History of Shaolin Kungfu

少林功夫是我国宝贵的文化遗产，是中华武术的重要组成部分。少林功夫历史悠久、源远流长。它发源于嵩山少林寺，并由此而得名。它内容广博、种类繁多、技法精湛、享誉中外，现已成为广为流传的健身运动。

一、初创

武术产生于中国古代，已有数千年的历史，是民族体育和搏斗的一种技艺。汉魏时期，武术运动在全国的传衍已相当广泛。北魏太和十九年（495年），少林寺创建后，我国古老的武术技艺便落迹寺院，并成为寺僧经常演练的一种业余活动。

在跋陀主持少林时，许多身怀武术技艺者入寺为僧，跋陀的弟子惠光、僧稠就是其中的代表人物。据南北朝梁初慧皎编著的《高僧传》载：跋陀在洛阳时，看见年仅12岁的惠光在天街井栏上反踢毽子，一连踢500下，跋陀及围观者都很惊讶。在此危险的地方反踢毽子，可见惠光有高超的技艺，这其中当含有武术的成分。跋陀看到惠光人小艺高，觉得是个奇才，于是为他剃度收为弟子，并带回少林寺。

跋陀在少林寺传法时所收的另一个弟子僧稠更是一个武功超群的僧人。唐张鷟著的《朝野佥载》记述了僧稠及僧众习武的情况：僧稠幼时在少林寺落发为僧，在角力格斗时由于受到会武功的沙弥的殴击，于是开始发奋练功，最后练得"筋骨强劲""拳捷骁武""引重千钧"。他甚至能"横踏壁行"而"跃至梁首"。先前曾以武功欺侮他的僧人观看了他的武功后"俯伏流汗"。相传，僧稠在王屋山见两虎争斗，竟用锡杖将二虎赶跑。这些关于僧稠习武的记述，当然有些夸张，但他精于武功当是可信的。僧稠、惠光等一批懂武术者聚集于少林寺，说明寺院创立之后，中华传统武术已落迹少林寺。这为少林功夫的形成奠定了基础。

Shaolin Kungfu,regarded as one of China's most precious cultural heritages, is an important component among a myriad of Chinese Martial Arts schools. Originated at the Shaolin Temple located at Mount Song, Henan province, Shaolin Kungfu enjoys an enduring reputation with its long history. It is extensive in its content, rich in varieties and exquisite in its techniques, that's why its reputation is enjoyed domestically and abroad. Currently, Shaolin Kungfu has developed into a popular form of bodybuilding and self-defense.

Ⅰ. Origins

Originated in ancient China with thousands of years of history, Wushu (Chinese Martial Arts) has developed into an art form of physical exercises and wrestling. From the Western Han dynasty (202 BCE) to the Northern Wei dynasty (495 CE), Wushu, as a form of sports, spread tremendously and developed nationwide. According to the historical records, the Shaolin Temple, known as one of China's most renowned ancient temples, was built in the 19th year of Taihe Emperor [Taihe Emperor: (September 20, 471CE—April 26, 499 CE) Ruled by Emperor Xiaowen of Northern Wei 北魏孝文帝) (October 13, 467—April 26, 499), personal name: Tuoba Hong (拓跋宏), later Yuan Hong (元宏), or Tuoba Hung Ⅱ.] reign (495 CE) of the Northern Wei dynasty. Ever since then, the ancient Chinese martial arts skills left their feet in the temples and became a kind of amateur activity commonly practiced by the monks.

When Ba Tuo (also called Fotuo or Buddhabhadra, the first Abbot of the Shaolin Temple in 495 CE) was in charge of the Shaolin Temple, many disciples with Kungfu skills followed him, among whom Hui Guang and Seng Chou were the most well-known. The Buddhist classic *Biographies of Eminent Monks* written by Hui Jiao in the early Liang period of the Northern and Southern dynasties (420—589 CE) recounts a story as follows: Once in Luoyang, Ba Tuo saw 12-year-old Hui Guang kicking a shuttlecock skillfully on the edge of the Tianjie well. Surprisingly, this 12-year-old boy could juggle the shuttlecock back and forth over his shoulder 500 times in a row, particularly in such a dangerous place. Ba Tuo was deeply impressed by Hui Guang's superb skill, which involved Kungfu movements. He immediately decided to take him back to the Shaolin

少林寺创立之后，寺僧开始习武的原因，除了展示本领外，还有一个很重要的原因就是适应自然环境。地处嵩山深处的少林寺，山势险峻，自然条件恶劣。为了生存，寺僧就必须有强健的体魄，因而习武健身成为寺僧必不可少的活动。同时，少林地区，林木茂密，猛兽出没，这对少林僧众也构成了极大威胁。为了抵御猛兽的攻击，寺僧不得不通过习武来增强他们抗御猛兽的能力。

当然，在跋陀之后，随着禅坐在少林寺的逐渐流传，寺僧在长期打坐后，由于身体困倦，静坐后起来活动筋骨或习武以强身也是可能的，在一定程度上也推动了寺僧习武活动的开展。但后来演变成为达摩倡导、组织弟子习武并创拳，则完全是附会，绝无此事。

图1-1 十三棍僧救唐王（之一）
One of the Episode of Thirteen Cudgel Warrior Monks Saving the Emperor of the Tang Dynasty

Temple as his disciple after Hui Guang's customary shaving of the head.

Another well-known disciple of Ba Tuo is Seng Chou, who was also extremely skillful in Kungfu. *Anecdotes in Court and Commonalty*, compiled by Zhang Zhuo, narrates the story of Seng Chou practicing Wushu: When Seng Chou was brought to the Shaolin Temple as a disciple, he was only a child, therefore, he was always bullied by the fellow monks with skillful Kungfu. Afterwards, he practiced Kungfu diligently and finally highly skilled in it. He could even climb across the wall and leap to the beam of rooftop. When seeing this, the fellow monks who had bullied him prostrated before him sweating. No one dared to challenge or insult him anymore. Legend has it that Seng Chou once saw two tigers fighting and drove them away with a powerful blow by his khakkara. Although the legend is sort of exaggerated, his skillful Kungfu is authentic. A group of Kungfu masters like Seng Chou and Hui Guang gathered at the Shaolin Temple, which shows that Chinese Traditional Wushu can trace its roots to the Shaolin Temple, thus laying the foundation for Shaolin Kungfu.

Since the foundation of the Shaolin Temple, another reason for the monks to practice Kungfu, besides skills, is to adapt to the natural environment. Geographically, the Shaolin Temple is located among the dense forest of the Mount Song, flooded with precipitous cliffs. Due to the worst natural conditions, the monks had to maintain a strong body and keep fit for survival. Therefore, practicing Kungfu gradually became an indispensable part of daily life for the monks. Meanwhile, wild animals such as tigers, wolves and leopards in the mountains and bushes viciously threatened monks' lives. Under such living conditions, the monks had to practice Kungfu by imitating the moves of wild animals and flying birds for self-defense.

Of course, with the gradual spread of meditation in the temple after Ba Tuo, it was also possible for the monks in long-time sitting meditation to relieve physical drowsiness and strengthen their bodies by exercising their muscles and bones through practicing Kungfu, which, to a certain extent, promoted the development of Kungfu. In fact, it is completely far-fetched that a later deduction goes that it was Dharma who advocated and organized his disciples to practice Kungfu and thus created boxing.

Kungfu practice of the monks developed profoundly as time passing by.

僧众的习武活动，随着时间的推移，逐步走向深入。到了隋末唐初，由于特定的历史条件，少林寺僧以武显于世。

隋王朝建立后，文帝颇重佛教，开皇时特赐少林寺田地100顷，从此少林寺成为拥有大量田产的庄园，寺僧也成了庄园主。

隋朝末年，天下大乱，战争频起，加上饥荒，少林寺这个拥有庞大田产的庄园，成为由饥民组成的农民军攻取的对象。当时，强大的农民军曾一度攻入少林寺，把少林寺烧得只剩一座孤塔。在少林寺遭到攻击的情况下，本来就习武的僧人自然不会袖手旁观，于是他们开始组织武僧以拒之，后来发展到训练僧兵武装，最后十三武僧还参与助唐平定王世充的战争。

隋末唐初，原隋大将军王世充拥兵洛阳称帝，派其侄王仁则率重兵驻守少林寺，封地柏谷庄，并侵占了少林寺大量田地。驻守在那里的少林武僧志操、昙宗、惠玚等十三武僧因不满王仁则霸占其田地，于是率众一举生擒王仁则而献之于唐军，为唐王朝平定王世充立下了赫赫战功。为此秦王李世民特给少林寺颁发《告柏谷坞少林寺上座书》。在这封书信中，李世民如是说：

当今天下大乱，群魔峰起，世道丧乱，民不聊生。我大唐应天受命，护持正法。奸贼王世充，乃窃同大盗，多行违天意之事。如今，你们少林寺僧人能深悟世道的变化，知道我大唐皇帝乃真命天子，于是率众僧兵，擒拿贼大将王仁则，并献之于大唐。这是顺应天意之事，你们为国家立了大功。现在东都洛阳不日即被攻破，这里有你们巨大的功劳，应当予以嘉奖。因此特派上柱国安远前往你处，宣读我的嘉奖和感激之情。另外，司令一两个立功德僧人来见我。

战后李世民还对少林十三武僧的义举大加封赏，赐地40顷，水碾一具。由于受到李唐王朝的封赏，少林寺不仅获得了无上的荣耀，同时少林武僧的武功也名扬天下。正如明傅梅诗云："地从梁魏标灵异，僧自隋唐好武名。"武僧助唐受嘉奖的行动是对慈悲为怀的僧人以武来捍卫

During the end of the Sui dynasty (581—618 CE) and the early Tang dynasty (618—907 CE), owing to the special historical circumstances, the Shaolin monks became well-known for their marvelous Kungfu expertise.

Since the foundation of the Sui dynasty, Emperor Wen, a worshiper of Buddhism, bestowed upon the Shaolin Temple 100 qing (approximately 666 hectares) land. The Shaolin Temple henceforth turned into a large manor with a substantial estate and the Shaolin monks became the manor owners.

Towards the end of the Sui dynasty, the whole country was thrown into disorder by wars and famine. The Shaolin Temple became a target of the peasant army, who once raided the temple and burned it to the ground. Under such a heavy attack, the monks who were good at Kungfu couldn't just look on with folded arms indifferently, therefore, they started to call on Kungfu monks and train monk warriors for fighting, culminating in the war of the 13 Shaolin Kungfu monks to fight against the self-appointed Prince of Zheng, Wang Shichong.

At the end of the Sui dynasty and the beginning of the Tang dynasty (618—907 CE), Wang Shichong dispatched Wang Renze, his nephew, to garrison Baigu Village, the fief of the Shaolin Temple, with massive forces encroaching upon a lot of fields. Zhi Cao, Tan Zong, Hui Yang and the other 10 Shaolin Kungfu monks, resentful of their dominance, took the side of the Prince of Qin, Li Shimin (the 2nd Emperor Taizong of Tang dynasty 626—649CE) and helped him capture Wang Renze alive to force the self-appointed prince to surrender. Thanks to the prominent military merits and the contributions made by the 13 Shaolin Kungfu monks, Li Shimin awarded the Shaolin Temple with an epistle called *Letter to Seniors of Baiguwu Shaolin Temple*, in which he writes:

Today's turmoil raises the demons, which makes people live hard. The Great Tang dynasty is endowed with the Mandate of Heaven to protect the proper law. Wang Shichong, a traitor, is a thief who goes against the Will of Heaven. Presently, you Shaolin monks deeply understand the changes of the empire, knowing that the Emperor of the Tang dynasty is the true Son of Heaven. Therefore, you led a number of monk warriors to capture the thief General Wang Renze, and dedicated yourselves to the Royal Court. Your heroic feat is compliant with the Will of Heaven. It is indeed a great labor for the whole empire. Now, Luoyang has fallen within just a few days, and has witnessed the full credit going

图1-2 十三棍僧救唐王（之二）
One of the Episode of Thirteen Cudgel Warrior Monks Saving the Emperor of the Tang Dynasty

自己利益的充分肯定，这为寺僧习武之风的形成提供了有力的保障。同时，随着大乘禅法"禁人为恶"主张的盛行，又为寺僧习武提供了理论依据。

　　唐初少林寺僧虽以武显于世，但未形成少林功夫体系。其原因是，此时少林寺僧所演习的武功仍是中国传统的武术，不是具有特色的武术流派。唐初十三武僧助唐击败王世充说明当时少林寺演武活动已非常兴盛。

　　李世民赐封少林寺后，寺院备受唐王朝的崇敬，高宗李治、武则天

to you. For the sake of commendation, I send An Yuan, the commander in chief, to express my gratitude in my name. In addition, I request the presence of one or two meritorious monks.

After the war, Emperor Li Shimin also rewarded the 13 Shaolin Kungfu monks for their heroic feat, offering 40 qing (266 hectares) land and a water-powered roller. The award of the Tang court not only endowed the Shaolin Temple with paramount glory, but also positioned the Shaolin monks well-known for their Kungfu. Just like Fu Mei (1565—1642 CE, a talented person in the Ming dynasty)'s remarks, "The Temple becomes extrodinary since the Liang (502—557 CE) and Wei dynasty (386—534 CE); The monks advocate Kungfu from the Sui (581—618 CE) and Tang dynasty (618—907 CE)." The royal reward for the feat of the monks is a full affirmation of the practice made by the lenient Buddhists to defend their own interests by turning to Kungfu, which has strongly guaranteed the formation of Kungfu practice style. At the same time, the prevalence of Mahayana Chan's principle of "Prohibition of Evildoings" also provides a theoretical basis for the monks to practice Kungfu.

In the early Tang dynasty, even though the Shaolin monks were prominent in Kungfu, a mature Shaolin Kungfu system had not been formed, because its attribute was still the Chinese Traditional Wushu, not having fully developed into a featured school of Wushu. The anecdote of the 13 Shaolin Kungfu monks defeating Wang Shichong indicated that the martial arts flourished at that time.

After Li Shimin conferred the Shaolin Temple with his praise and support, it was highly respected by the imperial court. Emperor Li Zhi (Emperor Gaozong of Tang 628—683 CE) and Empress Wu Zetian as well as others honored the temple with their visits. Xuanzong even had a stele erected in the temple as a memorial. Although, from the early years to the flourishing period of the Tang dynasty, owing to the stability of society and the Buddha's holiness of the Shaolin Temple, there were few historical records left for Shaolin monks' Kungfu practice, it was never interrupted. According to the annals of history, succeeding the Anshi Rebellion, Shaolin monks' Kungfu practice had revived due to the situation of feudal separatist regimes and the rise of war.

The Old Book of Tang records that, in the 10th year of Yuanhe Emperor reign (815 CE), Li Shidao, a local separatist warlord who opposed Emperor

图1-3 唐赐田牒
Stele of the Farmland Granting Certificate

等多次驾幸少林,玄宗也立碑于寺院。但从初唐到盛唐,由于社会比较稳定,加之少林寺仍为佛门之地,所以这期间,有关少林寺的史册未见记载寺僧习武情况。然而,少林寺僧的习武未中断,仍在继续。"安史之乱"后,随着藩镇割据的形成及战事的又起,少林寺僧习武活动又见于史册。

据《旧唐书》载,元和十年(815年),李师道因反对唐宪宗讨伐吴元济,密结武僧圆净反唐,并准备焚烧东都宫殿,后失密。留守东都的吕元鹰调兵围剿,谋反者逃入嵩岳山棚,后被擒获,审讯得知主谋为嵩山少林寺僧圆净。时圆净年八十,精武功,被捉住时,官兵"使巨力者奋锤不能折其胫"。而圆净骂道:"鼠子,斩人足犹不能,敢称健儿乎!"关于圆净反唐之事,由于唐王朝与少林寺关系甚密,故除《旧唐书》对此事有记载外,其他史志均未记载。少林武僧圆净反唐之事及圆净高深的武功,反映出唐初至中唐时寺僧习武仍不间断。圆净反唐,还说明寺僧习武的显现,往往是与战争有关系的。

Xianzong (the 11th Emperor of the Tang dynasty 805—820 CE)'s attack on Wu Yuanji, another local separatist warlord, secretly colluded with a Kungfu monk named Yuanjing at Mount Song, to burn the palace of the Tang court at Luoyang. But eventually, the plot was disclosed. Lv Yuanying, the governor of Luoyang, deployed troops to encircle and suppress the rebels. Shortly, the rebels were captured under the shed of Mount Song. After the interrogation, it was disclosed that the main plotter was Yuanjing, an eighty-year-old man, who was a Kungfu master. As he was captured, it was hard for the soldiers to break his legs even forcibly with a hammer. Yuanjing cursed the soldiers, "Cowards! You cannot even chop my feet! How dare you call yourselves fighters!" Due to the close relationship between the Tang court and the Shaolin Temple, Yuanjing's revolt against the Tang dynasty is recorded in *The Old Book of Tang* but not found in other historical records. Yuanjing's revolt and his profound Kungfu skills reflected the nonstop Kungfu practice by the Shaolin monks from the early to the middle of the Tang dynasty, along with the causal link between Kungfu practice and war.

Since the mid-Tang dynasty, owing to people's esteem for Chan Buddhism and to the founder status of the Chan Buddhist Temple, the Shaolin Temple became the center of Chan Buddhism. The advocacy on Chan Buddhist Temple thus became a main stream since then. Furthermore, to the end of the Song dynasty, even though there was no record left of the Shaolin monks' Kungfu practice, in fact, it still continued.

At the end of the Song dynasty (960—1279 CE), the records of the Shaolin monks' Kungfu practice were found again in *the History of Song – The Legend of Fan Zhixu*. It records that, during Emperor Huizong's reign (1100—1125 CE), Fan Zhixu, the governor of Henan county, dispatched the monk Zhao Zongyin to serve as the council officer of Xuanfusi, a local administrative department, and Jiedu (an ancient official title) for military moderating. Zhao Zongyin formed a monk troop, namely "Zunsheng Team", to fight against the Jin army. At that time, because the Shaolin Temple was under the administration of Fan Zhixu, he had a close relationship with the Shaolin Temple, even had the tablet *Pagoda for Wall-gazing and Mediation* built at the Shaolin Temple. At this point, the Kungfu monks were the strong backbone of Fan's troop of monk warriors. As a matter of fact, the way of organizing monk warriors by Zongyin inherited from the

中唐以后,随着对禅宗的推崇及少林寺祖庭地位的确立,少林寺成为禅学的中心,对禅宗祖庭的宣扬成为主流,故此后到宋末,有关史志未见记述寺僧习武情况,但寺僧的习武活动仍然继续传承。

在宋末,寺僧习武活动又见于史册。据《宋史·范致虚传》载,徽宗时,河南尹范致虚以僧赵宗印充任宣抚司参议官,并节度军马,宗印把武僧组成一支军队去抗击金兵,僧兵名"尊胜队"。而范致虚在徽宗时任河南尹,少林寺就在范的领地之内。范素与少林寺关系密切,曾立《面壁之塔》碑于少林寺,故范所组织的僧兵队伍当是以少林武僧为骨干。实际上,宗印统领的僧兵乃是唐代少林僧兵的延续。此外,现今流传的清末时期抄本《少林拳法》称北宋初年少林僧福居,曾邀请民间武术家到少林寺交流武艺,清《拳经》云宋朝开国皇帝赵匡胤亦精于少林拳法,后世还传有少林太祖长拳。此说虽不能以有力的史实予以佐证,但作为人们长期流传的一种说法,应当与少林寺武术有一定的渊源关系。宋代既然有僧兵,说明宋代寺僧习武是可以肯定的。

元朝建立后,少林寺得到了元廷的大力推崇,使之成为拥有至高无上地位的佛教寺院,少林寺由此也极力维护元朝的统治,并成为其忠实的卫士。在反元斗争充斥的时代,少林寺不断受到威胁,这一点有

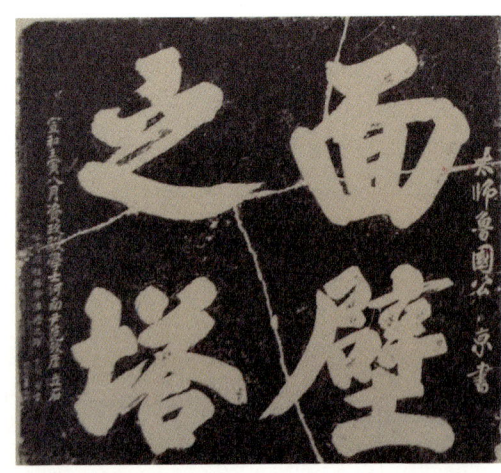

图1-4 面壁之塔

Pagoda for Wall-gazing and Mediation

Tang dynasty. In addition, the popular copy of *Shaolin Fist Position*, circulated at the end of the Qing dynasty, records that in the early years of the Northern Song dynasty, the Shaolin monk Fu Ju once invited the folk martial artists to the Shaolin Temple for martial arts exchange. *The Boxing Scripture* of the Qing dynasty writes that Zhao Kuangyin (Emperor Taizu of the Song dynasty; the founder and first Emperor of the Song dynasty in China 960—976CE), was also skilled at Shaolin Boxing and Shaolin Taizu Long Boxing (Taizu Changquan) in later generations. Although there is no supportive evidence in the annals for these, as popular sayings spreading over such a long time, there might be possibilities that the sayings had certain relationships with Shaolin Kungfu. Obviously, the existence of monk warriors during the Song dynasty proved the truth of Shaolin monks' Kungfu practice at that time.

Since the foundation of the Yuan dynasty, the Shaolin Temple was highly esteemed by the imperial court of Yuan, positioning it as a Buddhist monastery with supreme status. In turn, the Shaolin Temple also strived to guard the ruling power of the Yuan dynasty serving loyally. Recorded in the historical materials, the Shaolin Temple was threatened at times by fights against the Yuan dynasty. It is also recorded in *Inscription of Declaration and Grant to Master Zang Yun's Shan Gong An as the Major Pagoda*, that, in the 31st year of Zhiyuan Emperor reign (1294 CE) and the 1st year of Zhida Emperor reign (1308 CE), the master Zang Yun proposed decrees twice to the Emperor, the crown prince, the princes of the vassal states, the Emperor's teacher and the Ministry of Monk Administration (Dusengsheng) for the protection of the Shaolin Temple. The Yuan court once issued the prohibition of folks' casting weapons and practicing martial arts. However, because of the close relationship between the Shaolin Temple and the Yuan government, the Shaolin monks, as loyal guardians, were excluded from the prohibition against practicing Kungfu for self-defense. *The Qing Gong Stele* built in the 5th year of Yanyou Emperor reign (1318 CE) of the Yuan dynasty records that, "In year of Yichou (1265 CE), the Shaolin Temple at Mount Song had to conduct self-defense actions for invaders. Hui Qing, the disciple of Xue Ting, was appointed the assistant of abbot (Fusi) and in Renshen (1272 CE) was promoted to the head of monks (Tidian)." This evidently proves that the Shaolin monks of the Yuan dynasty used Kungfu to defend themselves. And the Shaolin monks

史料可以佐证。据《宣授少林寺提举藏云大师山公庵主塔铭》载，至元三十一年（1294年）和至大元年（1308年）藏云两次奏请皇帝、皇储、诸王、帝师及都僧省发圣旨、令旨等保护少林寺。元朝曾下令民间禁止铸造兵器，不准民间习武。但少林寺由于与元王朝关系密切，作为元朝统治者的忠实卫士，虽禁止民间习武，但并不禁止少林寺习武用以自卫。这从元延祐五年（1318年）《庆公碑》所载可证："乙丑，嵩少有御寇之扰，雪庭以师（慧庆）供副寺，壬申寻升提点。"让慧庆充任副寺、提点来"御寇"，当是以武力来御敌。此足以证明元代少林寺僧习武以自卫。此外，元代只有官府中才有的名称，在少林寺出现许多，比如"提点""都提举"等。从明朝武僧周参、广顺、玄机曾任过此职看，这几个职务极可能就是武僧的头领。

元朝末年，天下大乱，元朝护卫者少林寺与反元者的冲突已不可避免。在少林寺与农民军的对抗中，少林寺曾组织僧兵反击红巾军，但最终还是被强大的农民军打败，少林寺也被攻陷。此事记载于明洪武六年

图1-5 紧那罗王御红巾壁画（之一）
Mural of the King Jin Na Luo against the Red Turbans

were entitled as "tidian" "dutiju" or some other official titles, which were exclusively used in the Yuan court. In addition, judging from the responsibilities of Zhou Can, Guang Shun and Xuan Ji who were entitled, those titles possibly referred to the chief Kungfu monks.

At the end of the Yuan dynasty, there was a state of chaos, the conflicts between the Shaolin Temple and the rebels who were fighting against the Yuan dynasty were triggered. Among the rebels, there was a rebelled peasant army called the Red Turban Army (Hong Jin Jun). Eventually, the monk warriors were defeated by the Red Turban Army, thus the Shaolin Temple was captured by their assaults. This event is recorded in the *Inscription of Pagoda for Monk Song Yan Jun Gong* in the 6th year of Hongwu Emperor reign (1373 CE) of the Ming dynasty, "The end of the Yuan dynasty led the land into chaos; the temple had fallen." Afterwards, the war between the Kungfu monks and the peasant army at the end of the Yuan dynasty evolved into the myth of the Kinnara (Jinnaluo Wang) against the Red Turbans. It is said that when the Red Turban Army attacked the Shaolin Temple, Kinnara, a fire monk, was holding a fire stick, standing between the two mountains and scared off the Red Turban Army. Contrary to the legend, the fact is that it was not Kinnara who defeated the Red Turban Army, but the Red Turban Army that defeated the Shaolin Kungfu monks and captured the Shaolin Temple. Consequently, the Shaolin Temple regarded Kinnara as a master of the staff techniques. What's more, assigning according to seniority, the Kungfu monks even regarded Kinnara as the junior monk master, next only to the most senior monk master, Tanzong, the General of the Tang dynasty.

From the Northern Wei dynasty (386—534 CE) to the Yuan dynasty (1271—1368 CE), the scattered records of Shaolin monks' Kungfu practice were found throughout the history books and inscriptions rather than the special records in historical annals. Judging from the above stories, it is also evident that the Shaolin monks' Kungfu practice developed forward without being interrupted during this period. From the perspective of the contents of Shaolin Kungfu, it was still defined as a kind of folk martial arts while not forming into a complete system, i.e., a school of Kungfu with distinctive characteristics. In conclusion, this is defined as the initial stage or the foundation period of Shaolin Kungfu.

（1373年）《嵩岩俊公和尚塔铭》中："至正之末，天下大乱，兹寺失守。"关于元末少林武僧与农民军进行的战争，后来演化成了"紧那罗王御红巾"的神话。传说，红巾军进攻少林寺时，烧火僧紧那罗王手持烧火棍，站于两山之间吓退了红巾军。然而事实与传说恰相反，不是少林棍僧紧那罗王打败了红巾军，而是红巾军击败了少林武僧，并攻占了少林寺。后来少林寺还把紧那罗王奉为棍术大师，武僧则把唐代的大将军僧昙宗称为头辈武僧师爷，把紧那罗王称为二辈师爷。

纵观北魏到元代少林寺僧习武情况，史志没有专门记述，其习武活动是散见于史册、碑刻字里行间的。僧稠习武、十三武僧助唐、圆净反唐、宋代僧兵、元代御红巾等，可证少林寺僧在这期间习武未间断，并向前发展。但从这些时期少林寺僧习武的内容上看，仍是民间武术，并未形成完整的少林功夫体系，也就是说未形成带有鲜明特点的武术流派。由此，这一阶段是少林功夫的初创时期或称奠基时期。

二、形成

少林寺僧在经历了北魏至元代长期的习武之后，到了明代，经过武僧不断的演练、综合、提高，形成了完整的少林功夫体系。从武术门派角度来说，明代是少林功夫流派的形成时期，也是少林功夫的定名时期，即明代少林武僧所演练的武功才被正式定以"少林"之名。

明朝建立之后，寺僧习武活动开始向纵深发展。在元末遭重创的武僧习武活动，到明代中期的成化至弘治时，已形成大规模、有规律的演武活动。明正德八年（1513年）都穆《游嵩山记》："少林僧至今以武勇闻，则其所从来远矣。"明成化时入寺为僧的周友（三奇）和尚，武功高超，他在正德时（1506—1521年）曾统领少林僧兵南征北战，其武术弟子遍天下。这两个记载可证从明初开始复兴的演武活动，到中叶已达到相当高的程度。

II. Taking Shape

From the Northern Wei dynasty to the Yuan dynasty, the Shaolin monks went through a long history of Kungfu practice. Until the Ming dynasty, Shaolin Kungfu formed into a complete system due to the great efforts in Shaolin monks' Kungfu practice, integration and improvement. Therefore, the Ming dynasty is regarded as the key period for the formation of Shaolin Kungfu schools and its definition, which means that only the Kungfu practiced by Shaolin monks during the Ming dynasty were formally designated as "Shaolin Kungfu".

With the establishment of the Ming dynasty, the Shaolin monks' Kungfu practice was developed both extensively and intensively. Although suffering a heavy damage during the late Yuan dynasty, the Shaolin monks' Kungfu practice had been formalized and practiced on a large scale under the Emperor reign of Chenghua (1465—1487 CE) and Hongzhi Emperor reign (1488—1505 CE) of the mid-Ming dynasty. *Mount Song Travel Notes*, written by Du Mu in the 8th year of Zhengde Emperor reign (1513 CE) of the Ming dynasty, records, "It has been a long time since the Shaolin monks were renowned for their extraordinary braveness and superb martial arts skill from all over the world." The monk Zhou You (also named San Qi), under the Chenghua's Emperor reign, was an excellent Kungfu master with numerous disciples. He ever led Shaolin monks for the national military battles during the Zhengde Emperor reign (1506—1521 CE). These two records demonstrate that the Kungfu practice revived from the beginning of the Ming dynasty and reached a high level till the mid-Ming dynasty.

It was the staff techniques that first became famous among Shaolin Kungfu techniques during the Ming dynasty. According to Cheng Zongyou's *Introduction to Shaolin Cudgel Technigues* (*Shaolin Gunfa Chanzong*), during the Wanli Emperor reign (1563—1620 CE) of the Ming dynasty, Master Hama, the offspring of Kinnara, used to coach the monk Bian Tun boxing and staff techniques at the end of the Yuan dynasty. During the Jiajing (the 11th Emperor of the Ming dynasty 1522—1566 CE) Emperor reign, Yu Dayou, the famous general of the anti-Wokou army, wrote the following words in *Inscriptions of the Newly Built Shifang Chan Temple*, "We've heard that there are staff techniques descended from Kinnara at the Shaolin

明代少林功夫最先成名的是棍法。据明万历时程宗猷所著的《少林棍法阐宗》载，元末紧那罗王的后嗣哈嘛师，以拳棍授以匾囤和尚。明嘉靖时抗倭明将俞大猷在《新建十方禅院碑》中载："予昔闻河南少林寺，有神传长剑技。"长剑即棍，所谓神即元末紧那罗王。当然，紧那罗王持棍御红巾之神话不足信。但从二者的记载看，元末明初时少林寺僧已开始演练棍法当是史实，只不过是以神话与史实相杂的方式出现。也就是说少林棍法，创始于元末明初。到了明代中后期，少林棍法已发展到了相当成熟的阶段。嘉靖至万历时的少林武僧洪转，为一代著名棍术大师，"棍法神异，寺众推尊"（《少林棍法阐宗》）。洪转还著有棍、枪相融的《梦绿堂枪法》一卷传世。嘉靖、万历时的少林武僧洪纪、宗想、宗岱、广按、普从、宗擎等，皆是精通少林棍法的大师。明代少林棍法不仅习之者众多，而且形成了完整的理论体系。万历时，民间武术家程宗猷（字冲斗），曾先后到少林寺从洪转、宗想、宗岱等习棍达十余年之久。后来程宗猷于万历四十四年（1616年）写成了著名的《少林棍法阐宗》一书。该书对少林棍术的起源、内容及理论都作了比较详尽的记述，是人们研究少林棍法珍贵的史料。

继棍术扬名之后，少林拳法体系也走向成熟并风行海内。明万历九年（1581年）王士性《嵩游记》载："山下再宿，武僧又各来以技献，拳棍搏击如飞，他教师所束手视，中有为猴击者，盘旋踔跃，宛然一猴也。"从"拳棍搏击如飞"看，当时少林寺不仅棍术名扬四方，拳术也达到了相当高的境界。再从"盘旋踔跃"者所练的猴拳看，当时少林拳的种类是相当广泛的，已产生了猴拳。明代的少林拳主要是格斗搏击的实战技法。明万历三十六年（1608年）金忠士在其所写的《游嵩山少林寺记》中载："午刻，少参君招饮溪南方丈中，观群僧角艺。"万历三十九年（1611年）袁宏道在其《嵩游记》中载："晓起出门，童白分棚立，乞观手搏，主者曰：'山中故事也。'试之多绝技。"此可证，明代以搏击为主的拳法，技艺相当高超。明代拳法与棍法体系的形成时

Temple of Henan." Although the myth of Kinnara is unbelievable, the records of Cheng Zongyou and Yu Dayou have obviously proved the start of staff techniques practice of the Shaolin monks at the end of the Yuan dynasty and the beginning of the Ming dynasty. That is to say, the Shaolin staff techniques originated during the late Yuan and the early Ming dynasties. By the mid-late Ming dynasty, Shaolin staff techniques had developed to a fairly mature stage. Hongzhuan, a Shaolin monk from the Jiajing to Wanli Emperor reign, was a grand staff master. "The staff technique is magical, and the temples hold high esteem." *Introduction to Shaolin Cudgel Technigues (Shaolin Gunfa Chanzong)* Hongzhuan also wrote a book *Meng Lv Tang Spear Techniques*, which is a combination of staff and spear techniques, inheriting to generations. Hongji, Zongxiang, Zongdai, Guang'an, Pucong and Zongqing were all masters of Shaolin staff techniques during that period. The Shaolin staff techniques of the Ming dynasty not only attracted a great number of practisers, but also formed into a complete theoretical system. During the reign of Wanli Emperor, the folk Wushu master Cheng Zongyou (style name Chong Dou) practiced the staff techniques at Shaolin Temple for over ten years with Hongzhuan, Zongxiang and Zongdai successively. Later on, Cheng Zongyou completed the famous book Introduction to *Shaolin Saber Staff (Shaolin Gunfa Chanzong)* in the 44th year of Wanli Emperor reign (1616 CE). The book depicts the origin, content and theory of Shaolin staff techniques, which is a valuable historical material for those who prefer to learn Shaolin staff techniques.

Following the reputation of the staff techniques, Shaolin boxing techniques also received nationwide recognition. In the 9th year of Wanli Emperor reign (1581 CE) of the Ming dynasty, Wang Shixing's *Mount Song Travel Notes* records, "When coming down from the mountain, we lodged in the Shaolin Temple. The monks performed their techniques of boxing and staff like something flying. The Master in the middle of them, with hands bound and blindfolded, moving in spirals – vividly like a monkey!" From the records, it can be concluded that the Shaolin Temple is famous for both staff techniques and boxing techniques that reached a considerably high level. Furthermore, a wide variety of Shaolin boxing and the Monkey boxing (Hou Quan) emerged during that time. The main function of Shaolin boxing in the Ming dynasty was for fighting. In the 36th year of the Wanli Emperor reign (1608 CE) of the Ming

间相差不是很远，但拳术没有棍术闻名天下早。这从程宗猷《少林棍法阐宗》问答篇中可知："棍尚少林，今寺僧多攻拳而不攻棍者何也？余曰：少林棍名夜叉，乃紧那罗王之圣传，至今称为上菩提矣。而拳犹未盛行海内，今专攻于拳者，欲使与棍同登彼岸。"宗猷所言非常明确，其棍乃是"圣人"紧那罗王所传，名扬四方；而拳则不是，故不能与棍"同登彼岸"。这里要说明的是，现在许多人据此认为少林拳法是继棍法之后而形成的。事实上，程宗猷所说的并不是棍术比拳术产生早，而是说少林棍术比拳术名扬天下早。

明代少林拳法的成熟还有许多例证。嘉靖时著名将领唐顺之的《峨眉道人拳歌》云："浮屠善幻多技能，少林拳法世稀有。"清初黄宗羲《王征南墓志铭》："少林拳勇名天下。"从唐顺之、黄宗羲的话中看，虽然词句有些夸张，但绝非戏言。这些赞美诗句的出现，说明嘉靖至明末时少林拳法已相当成熟，并且已具有相当的影响力。明代的少林寺拳法和棍术一样都形成了完整的理论体系。明末少林寺著名拳法大

图1-6 少林棍
Shaolin Cudgel Techniques

Temple of Henan." Although the myth of Kinnara is unbelievable, the records of Cheng Zongyou and Yu Dayou have obviously proved the start of staff techniques practice of the Shaolin monks at the end of the Yuan dynasty and the beginning of the Ming dynasty. That is to say, the Shaolin staff techniques originated during the late Yuan and the early Ming dynasties. By the mid-late Ming dynasty, Shaolin staff techniques had developed to a fairly mature stage. Hongzhuan, a Shaolin monk from the Jiajing to Wanli Emperor reign, was a grand staff master. "The staff technique is magical, and the temples hold high esteem." *Introduction to Shaolin Cudgel Technigues (Shaolin Gunfa Chanzong)* Hongzhuan also wrote a book *Meng Lv Tang Spear Techniques*, which is a combination of staff and spear techniques, inheriting to generations. Hongji, Zongxiang, Zongdai, Guang'an, Pucong and Zongqing were all masters of Shaolin staff techniques during that period. The Shaolin staff techniques of the Ming dynasty not only attracted a great number of practisers, but also formed into a complete theoretical system. During the reign of Wanli Emperor, the folk Wushu master Cheng Zongyou (style name Chong Dou) practiced the staff techniques at Shaolin Temple for over ten years with Hongzhuan, Zongxiang and Zongdai successively. Later on, Cheng Zongyou completed the famous book Introduction to *Shaolin Saber Staff (Shaolin Gunfa Chanzong)* in the 44th year of Wanli Emperor reign (1616 CE). The book depicts the origin, content and theory of Shaolin staff techniques, which is a valuable historical material for those who prefer to learn Shaolin staff techniques.

Following the reputation of the staff techniques, Shaolin boxing techniques also received nationwide recognition. In the 9th year of Wanli Emperor reign (1581 CE) of the Ming dynasty, Wang Shixing's *Mount Song Travel Notes* records, "When coming down from the mountain, we lodged in the Shaolin Temple. The monks performed their techniques of boxing and staff like something flying. The Master in the middle of them, with hands bound and blindfolded, moving in spirals – vividly like a monkey!" From the records, it can be concluded that the Shaolin Temple is famous for both staff techniques and boxing techniques that reached a considerably high level. Furthermore, a wide variety of Shaolin boxing and the Monkey boxing (Hou Quan) emerged during that time. The main function of Shaolin boxing in the Ming dynasty was for fighting. In the 36th year of the Wanli Emperor reign (1608 CE) of the Ming

间相差不是很远，但拳术没有棍术闻名天下早。这从程宗猷《少林棍法阐宗》问答篇中可知："棍尚少林，今寺僧多攻拳而不攻棍者何也？余曰：少林棍名夜叉，乃紧那罗王之圣传，至今称为上菩提矣。而拳犹未盛行海内，今专攻于拳者，欲使与棍同登彼岸。"宗猷所言非常明确，其棍乃是"圣人"紧那罗王所传，名扬四方；而拳则不是，故不能与棍"同登彼岸"。这里要说明的是，现在许多人据此认为少林拳法是继棍法之后而形成的。事实上，程宗猷所说的并不是棍术比拳术产生早，而是说少林棍术比拳术名扬天下早。

　　明代少林拳法的成熟还有许多例证。嘉靖时著名将领唐顺之的《峨眉道人拳歌》云："浮屠善幻多技能，少林拳法世稀有。"清初黄宗羲《王征南墓志铭》："少林拳勇名天下。"从唐顺之、黄宗羲的话中看，虽然词句有些夸张，但绝非戏言。这些赞美诗句的出现，说明嘉靖至明末时少林拳法已相当成熟，并且已具有相当的影响力。明代的少林寺拳法和棍术一样都形成了完整的理论体系。明末少林寺著名拳法大

图1-6 少林棍
Shaolin Cudgel Techniques

dynasty, Jin Zhongshi writes in his *Travel Notes of Mount Song*, "At noon, Shao Canjun invited Abbot Xi Nan to watch the monks' Kungfu performance." Three years later, Yuan Hongdao noted in his article *Mount Song Travel Notes*, "In the morning, while going out, I saw some young and senior monks clasping hands and standing on one foot. I invited them to show an unarmed combat performance. The head monk replied, 'This is the tradition of the Shaolin Temple,' for testing their skills." This shows that, during the Ming dynasty, the boxing techniques were quite exquisite with the function of fighting. The formation period of the boxing and staff techniques were not all that far apart, however, the nationwide recognition of the staff techniques preceded the former one. Besides, the chapter "Questions and Answers" of Cheng Zongyou's *Introduction to Shaolin Cudgel Technigues (Shaolin Gunfa Chanzong)* writes, "The staff techniques still belong to Shaolin, but why do the Shaolin monks practice boxing techniques more than that? I answered, The name of the Shaolin staff is Ye Cha, which is originated from a sacred tradition of Kinnara, named as the holy Bodhi. Now, although the boxing techniques are still not prevalent widely, practisers are trying to make it equal in status to the staff techniques." Zongyou's remarks clearly implied that the staff techniques inherited from Kinnara, known as the Sage, had spread extensively. Thus, the fame of the boxing techniques was not equal to that of the staff techniques. It needs to be explained that, based on the above evidence, many people think that the Shaolin boxing techniques were formed succeeding the staff techniques. However, Cheng Zongyou's remarks do not actually imply that the creation of the staff techniques is prior to the boxing techniques, but that the staff techniques became famous earlier than the boxing techniques.

    Lots of evidences attest the maturity of Shaolin boxing techniques of the Ming dynasty. During the reign of the Jiajing Emperor, the famous general Tang Shunzhi wrote in *Emei Taoist Boxing Verses*, "Buddhist monks are skillful at Kungfu in a magical way. The Shaolin boxing techniques are rare in the whole country." Huang Zongxi's *Epitaph of Wang Zhengnan* from the early Qing dynasty records that "Shaolin Boxing is famous for its reputation all over the country". The words of Tang Shunzhi and Huang Zongxi are somewhat exaggerated, though not joking. The above passages indicate that the Shaolin boxing techniques had become considerably mature and influential from the

师玄机和尚,将拳法传于陈松泉,陈又传张鸣鹗,清初张孔昭据张鸣鹗所传玄机遗法写成了《拳经》一书。该书不仅有少林拳的练法而且有理论,是少林拳法的经典。

明代少林功夫,不仅仅包括棍法和拳法,而是一个内容相当广泛的武术体系。明万历四十三年(1615年)文翔凤在其《嵩游记》中写道:"归观六十僧,以掌搏者、剑者、鞭者、戟者……"从这个记述看,明代少林功夫不仅有拳有棍,而且有剑、鞭、戟,等等。清洪亮吉《登封县志》载明末郜如城:"习拳棒于少林寺僧,尤娴大刀。"可见大刀在明代已被列入少林重要兵器。明天启五年(1625年),河南巡抚程绍在

图1-7 少林兵器

Shaolin Weapons Forms

Emperor Jiajing's reign to the end of the Ming dynasty. The Shaolin boxing techniques and staff techniques in the Ming dynasty thus both formed a complete theoretical system. The Shaolin monk Xuanji, a famous boxing master of the late Ming dynasty, handed down the boxing techniques to Chen Songquan, who in turn coached to Zhang Minge. During the early Qing dynasty, Zhang Kongzhao completed a classic The Book of *the Fist Techniques* according to Zhang Minge's techniques bequeathed from Xuan Ji, the techniques and theories of Shaolin boxing included.

In the Ming dynasty, Shaolin Kungfu including the staff techniques and the boxing techniques formed quite an extensive Kungfu system. In the 43rd year of the Wanli Emperor reign (1615 CE) of the Ming dynasty, Wen Xiangfeng wrote in his *Mount Song Travel*, "When I was back [at the Shaolin Temple], I saw sixty monks practicing Kungfu with the fist, the sword, the whip and the halberd..." This illustrates that Shaolin Kungfu in the Ming dynasty not only included the boxing and staff techniques, but also included the sword, whip, halberd and so on. *Dengfeng County Annals* written by Hong Liangji of the Qing dynasty cited the remarks of Gao Rucheng of the Ming dynasty, "Shaolin monks are good at not only boxing and staff but also the broadsword." It can be judged that the broadsword had been listed as one of the important weapons in the Shaolin Temple during the Ming dynasty. In the 5th year of the Tianqi Emperor reign (1625 CE) of the Ming dynasty, the governor of Henan province, Cheng Shao, wrote *A Poem of Shaolin Kungfu Appreciation* after watching a Kungfu performance at the Shaolin Temple, "Resting from watching the performance of Shaolin monks; feeling impressed by the superb skills of Kungfu weapons and staffs." During the Wanli Emperor's reign of the Ming dynasty, the assistant minister of the Ministry of Rites Gongding's *Verses of Watching Martial Arts Competing* also described scenes similar to those of other authors. The above poems or verses clearly prove that there was a fairly large variety of boxing techniques and weapons of Shaolin Kungfu during the Ming dynasty.

During the Ming dynasty, the development of Shaolin Kungfu and the improvement of its techniques, especially the staff techniques, were closely related to the participation of Kungfu monks in war. During the years of the Zhengde (the 10th Emperor of the Ming dynasty 1506—1521 CE) Emperor

少林寺观武僧演武后写的《少林观武诗》云:"暂憩招提试武僧,金戈铁棒技层层。"明万历时的礼部侍郎公鼐《少林观僧比武歌》:"复有戈剑光陆离,挥霍撞击纷飙驰。"以上这些,足可证实明代少林功夫的拳术、器械种类相当多。

明代少林功夫的发展和技法的提高,尤其是棍术的提高,与武僧参战关系密切。正德时少林武僧周友曾率僧兵镇守山陕边关并征讨云南,嘉靖时少林武僧也曾大规模参与抗倭战争和镇压农民起义战争。战争的洗礼使少林功夫得到了长足发展。明嘉靖时,抗倭明将俞大猷自云中(山西大同)归沿海抗倭前线,路经少林寺,临走时将少林武僧普从、宗擎带到军中,习练实战少林棍法达三年之久。后二人回到少林寺,将实战棍法广传于寺内武僧。

明代少林寺的演武活动非常盛行,这也是少林功夫技法提高的一个重要途径。当时凡是有地位的名人到少林寺,寺僧皆以演武形式展示少林功夫。公鼐、程绍、王士性、金忠士、袁宏道、文翔凤等到少林,

图1-8 众武僧习武

Shaolin Warrior Monks' Practicing Martial Arts

reign, Shaolin monk Zhou You, led the other monks to defend the frontier of Shan-Shan (Shanxi and Shaanxi) and conduct a punitive expedition in Yunnan province. During the years of the Jiajing Emperor reign, the Shaolin monks also participated in the war against Wokou and a war suppressing large-scale peasant uprisings. These wars tested the mettle of the monks and spurred on the development of Shaolin Kungfu. Yu Dayou, a famous general against Wokou, returned from Yunzhong (Datong city, Shanxi province) to the front line of the coastal anti-Wokou war. On his way, he passed through the Shaolin Temple and recruited the Shaolin monks Pucong and Zongqing in the army. The two monks didn't go back to the Shaolin Temple until they had practiced and coached the Shaolin staff techniques for three years. After returning, they strove to coach the staff techniques to the other Shaolin monks.

The Kungfu performance at the Shaolin Temple, as an important way to improve the Shaolin Kungfu techniques, prevailed during the Ming dynasty. At that time, whenever famous celebrities visited the Shaolin Temple, the Shaolin monks displayed Shaolin Kungfu in a way of performance for them. Gong Ding, Cheng Shao, Wang Shixing, Jin Zhongshi, Yuan Hongdao, Wen Xiangfeng and so on, all watched the large-scale Kungfu performances. Only with superb skills the Kungfu monks were able to show the perfect performance.

Thus, Shaolin Kungfu has been widely disseminated nationwide since the Ming dynasty. Zhou You's disciples spread to dozens of prefectures and counties in Henan, Shandong and two Zhili provinces. During the reign of the Jiajing Emperor, the Kungfu monks, who were recruited in the anti-Japanese war with staffs, spread all over the southeastern coastal areas, which promoted Shaolin Kungfu to take root in the southeastern provinces of China. During the Ming dynasty, many secular disciples, such as Cheng Junxin, Cheng Hanchu and Cheng Zongyou, were recruited into the Shaolin Temple for Kungfu practice. After over ten years' Kungfu practice in the Shaolin Temple, Cheng Zongyou completed a Book named *Introduction to Shaolin Cudgel Technigues* (*Shaolin Gunfa Chanzong*), which saw the proliferation of Shaolin staff techniques to the nation. Similarly, also during the Ming dynasty, Xuan Ji passed the boxing techniques down to secular disciples in order to spread the techniques widely. At the end of the Ming dynasty, the Ming generals also recruited Shaolin monks frequently as

都观看了武僧大型的习武场面。武僧的演武促使其必须有一个良好的技艺，才能展示少林武功的高超。

少林功夫自明代扬名之后，即开始在国内广泛传播。明正德时镇守边关、征讨云南的著名武僧周友的武术弟子遍及河南、山东、两直隶四省的几十个州县。嘉靖时参加抗倭的众多手持棍棒的少林派武僧，遍及东南沿海，使少林功夫根植我国东南诸省。明代也有许多俗家弟子进入少林寺习武，如程君信、程涵初、程宗猷等，都曾到少林寺习武。程宗猷求学于少林寺十余年后写的《少林棍法阐宗》一书，使少林棍法广播四方。明代玄机传拳法于俗家弟子，使少林拳法广传于世。明末，明王朝将领还多次聘少林武僧为之训练军队，传授少林武功。

三、发展

明代是少林功夫发展史上的一个辉煌时期。这期间不仅少林寺繁荣，寺僧练武、演武、传武也很兴盛，甚至僧兵的参战也多受朝廷的调遣。进入清朝，少林功夫经历了曲折的发展道路。清初之后武僧练武由公开变成隐蔽，演武活动销声匿迹，直到清末。然而，在社会上，清朝建立后，少林功夫声誉更加卓著，流传更加广泛。少林功夫在清代出现这样的局面，与清廷禁止民间秘密结社性质的宗教组织有着极为密切的关系。

少林功夫在清代所走过的曲折道路肇始于满族的统治。明朝灭亡后，被称为"外夷"的清朝定鼎中原。由于历史上长期积存下来的对北方少数民族的敌视，所以清朝的建立，引起了广大汉族地区民众的不满，于是民间开始组织秘密结社性质的宗教组织来反清。面对汉族地区有组织的秘密反清活动，清朝一开始就予以严厉镇压。清顺治三年（1646年），世祖下令："如遇各色教门，即行严捕，处以重罪。"（《清实录》）

coaches to train the army and coach Shaolin Kungfu.

III. Development

During the Ming dynasty, a glorious period in the development history of Shaolin Kungfu, not only did the Shaolin Temple flourish, but also the Shaolin Kungfu was experiencing unprecedented prosperity in practice, performance and dissemination. Moreover, the monks were often dispatched to join wars as soldiers by the court. During the Qing dynasty, Shaolin Kungfu went through a tortuous development path. From the early till the end of the Qing dynasty, although Shaolin monks' Kungfu practice became hidden from the public, the reputation of Shaolin Kungfu became much more outstanding and proliferated. The status of Shaolin Kungfu in the Qing dynasty was closely connected to the Qing court's prohibition of local secret religious fraternities.

The ruling of Manchu in the Qing dynasty led Shaolin Kungfu to a tortuous path. After the demise of the Ming dynasty, the Manchu-led Qing court, considered as "foers", established its capital in the Central China, which raised the discontent of the majority of the Han people. With the long-standing hostility toward the Northern minorities, the Han people began to set up secret religious fraternities to oppose the government. But the opposition activities were severely suppressed by the government from the very beginning. In the 3rd year of the Shunzhi Emperor reign (1646 CE) of the Qing dynasty, Emperor Shizu ordered, "Once the religious fraternities were founded, the court must at once strictly arrest and enforce the law." (*The Memoir of the Qing Dynasty*)

In the early Qing dynasty, although the Qing court issued strict prohibitions on these religious fraternities, initially the Shaolin monks were not affected on Kungfu practice. One reason is that, the local religious fraternities and the various religious schools were not strong enough to take actions to oppose the Qing court, and the other one is that, there were no clues of the alliance between the Shaolin Temple and other organizations. On the contrary, in the early Qing dynasty, the govemment was quite supportive of the Buddhist Shaolin Temple. The Shaolin Temple even received similar political status like that of the Ming dynasty, "Ever

在清初之时，清廷虽有严格禁止民间宗教组织的法令，但当时民间的反清教会、教门并不太明显，力量也比较薄弱，而且这些初兴的民间宗教组织并未与少林寺及少林功夫有什么关系。所以，清初时，清廷并没有把少林武僧的聚众习武等同于民间秘密的反清组织，也没有采取限制和禁止措施。相反，在清初之时，朝廷对禅宗祖庭少林寺还是相当支持的，对寺院的政治待遇和明朝也差不多："河南嵩山少林禅寺，自达摩面壁传心之后，为天下佛门之祖庭。凡嗣位传法者，俱请钦依礼部札付主持少林，提衍禅学，嗣祖传灯，钤束僧众。如儒门之衍圣，道达之真人。千百年于兹，不随世代变迁者也。"（见《少林寺志·部札》）明末清初少林寺住持海宽，于崇祯十二年（1639年）得到明王朝钦命文书出任住持，清朝定鼎后，即于顺治三年（1646年），沿用明朝旧制给少林寺住持（方丈）海宽以钦命住持衔，因海宽足疾未赴京领命。顺治十三年（1656年）底，海宽赴京次年抵京后正式领取朝廷钦依礼部颁发的札子（公文），正式出任少林寺钦命住持。在顺治九年（1652

图1-9 少林棍法对练

Pair Practicing the Shaolin Cudgel Techniques

since Da Mo (Bodhidharma)'s wall-gazing meditation at the Shaolin Temple on Mount Song, located in Henan province, the Shaolin Temple thus became the ancestral home of Buddhism. Appointed by the Ministry of Rites to preside over the Shaolin Temple, the descendants' responsibilities were to teach Chan, to pass on the essence of Chan to their ancestors and to restrain the Shaolin monks' behavior. This custom had been carried forward for hundreds of years similar to the Confucian saint Yan Sheng (a title of the eldest direct descendant of Confucius of each generation) and the Taoist Saint who passed on the doctrines from masters to disciples."(See *Shaolin Temple Annals*) During the late Ming and the early Qing dynasties, Hai Kuan was appointed abbot of the Shaolin Temple by the imperial edict in the 12th year of the Chongzhen Emperor reign (1639 CE) of the Ming dynasty. After the establishment of the Qing dynasty, in the 3rd year of the Shunzhi Emperor reign (1646 CE), Hai Kuan was again entitled the rank of abbot of Shaolin Temple by the Qing dynasty maintaining the law of the Ming dynasty. But Hai Kuan was not present at the inauguration ceremony in Beijing (the current capital of China, Peking) because of his foot disease. At the end of the 13th year of the reign of the Emperor Shunzhi (1656 CE), Hai Kuan arrived at Beijing and received official documents issued by the Ministry of Rites of the Qing government. He thus officially took up the post as the imperial abbot of the Shaolin Temple. From the 9th year (1652 CE) to the 10th year of the Shunzhi Emperor, the Qing court also overhauled the Shaolin Temple (See Fu Jingxing's *Rebuilding the Shaolin Temple*). Under such a historical backdrop, at the beginning of the Qing dynasty, the Shaolin monks could practice Kungfu publicly as in the Ming Dynasty. These records can be found in many early historical annals of the Qing dynasty.

During the years of Shunzhi Emperor reign (1644—1661 CE) of the Qing dynasty, Jiao Fuheng's poem *Shaolin Temple* records, "The staff techniques are superb techniques; the successful outcomes belong to Bilian Palace." In the early Qing dynasty, Gu Zuyu's *Essentials of Historical Geography* records, "In the north was a Shaolin Temple, built in the Northern Wei dynasty and repaired in the subsequent dynasties, where the Shaolin monk warriors originated." In the 16th year of Kangxi (the 3rd emperor of the Qing dynasty) Emperor reign (1679 CE) of the Qing dynasty, Gu Yanwu visited the Shaolin Temple and wrote in

年）至十年时，清朝官府还大修了一次少林寺（见傅景星《重修少林寺记》）。由此，清初之时，少林寺武僧和明朝一样可以公开习武。这些，清初诸多史册的记载可证。

清顺治时焦复亨《少林寺》诗云："艺高白棓（棒）手，夏解碧莲宫。"清初顾祖禹《读史方舆纪要》："其北有少林寺，原魏所建，历代尝修治之，近代所称少林寺之僧兵也。"清康熙十六年（1679年）顾炎武游少林寺后，在其所写的《天下郡国利病书·嵩高》中写道："至今寺僧以技击闻，其由来久矣。"而其所写的《少林寺》诗中也写道："颇闻经律余，多亦谐武艺。"清康熙时进士景日昣在其所著《说嵩》一书中亦云："今寺僧矜尚白棓。"

从上述记载看，清初寺僧公开习武是毫无疑问的，但从史册的记述看，寺僧清初时以习棍为主，而不是明代"金戈铁棒持层层"（明程绍《少林观武》）那种场面，这是清代禁止民间拥有兵戈的结果。清初寺僧习武规模和人数较少的原因，在于明末战乱对少林寺的重创。清傅景星《重修少林寺记》记载了战乱对少林寺的影响："以末业式微，揭竿四起，野猿悲而出谷，飞鸟为之惊栖。于是风沙迷目，梵宇穿云，即缁流传侣衹，虞山不高，林不密矣。洞天福地，铁甲金戈。而少林千百年祖庭，遭赤眉夜占南山，祸及之险危哉！"

由于战争的重创，少林寺走向衰弱。清康熙初登封知县叶封《少林寺》诗描述了战后少林寺情景："乱余僧亦少，晚坐静无哗；古殿聊支水，丰碑漫似麻。"清康熙初进士王无忝《少林寺》诗亦有："寺破山僧少，人来夏涧幽。"由于寺僧大量减少，清初武僧习武规模虽小，然而是公开的。

进入清朝康熙中后期，随着民间反清教会力量的壮大，在"反清复明"的旗帜下，为了达到反清目的，民间教会便开始寻觅反清力量。于是久负盛名的少林功夫及少林僧兵成了民间秘密结社组织教门利用的对象。利用少林功夫作为反清武器的民间教会，最有代表性的是天地会和

his book *Pandect for Pros & Cons of Social, Political and Economic Conditions Throughout Ming Empire: Songgao*, "It has been a long time that the Shaolin monks are well-known for their superb Kungfu." His poem *Shaolin Temple* also reads, "While watching some monks meditating in the Shaolin Temple, the other monks were also seen practicing Kungfu techniques." During the Kangxi Emperor reign (1661—1722 CE) of the Qing dynasty, Jinshi (a successful candidate in the highest imperial examinations) Jing Rizhen wrote in his book *On Mount Song*, "The staff technique is still prominent among the Shaolin monks."

Judging from the above records, it is undoubted that the Shaolin monks could still practice Kungfu publicly and manily practice staff techniques during the early Qing dynasty, rather than the scene of "A numbers of sword and spear practiced" (Cheng Shao's *Shaolin Martial Arts Appreciation* in the Ming dynasty). This was a result of the Qing dynasty's prohibition of civilian possession of military weapons. The reason for the small size and number of Shaolin monks practicing Kungfu in the early Qing dynasty lay in the heavy casualties of the Shaolin Temple in the late Ming dynasty. Fu Jingxing (in the Qing dynasty)'s Records of *Rebuilding the Shaolin Temple* records the impacts of the war on the Shaolin Temple, "In the late Qing dynasty, the country's decline caused riots nationally. The wild apes, wailing, were driven out of the valley; the frightened birds, screaming, were flying around in a turmoil. Heavily, the Shaolin Temple was blown by the wind and dust. In such a Buddhist holy monastery, the Shaolin masters and monks were worrying about the lower mountain, the sparse forest. In the Buddhist Temple and the Taoist Abbey, the weapons and armors were waved everywhere. The southern mountain of the Shaolin Temple, with thousands of years' history, suffered the riots of peasant soldiers being captured and in imminent danger of disaster!"

The heavy impact of war caused the Shaolin Temple to a decline. In the years of Kangxi Emperor reign of the early Qing dynasty, the poem *Shaolin Temple* written by Ye Feng, a county magistrate of Dengfeng county, described the scene of the postwar at Shaolin Temple, "After the war, there were few monks remaining who were seated silently at night. The ancient palaces were idle like the little stream, and the huge stele was too blurry to be recognized." At the same time, another poem written by Jinshi Wang Wutian, recounts, "Few monks were left

图1-10 少林双拐
Shaolin Shuang Guai

白莲教。

天地会乃是起源于清康熙时的一个秘密反清教门，该教对外称"洪门"。所谓"洪门"，乃是以明太祖朱元璋"洪武"年号为名，入门者称"洪门""洪门兄弟"。天地会成立后，感到自身力量薄弱，为了激起更多的武林志士反清，开始利用在社会上具有相当影响力的少林功夫。

萧一山《近代秘密社会史料·洪门问答书》："武从何处学习？在少林寺学习。何艺为先？洪拳为先。有何为证？有诗为证：'猛勇洪拳四海闻，出在少林寺内僧；普天之下归洪姓，相扶明主定乾坤。'"又《近代秘密社会史料·洪拳诗》："武艺出在少林寺，洪门事务我精通；洪拳能破西达子，万载名标第一功。"天地会为了激起少林派弟子反清，还编造了一个神奇的"火焚少林寺"的故事。罗尔纲《清史资料丛刊·天地会》、肖一山《近代秘密社会史料》等都记载这个故事。说

in the Shaolin Temple after the temple fell into ruin, and the brook among the mountain was very peaceful in summer." Due to the decreasing number of monks at the temple, the scale of Kungfu practice in the early Qing dynasty was small, but people could practice Kungfu publicly.

During the mid-late years of Kangxi Emperor reign, the power of the local anti-Qing fraternities rose. Under the banner of "Oppose Qing and restore Ming", the local religious fraternities began to seek out other anti-Qing forces in order to achieve their goals. Hence, the renowned Shaolin Kungfu monks and warriors became the primary objective of these secret communities to utilize and organize into fraternities in order to oppose the Qing dynasty. The chief representatives of these fraternities were the Tiandihui and the White Lotus Society.

The Tiandihui, also publicly called "Hongmen", was a secret anti-Qing organization that was originated during the Kangxi Emperor reign of the Qing dynasty. "Hongmen", named after Zhu Yuanzhang's (the first Emperor of the Ming dynasty) name "Hongwu", recruited initiates who were eponymously called "Hongmen" and "Hongmen Brothers". Afterwards, in order to arouse more Kungfu heroes to join the anti-Qing activities, the Tiandihui started to utilize Shaolin Kungfu to bolster their strength, which had considerable influence nationally.

Xiao Yishan's *Historical Materials of Modern Secret Society: Hong Men's Q & A* writes, "Where is the best place for martial arts learning? Shaolin Temple. Which is the first technique for martial arts learning? Hong Quan. What is the evidence? The poem is the evidence: 'The powerful Hong Quan, which is famous nationwide, originated from the Shaolin monastery; In the name of Hong (re: Emperor Zhu Yuanzhang), it aids the Emperor of the Ming dynasty to govern the country.'" Moreover, the *Historical Materials of Modern Secret Society: Hong Quan Poem* writes that, "I am proficient in the history of Hongmen which originated from the Shaolin Temple. Hong Quan bearing powerful features is renowned as the first level technique in the history of martial arts." In order to arouse the passion of Shaolin disciples to oppose the Qing dynasty, the Tiandihui also fabricated a mysterious story called "Shaolin Temple's Burning" in order to rally supporters. Luo Ergang's *Qing Dynasty History Series*: *Tiandihui* and Xiao Yishan's *Historical Materials of Modern Secret Society* both record this story. It

是康熙时期，西鲁造反，清廷派御林军征讨却损兵折将。后皇帝下榜说，能征服西鲁者，封万户侯，赏金万两。少林寺武僧闻知扯榜，出征西鲁，大胜而归。后少林寺叛徒亚七诬告少林僧谋反。康熙帝不分青红皂白派御林军数万，夜赴少林寺，乘寺僧熟睡之机，一把火焚烧了少林寺，108名武僧仅余5人。洪门所说的清帝焚毁的为福建少林寺，实际上影射的是少林功夫发祥地嵩山少林寺。

　　清代另一个民间教会白莲教，也是一个利用少林功夫反清的组织。该教原来是起源于宋代的一个民间教派，元、明时曾多次发动反元、反明武装斗争。当进入清朝后，他们转而树起了"反清复明"的旗帜。同样，白莲教为了达到反清目的，也不断利用少林功夫作为号召。

　　面对汉族地区各种秘密教会的反清活动，清廷开始大规模查禁民间秘密教会组织，到乾隆时甚至把禁止天地会列入《大清律》之中。在这种情况下，作为民间教门反清武器的少林寺及少林寺武僧，开始受到清王朝的压制。

　　随着民间宗教组织利用少林功夫反清后，清廷对少林寺的态度发生了巨大的变化，由开始的支持变成削弱和压制。清康熙五年（1666年）海宽去世后，按旧制本应重新钦命住持，但清廷却终止了对少林寺住持的任命，使传承了数百年的钦命住持制度宣告终结。之后，在清廷的压制下，少林寺出现了相当混乱的局面，以致"法堂草长、宗徒雨散"（见张思明《重建慈云庵碑记》）。

　　到清朝雍正时，在清廷的压制下，少林寺败落更加明显，面对赫赫禅宗祖庭的凋零，河东总督王士俊感慨道："登封少林，乃系东土初祖道场，九年传冷坐之心，五叶启宗门之绪。法灵普覆，慧日光涵，缘自历代相沿，迄今实多颓圮。"（《河东总督王士俊檄》）为此，王士俊奏请皇上重修少林寺。在得到王士俊奏折后，雍正帝下圣旨批准重修少林寺。但在雍正批准重修少林寺的圣旨中，对少林的门头房（家族式庭院）却给以严厉训责："朕览图内，门头二十五房，距寺较远，零星散

was said that, under the reign of the Kangxi Emperor, the Qing court was defeated after dispatching the imperial Yulin Army to suppress troops of the Xilu Rebellion. Afterwards, Emperor Kangxi issued an imperial decree of money and land reward for those who captured the Xilu army. Immediately, the Shaolin monks tore the reward post and conquered the Xilu army with great success. After this, the traitorous monk Ya Qi falsely accused the Shaolin monks of conspiring against the empire, and Kangxi, unable to discern friend from foe among the fraternities, dispatched the Yulin army to set fire to the Shaolin Temple at night. In this fire, only five of the 108 Shaolin monks were alive. Although it was the Shaolin Temple of Fujian that the Hongmen alluded to in the tale, as a matter of fact, the burnt Shaolin Temple was the one at Mount Song, from where Shaolin Kungfu originated.

Another popular fraternity called the White Lotus Society in the Qing dynasty, originated from a folk school during the Song dynasty, also used Shaolin Kungfu to fight against the Qing court. The White Lotus Society launched many armed struggles against the Yuan and Ming dynasties. During the Qing dynasty, with the entry of the Manchu-led Qing government into the Central China, conversely, the White Lotus upheld the banner of "Oppose Qing and restore Ming". Meanwhile, in order to achieve the goal, the White Lotus still made full use of Shaolin Kungfu to attract more attention and supporters.

Considering the anti-Qing activities of various secret fraternities in the area of Han nationality, the Qing court commenced to ban them. Under the Qianlong Emperor reign (1735—1796 CE), the Qing government even listed a prohibition against the Tiandihui in *"The Law of Qing Dynasty"*. From then on, the Shaolin Temple and the Shaolin monks, used as the tools against the Qing dynasty by the secret fraternities, were suppressed by the Qing dynasty.

Due to the above reasons, the Qing imperial court's attitude toward the Shaolin Temple changed tremendously from supporting to weakening and suppressing. In the 5th year of Kangxi Emperor reign (1666 CE), after Hai Kuan's death, the Qing government terminated the appointment of the abbot at the Shaolin Temple rather than reappoint a new abbot based on the old rules. This ended the system of imperial abbots, which had been passed down for hundreds of years. Afterwards, under the oppression of the Qing dynasty, the Shaolin Temple went through a rather chaotic situation, resulting in "Weeds overgrown in Buddha's worshipping hall; The Shaolin

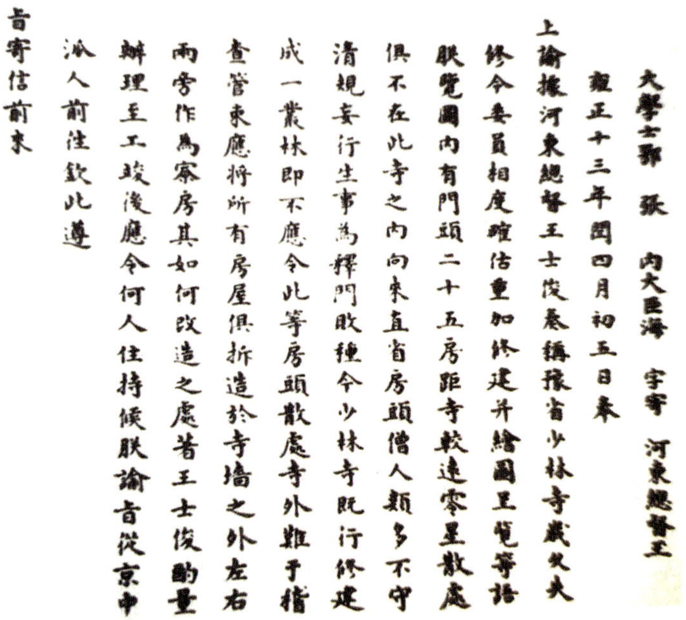

大學士鄂　張　內大臣海　字寄　河東總督王
雍正十三年閏四月初五日奉
上諭據河東總督王士俊奏稱豫省少林寺歲久失
修令委員相度確估重加修建并繪圖呈覽等語
朕覽圖內有門頭二十五房距寺較遠零星散處
俱不在此寺之內向來直省房頭僧人類多不守
清規妄行生事為釋門敗種令少林寺既行修建
成一叢林即不應令此等房頭散處寺外難于稽
查管束應將所有房屋俱拆造於寺墻之外左右
兩旁作為寮房其如何改造之處著王士俊酌量
辦理至工竣後應令何人住持候朕諭旨從京中
派人前往欽此遵
旨寄信前來

图1–11　雍正敕修少林寺上谕
Yongzheng's Imperial Edict

处，俱不在此寺内之内。向来直省房头僧人，类不守清规，妄行生事，为释门败种。”（见《少林寺志》所载雍正《上谕》）为此，雍正帝特下令拆除了少林寺周围二十五座远离寺院的“门头房”。这二十五座门头房，过去大多都是少林寺武僧的练功场。由于雍正对少林寺心怀不满，所以在上谕中甚至对寺院修好后由谁来作方丈一事，他也不同意由少林寺僧担任，而是想从京师中调帝王信任的僧人充任：“至工竣后，应令何人住持，候朕谕旨，从京中派人前往。”（雍正《上谕》）由此可知，雍正对少林寺的态度虽不像对民间教会那样严酷，但限制还是很多的。

随着民间教会利用少林功夫反清活动的高涨，雍乾之时，清廷甚至把少林武僧的演武和传武活动视为“邪教”的帮凶。清乾隆五年（1740年），河南巡抚雅尔图奏折可证：“豫有少壮之民，习于强悍，多学拳棒。如少林寺僧徒，向以教习拳棒为名，聚集无赖、凶狠不法之辈，效

monks scattered like raindrops". (See Zhang Siming's *Rebuilding the Stele of Ciyun Nunnery*).

By the time of the Yongzheng Emperor reign (1722—1735 CE) of the Qing dynasty, under the oppression of the Qing court, the ancestral Buddhist Shaolin Temple continued to decline, which aroused Wang Shijun (the governor of Hedong)'s lament, "Dengfeng Shaolin, the Buddhist site of the ancestor Bodhidharma with his sincere heart for his nine years' wall-gazing Chan meditation, inherited five sects to develop into a glorious stage. It is to be regretted that the Shaolin Temple wasted away." (By *Hedong Governor Wang Shijun*) Then, Wang Shijun appealed to Emperor Yongzheng to rebuild the Shaolin Temple. The Emperor approved his petition of the Shaolin Temple's restoration by imperial decree. However, the Emperor severely reprimanded the Shaolin gatehouse (a family-style courtyard), in which it is written, "When watching the picture, I can see twenty-five gatehouses along the roadside which are far away from the Shaolin Temple, scattered everywhere. Most Shaolin monks live in the detached houses, rather than abide by the religious rules. They disobeyed the rules mischievously." (See Emperor Yongzheng's Imperial Edict recorded in *Shaolin Temple Annals*)

Therefore, Emperor Yongzheng ordered the demolition of the twenty-five gatehouses around the Shaolin Temple, which are located relatively far from the temple. Most of these gatehouses were used as Shaolin monks' Kungfu practice courts. Due to Yongzheng's dissatisfaction with the Shaolin Temple, he preferred a reliable monk from the capital to take up the post of abbot after the rebuilding of the monasteries rather than select an abbot from the Shaolin Temple. "After the completion of the rebuilding, regarding the abbot candidate, you must wait for my order. I will assign someone from the capital to take up the post." (Emperor Yongzheng's Imperial Edict, *Shang Yu*) It can be concluded that, although Yongzheng's attitude towards the Shaolin Temple was not as harsh as that towards the local secret fraternities, he had many restrictions on the Shaolin Temple.

Because the secret fraternities used Shaolin Kungfu to organize anti-Qing activities, the Qing government even regarded the Shaolin monks' Kungfu performance and coaching as accomplices of "heresy" during the reign of Yongzheng and Qianlong Emperor. In the 5th year of Qianlong Emperor reign

尤成风。邪教之人传意诱骗此等入伙,以张羽翼。"(见《朱批档》)从雍正开始,在清廷及官府禁止少林寺僧人聚众习武和传武的情况下,少林寺僧人为了保全自己,避开清廷的追查,于是习武活动从公开变成秘密。

  从雍正时期开始,在少林寺已基本上见不到武僧公开习武、演武的场面。雍正到道光初人文墨客游少林寺后所写的各种游记、纪胜诗及所立碑刻等,基本上都找不到寺僧习武演武的记载。清雍正十三年(1735年)至乾隆五年(1740年)任登封知县的施奕簪,在游少林寺后所写的《偕友游少林寺》诗中,描述了当时寺僧习武及少林寺的状况:"武功魔渐息,禅律讲何曾。吴画委荒草,唐文叠石层。琼楼藏鼠雀,丽宇聚蜂蝇。无复前朝树,空闻古涧藤。"由上可知,当时少林寺僧习武活动受到了空前的抑制。

图1-12 少林寺千佛殿脚坑
Foot Pits in Hall of One Thousand Buddhas of Shaolin Temple

(1740 CE) of the Qing dynasty, the memorial to throne by Ya Ertu, the governor of Henan province shows that, "Many young and strong natives of Henan province with brutal characters were learning Kungfu. Shaolin monks, in the name of coaching Kungfu, gathered bullies and fierce criminals to spread Kungfu, which was rather popular among the folks. The heretics used Kungfu to lure more people to join their groups to expand the influence." (See *Zhupidang*) Under the rule of Emperor Yongzheng, the Qing court and the local government prohibited Shaolin monks from gathering to practice and spread Kungfu. In such a situation, in order to self-protect and avoid the Qing court's capture, the Shaolin monks began to practice Kungfu secretly.

Under the reign of the Yongzheng Emperor (1723—1735CE), there were almost no scenes of Shaolin monks' Kungfu practice and performance at the Shaolin Temple. During the rule of Emperor Yongzheng to the early rule of Emperor Daoguang, few travel notes, poems and inscriptions recorded the Shaolin monks' Kungfu practice and performance. From the 13th year of the Yongzheng Emperor reign (1735 CE) to the 5th year of Qianlong Emperor reign (1740 CE), Shi Yizan, Dengfeng county's magistrate, described the situation of the Shaolin Temple in the poem of *Tour of Shaolin Temple with Friends*, "The super natural spirit of Kungfu has gradually decayed; Who knows if the Chan center has ever been located here. The beautiful wall-paintings of Shaolin Temple were abandoned in the weeds, and the valuable steles of the Tang dynasty were left about among the stones. Rats scampered in the magnificent buildings and the bees flew around in the palace. The days of glory vanished with only the creepers left scattering everywhere." This poem shows that the Shaolin monks' Kungfu practice was unprecedentedly suppressed.

To the Shaolin Monks, Kungfu practice was a unique style of Buddhism sect that could never be given up regardless of the Qing court's stringent suppression. In order to avoid being noticed by the Qing court, the Shaolin monks practiced Kungfu secretly at night. Since the reign of the Yongzheng Emperor, they usually practiced Kungfu at the Pilu Hall (Hall of One Thousand Buddhas) of Shaolin Temple, which was built in the late Ming dynasty and originally used for storing scriptures and statues. In the 26th year of the Daoguang Emperor reign (1846 CE), "The Strategy of Kungfu Night Performance" contained in *The Tablet of*

在少林寺习武受到清廷压制之后，作为一直把习武作为宗风的少林寺僧来说，虽然清廷对寺僧的习武施以高压，但习武仍未停止。他们为了避开清廷的查究，习武活动改在夜间秘密进行。建于明末的少林寺毗卢殿（千佛殿）原为储存藏经和佛像的场所，从雍正开始，这里变成了少林寺的秘密夜间练功房。道光二十六年（1846年）《西来堂志善碑》所载的"夜演武略"就是寺僧练功由公开变成秘密的真实写照。清席书锦于光绪二十年（1894年）撰的《嵩岳游记》记述了寺僧在千佛殿习武留下印记的情况："今后殿壁，绘罗汉手搏像。屋地下陷，深数寸，传为习武场。"由于寺僧长期不断地在千佛殿内练功，殿内地下被脚踩出了48个深深的脚坑。据寺僧德禅、行正讲，此坑是清代少林武僧演练内功心意把留下的。从脚坑的深度看，它不仅表示练功时间较长，而且表明清代少林功法也是注重内功的。

清代少林武僧的秘密练功场，除了千佛殿外，处于偏远地区众多的少林寺下院也是武僧习武的重要场所。少林老僧德禅生前曾数次给笔者

图1-13 石沟寺演古窑
Cave-houses of the Shigou Temple

Xilaitang Zhishan is a true portrayal of the Shaolin monks' practice from openness to secret. *Travel Notes of Song Yue*, written by Xi Shujin of the Qing dynasty in the 20th year of the Guangxu Emperor reign (1894 CE), records the imprints of the monks in the Hall of One Thousand Buddhas, "Now on the walls of the palace there are paintings of monk warriors in boxing action. On the floor of the hall lie footpits a few inches deep where it is said to be the place for practicing Kungfu in the court." Because the Shaolin monks had practiced in the Hall of One Thousand Buddhas for a long time, 48 deep foot pits were imprinted into the ground. According to the monks De Chan and Xing Zheng, the pits were drilled into the ground by the Shaolin monks who practiced the internal force Xinyiba during the Qing dynasty. The deep footpits not only indicate that the monks practiced Kungfu for a long time, but also show that the internal force was very important at that time.

Except for the Hall of One Thousand Buddhas, the remote Shaolin Temples were also important places for Shaolin monks' Kungfu practice. The senior Shaolin monk De Chan once told the author several times that, in order to avoid the Qing court's investigation during the Daoguang Emperor reign (1821—1850 CE), the ancestors Hai Fa, Zhan Mo and Zhan Ju practiced Kungfu at the Shigou Temple of Yanshi. Till now, the *Inscriptions of Rebuilding Shigou Temple* built by Hai Fa and Zhan Mo in the 10th year of the Daoguang Emperor reign (1830 CE) still exists. Additionally, the ancient cave-houses where Hai Fa and Zhan Mo practiced Kungfu still exist north inside the temple.

Among the villagers of Shigou Temple, many legends about monks are still widely spread, such as Hai Fa, Zhan Mo and Ji Qin practicing Kungfu at the temple. The legends tell of Zhan Mo's "Crossing the River without Wetting Shoes", Ji Qin's "Crushing Stones into Powder" and so on. According to the author's research, the Shaolin monks like Hai Fa and Zhan Mo, who had practiced Kungfu at the Shigou Temple under the Daoguang Emperor reign, become the important roles of the Shaolin Kungfu legacy. Masters thereafter such as Zhan Ju, Ji Qin, Wu Shanlin (Ji Qin's secular disciple), Zhen Jun and De Gen are successively regarded as the important inheritors of Shaolin Kungfu in modern times. It is said that the current Kungfu taught at the Shaolin Temple in Dengfeng, Yanshi and Gongyi are descended from Wu Shanlin, who shares the

讲，其先祖海发、湛谟、湛举等，在道光时为避清廷追查曾隐居偃师少林寺下院石沟寺练功。至今寺院中海发、湛谟于道光十年（1830年）立的《重修石沟寺碑记》尚存。寺院北侧海发、湛谟练功的几孔古窑洞至今也尚存在。

在石沟寺村民中，至今还流传着许多海发、湛谟、寂勤等武僧在寺院练武的传奇故事。什么湛谟"过河不湿鞋"、寂勤"挟石成粉"等。据笔者调查，道光时在石沟寺练武的海发、湛谟一系武僧，后来成为少林寺武功的重要传人。海发、湛谟之后的湛举、寂勤、吴山林（寂勤俗子）、贞俊、德根等乃少林寺近现代重要的少林武功传人。现在寺院及登封、偃师、巩义一带社会上所传的许多功法，都是海发、湛谟一系的吴山林传下来的。而吴山林的后人吴南方也是传承其功夫的大师。

清朝后期，随着社会的动荡，清廷已自顾不暇，雍乾时期禁教的高压政策到道光时已大为削弱。但寺僧仍惧怕清廷追究，所以秘密习武，到道光初仍沿袭不变。道光八年（1828年）三月，满族大员麟庆代巡抚杨海梁祭中岳。3月25日，麟庆走马至少林寺，在参观了少林寺后，因久闻少林武功名冠天下，遂让寺主僧组织武僧为之演武。寺主僧见麟庆为满族大员，又因清廷禁止聚众习武，于是矢口否认寺僧练武。麟庆听后，立即明白寺主僧是惧怕清廷的追究，于是对少林寺僧习武作出了具有定性意义的解答："谕以少林拳勇，自昔有闻，只在谨守清规，保护名山，正不必打诳语。"（麟庆《鸿雪因缘图记·少林校拳》）寺主僧在听了麟庆这种平反式的话语后才放心。于是，主僧挑选功夫高超的武僧在紧那罗殿前为麟庆进行表演。麟庆在看了武僧表演后赞道："熊经鸟伸，果然矫捷。"（《鸿雪因缘图记·少林校拳》）。

寺僧为麟庆所举行的演武活动，是自康熙后期至道光初在少林寺内唯一可查的公开的大型演武活动。自麟庆对少林武僧演武"正名"后，再加上清朝后期对聚众习武限制的放宽，少林寺自道光后期便公开了其自雍正时"夜演武略"的秘密。清道光二十六年（1846年）立的《西来

same school of Hai Fa and Zhan Mo and his descendant Wu Nanfang.

When the late Qing dynasty was in turmoil, the Qing government was concentrating on the governing of the imperial stability. The high-pressure policy on religion implemented during the Yongzheng and Qianlong Emperor reign had been greatly weakened under the the Daoguang Emperor reign. However, the Shaolin monks were still afraid of the Qing court's investigation, so they kept on Kungfu practicing secretly until the early Daoguang Emperor reign. In March of the 8th year of the Daoguang Emperor reign (1828 CE), a Manchu official, Lin Qing was substituted for the provincial governor Yang Hailiang to hold a sacrificial ceremony at Mount Song. On March 25, when visiting the Shaolin Temple, Lin Qing requested a Kungfu performance, because he had already heard of Shaolin Kungfu's reputation. Considering Lin Qing's Manchu official status and the Qing government's prohibition, the abbot of Shaolin Temple denied the request, pretending that there were no Shaolin monks practicing Shaolin Kungfu. Hearing this, Lin Qing immediately understood that the abbot was afraid of the investigation from the Qing court, so he gave a confirmative answer, "Tell the abbot that I have already heard that the Shaolin monks have been proficient at Kungfu for a long time. I know that their purpose is to obey religious precepts and protect the famous mountains, so it is unnecessary to lie." (Lin Qing's *Hongxueyinyuan Painting Notes of Shaolin Fist*) The abbot was relieved by the accusation-free remarks and thus, he selected some Shaolin monks with superb Kungfu skills to perform for Lin Qing in front of the Kinnara's palace. The amazing performance gained Lin Qing's praise, "The movements are like bears stamping and birds flying, powerful and agile." (See Lin Qing's *Hongxueyinyuan Painting Notes of Shaolin Fist*)

It is recorded that the Kungfu performance for Lin Qing was the only large-scale open one from the late years of the Kangxi Emperor reign to the early years of the Daoguang Emperor reign at the Shaolin Temple. Due to Lin Qing's redressing the wrongs done to the Shaolin monks' Kungfu practice and less restrictions on public Kungfu practice in the late Qing dynasty, the Shaolin Temple, in the late years of the Daoguang Emperor reign, disclosed its secret "Night Kungfu Strategy" that had endured since the Yongzheng Emperor reign. *The Stele of Xilaitang Zhishan*, erected in 26th year of the Daoguang Emperor

堂志善碑》记载的武僧湛声等习武情况可证："余自祝发禅门，禀师敬之重，修弟子之职，昼习经典，夜演武略，亦祗恪守，少林宗风，修文不废武备耳！"

道光之后，由于清廷腐败社会更加动荡，禁教习武的法令已形同虚设。再者，少林寺有麟庆对寺僧习武的肯定，所以习武已不再秘密进行了。清末时，寺僧甚至将麟庆观武的场面，以大型壁画的形式公开绘于白衣殿的北壁上，至今犹存。据寺僧德禅讲，在壁画中指挥练功的就是曾隐居石沟寺练功的湛举。在绘此壁画时，毫无顾忌的寺僧甚至演化出了乾隆帝游少林寺观武的场面，并将其绘于南壁上，至今犹存。

乾隆游少林寺的情况，清洪亮吉《登封县志》记载的非常详尽，寺僧根本没有为乾隆演武。事实上，武僧当时也根本不敢演武。不仅如此，乾隆游少林寺时还对少林寺奉为圣物的面壁石提出了质疑："九年面壁却何曾？片石无端留色相。"（乾隆《题面壁石诗》）然而，南墙壁画中，身着皇帝服饰者，显然就是乾隆。因为清朝只有乾隆帝到过少林寺。寺僧演化出乾隆观武，显然表明乾隆帝也是支持寺僧练武的。这幅壁画反映了清末时期，清朝实行的禁教政策已完全不再适用于少林武僧的习武和传武活动。

清末不仅寺僧习武没有顾忌，俗家弟子到寺院公开学武也很普遍。道光二十六年立的《西来堂志善碑》中就记载了俗家弟子王生随武僧习武情况。清咸丰四年（1854年），福山王祖源偕关中力士周斌同往少林寺学艺："尽得其《内功图》及《枪棒谱》以归。"（王祖源《内功图说序》）光绪七年（1881年）王祖源根据其在少林寺所学之内功，还著成《内功图说》一书刊行于世。

少林功夫在明代开始向社会传播后，到清代由于禁教而遭到压制和禁止。但少林功夫在社会上的传播却没有因禁教而终止，也没有因压制而停步，而是传播规模和范围更大，甚至超过明代。

少林功夫在社会上流传的加快，很重要的原因在于民间秘密结社

regin (1846 CE) of the Qing dynasty, records the Shaolin monk Zhan Sheng's Kungfu practice, "Since I was tonsured as a Shaolin disciple, respecting masters and obeying the rules, I meditated during the day and practiced Shaolin Kungfu at night in order to adhere to the Buddhist religion."

Succeedingly, the corruption of the Qing dynasty led the whole community into a more turbulent state and the prohibitions against coaching and practicing Kungfu were not effective. Moreover, Lin Qing's affirmation of the monks at the Shaolin Temple made Kungfu practice no longer a secret activity. In the late Qing dynasty, the Shaolin monks even painted the scenes of Lin Qing watching Kungfu performance on the northern wall of the Baiyi Palace, which remains till now. According to Dechan's remarks, the figure in the murals who was coaching the monks practicing Kungfu was Zhan Ju, once secluded at the Shigou Temple. In the process of painting, the unfettered monks even depicted the scene of Emperor Qianlong's visit to the Shaolin Temple in another mural on the southern wall, which also remains to this day.

However, Hong Liangji's *Dengfeng County Annals* records the tour of Emperor Qianlong at the Shaolin Temple in details, which stated that the Shaolin monks did not perform Kungfu for him at all. The fact is that the monks did not dare to perform Kungfu at that time. The records also tell the story that, when Emperor Qianlong visited the Shaolin Temple, he questioned the sacred wall stone of the Shaolin Temple, "Is the story of the nine-year wall-gazing true? The stone wall inherited Dharma's immortal image." (Qianlong's Inscription on *Wall Stone Poem*) However, on the south wall of the murals, the figure dressed in imperial costumes is evidently Emperor Qianlong, as he was the only Emperor who had ever visited the Shaolin Temple during the Qing dynasty. In addition, the depiction of his watching Kungfu obviously indicated that Emperor Qianlong also supported the monks' Kungfu practice. This mural reflects that the prohibition of the Qing dynasty could no longer limit the Shaolin monks' Kungfu practicing and coaching at the end of the Qing dynasty.

Meanwhile, the Shaolin monks had no more scruples about Kungfu practice, and it was also very common for the secular disciples to practice Kungfu at the Shaolin Temple publicly. *The Stele of Xilaitang Zhishan* established in the 26th year of the Daoguang Emperor reign (1846 CE) of the Qing dynasty records the

性质的反清教会、帮会利用少林功夫、宣传少林功夫。天地会的"武艺出在少林寺"就是民间教会利用少林功夫的代表。在康熙后期，少林功夫在社会上的传播已相当广泛，不仅天地会说武艺出在少林寺，民间习武者也沿袭教会、帮会的说法，说自己的武艺出自知名的少林寺。清康熙时长洲人褚人穫《坚瓠集》："今人谈武艺，辄曰：'从少林寺出来'。"这句话实际上就是后来所说的"天下功夫出少林"的早期表述。当然，天下功夫出少林这是不可能的，也是不准确的，但褚人穫的记载，反映了清代少林功夫在社会上影响和流传的程度。

　　清代虽然禁止民间教会、帮会习武，并一度将少林武僧聚众传武视为"邪教"帮凶，但事实上清廷是愈禁反而传得愈广。同时，鉴于少林功夫在民间流传已不能完全禁止的现状，清廷对民间传习少林功夫并没有予以严格禁止，甚至对少林寺僧在社会上一些传武活动也是容忍和许可的。这反映了清朝禁教的本意，即主要是禁止公开进行"反清复明"教会的，而不是禁止一切传武活动。清代少林武僧频繁在民间的传武活动可证。《郑板桥笔记》中就记载了湖北魏子兆学艺于少林寺僧的情况："遇少林寺僧，授以练气运神之诀，魏习之数年，周身坚硬如铁，值运气时，气之所至，虽刀斧勿能伤也。"郑的描述当然有些夸张，但能证明的是少林寺僧敢在社会上传艺。此外，王韬的《遁窟谰言》、俞樾的《荟蕞编》、徐珂的《清稗类钞》等都有少林寺僧在民间传武的记载，其中《清稗类钞》记载尤多。不仅如此，甚至清代的神话小说《聊斋志异》等都写有少林寺僧在民间传武。这反映出清代少林武僧在社会上传武是很普遍的。到清代后期，随着民间教会"反清复明"势力的削弱，清廷禁令形同虚设。不仅如此，清廷还利用民间的乡勇湘军镇压太平天国，利用义和团反对洋人。这说明清廷在形势逼迫下政策已发生了变化，即由初期的反对民间聚众习武，到后期有选择性地利用民间武术组织，这种变化对少林功夫的广传也起到了积极作用。

　　随着少林功夫在社会上的广传，清代社会上流传的少林功夫开始

secular disciple Wang Sheng's Kungfu practice with the monks. In the 4th year of the Xianfeng Emperor reign (1854 CE) of the Qing dynasty, Wang Zuyuan from Fushan and Zhou Bin, a strongman from Guanzhong, went to the Shaolin Temple to study Kungfu, "They finally returned to their native places from the Shaolin Temple with *the Inner Power Illustrated Handbook* and *the Spear and Staff Guidebook*." (*Preface to the Inner Power Illustrated Handbook* by Wang Zuyuan) In the 7th year of the Guangxu Emperor reign (1881 CE), Wang Zuyuan completed a book named *the Inner Power Illustrated Handbook* based on what he had learned at the Shaolin Temple.

Shaolin Kungfu began to spread from the Ming dynasty, and was suppressed and prohibited in the Qing dynasty due to the Qing court's prohibition against religion. In spite of the heavy suppression, the spread of Shaolin Kungfu was even more extensive both in scale and scope than that of the Ming dynasty.

The rapid spread of Shaolin Kungfu is due to the anti-Qing fraternities' utilizing and publicizing of Shaolin Kungfu, which was illustrated by the saying from the Tiandihui, "Kungfu was originated from the Shaolin Temple." In the late years of the Kangxi Emperor reign, Shaolin Kungfu had widely spread. Not only did the Tiandihui say so, but also the Kungfu practisers from the Shaolin Temples. During the reign of the Kangxi Emperor of the Qing dynasty, Chu Renyue, a native of Changzhou, wrote in his *Collection of Jian Hu*, "Currently, when people talk about Kungfu, everyone says that it comes from the Shaolin Temple." This saying is the initial expression of "Kungfu is originated from Shaolin." Although Chu Renyue's saying is impossible and inaccurate, the record of it reflects the deep influence and wide spread of Shaolin Kungfu during the Qing dynasty.

Although the Qing court prohibited religious fraternities from practicing Kungfu, and regarded Kungfu monks as "heretics", conversely, the prohibition didn't suppress the Kungfu practice as expected. At the same time, considering the high recognition and publicity of Shaolin Kungfu among the common people, the Qing court didn't strictly prohibit Shaolin Kungfu, but permitted its practice and performance publicly with a tolerant attitude. This reflects that the Qing court's original intention was to prohibit the ecclesial organizations from publicly conducting "Oppose Qing and restore Ming" activities, rather than prohibit all Kungfu activities. The high frequency of Shaolin Kungfu performances in the

分派。黄宗羲《王征南墓志铭》称:"张三丰精于少林,复从而翻之,名为内家。"内家出现后,便称少林为外家。少林功夫在社会上广传之后,清末时南方流传的少林功夫开始称为南派,北方流传的称为北派,由于北派重脚,南派重拳,故有"南拳北脚"之说。此外,清末时还把少林功夫分为广东少林、峨眉少林、福建少林等等。这些都是清代以前的史册根本找不到的。事实上,清代民间流传的各派少林功夫,与少林寺传统的"拳打一条线""拳打卧牛之地"等已有明显的差别。这是因为清末的少林功夫,有许多虽署少林之名,但实际上是民间武术,而非少林功夫。

　　清代少林功夫在民间的广传,表现在多个方面。在图书的出版上,清廷禁教虽有负面影响,但少林功夫书籍还是出了不少。清代最知名的少林功夫书籍当是《拳经·拳法备要》。该书所载拳法乃明末清初少林寺著名武僧玄机和尚遗法。清康熙时经张孔昭整理而成《拳经》一书,乾隆时曹焕斗又作注,更名《拳经·拳法备要》。该书撰成后,未能刊印,一直以手抄本传世,直到民国十八年(1929年)方由大声书局石

图1-14 白衣殿北壁画
Mural On the North Walls of the Baiyi Palace

Qing dynasty was the strongest proof. *The Notes of Zheng Banqiao* records the story about Wei Zizhao, a native of Hubei province, who was practicing Kungfu at the Shaolin Temple, "When meeting a monk at the Shaolin Temple, he was taught the secret of harnessing Qi (Yun Qi). After several years of practice, Wei Zizhao was so strong as iron and could not even be hurt by an axe or a knife." Of course, Zheng Banqiao's description is sort of exaggerated, but it demonstrates that the Shaolin monks had dared to spread Kungfu publicly. This was also recorded in Wang Tao's *Dun Ku Lan Yan*, Yu Yue's *Hui Zui Bian* and mostly in Xu Ke's *Qing Bi Lei Chao*. Furthermore, even the mythological novels in the Qing dynasty, such as Strange Stories from a Chinese Studio (*Liao Zhai Zhi Yi*) told the stories of the Shaolin monks' Kungfu practice, implying the fact that Shaolin monks' Kungfu practice during the Qing dynasty prevailed widely in the country. In the late Qing dynasty, with the weakening of the religious fraternities' forces of "Oppose Qing and restore Ming", the prohibition by the Qing court became virtually useless. Additionally, the Qing court even recruited the local army from Hunan province to suppress the Taiping Rebellion and made use of the Boxer (Yihetuan, the League of Harmony and Justice) Movement to oppose foreigners. This shows that the policy of Qing court had been changed from the initial prohibition on Kungfu practice to the selective use of folk Kungfu organizations, which also played a positive role in the spread of Shaolin Kungfu.

During the rule of the Qing dynasty, the proliferation of Shaolin Kungfu led it into different sects. Huang Zongxi's *Wang Zhengnan Epitaph* records, "Zhang Sanfeng who is proficient in the Shaolin boxing technique transformed Shaolin boxing into Neijia boxing." Hence, Shaolin boxing was renamed Waijia after the emergence of Neijia boxing. With the proliferation of Shaolin Kungfu to the southern China during the late Qing dynasty, Shaolin Kungfu was called the Southern School, and in the northern China, it was called the Northern School. Since the Northern school primarily stressed on the kick techniques while the Southern school stressed on fist techniques, the saying "Southern fists and Northern kicks (Nan Quan Bei Jiao)" came into being. In addition, at the end of the Qing dynasty, Shaolin Kungfu was divided into different schools such as Guangdong Shaolin, Emei Shaolin and Fujian Shaolin, which were not available in the annals before the Qing dynasty. Practically speaking, the various schools of

印出版，1936年蟫隐庐又据最完备手抄本刊印。清乾隆二十七年（1762年）刊印的《少林衣钵》也是清代较早的少林功夫著述，其内容记载有少林衣钵真传、罗汉短打图、罗汉兵刀、器械、罗汉行动全谱、口诀等。这部署名"升霄道人"撰的《少林衣钵》，其内容是否为少林寺所传武功尚存争议，但它以"少林衣钵"刊行，表明少林功夫的影响力还是较大的。此外，清初吴殳的《手臂录》中已记载有少林武僧洪转的枪法和程宗猷著的少林棍法。清代后期，社会上关于少林功夫方面的书籍更多，咸丰时王祖源的《内功图说》、咸丰末蒋鹏的《少林单刀谱》等纷纷刊行。甚至到了宣统三年（1911年）时，上海的《天铎报》公开刊登具有反清性质的《少林宗法》。当然，少林宗法的内容也并非全是少林功夫，但它的刊行表明少林功夫更加广泛地融入社会，深入到群众中。

综上所述，清朝的禁教对少林功夫的传播和发展产生了重大影响，其总体情况是这样的：清廷的禁教在初期是针对民间秘密反清组织的，对少林寺僧习武没有限制，寺僧仍然公开习武，但规模不大。从雍正开

图1-15 白衣殿南壁画

Mural On the South Walls of the Baiyi Palace

Shaolin Kungfu popular in different regions during the Qing dynasty obviously differ from the traditional Shaolin Kungfu, which featured as "boxing of the crow-fly movement" and "to box in a place as small as where an ox lies down". The reason is that, although many various Shaolin Kungfu schools at the end of the Qing dynasty called themselves Shaolin Kungfu, it was in fact folk Wushu, while not the genuine Shaolin Kungfu.

The wide spread of Shaolin Kungfu during the Qing dynasty is reflected in many aspects. In terms of publication, although the prohibition against religion by the Qing court had a negative effect, there were still a great number of books on Shaolin Kungfu published. The most outstanding book on Shaolin Kungfu in the Qing dynasty was *Book of Boxing-Brief of Fist Techniques*, which recorded the remaining boxing techniques of the famous Shaolin monk Xuan Ji in the late Ming and early Qing dynasty. During the reign of Kangxi Emperor of the Qing dynasty, Zhang Kongzhao compiled the book *The Classic of Fist*. During the reign of Qianlong Emperor, Cao Huandou had its name changed to *Book of Boxing-Brief of Fist Techniques*. After completion, the book failed to be published for unknown reasons. But the book was handed down in manuscripts until the 18th year of the Republic of China (1929 CE), when it was published by Shiyin Press of Dasheng Book Bureau. In 1936, Tan Yinlu published another one according to the completed manuscripts. *Shaolin Legacy*, published in the 27th year of the Qianlong Emperor reign (1762 CE) of the Qing dynasty, is also an early work of Shaolin Kungfu, which contains the true biography of Shaolin's legacy, depictions of an Arhat's close combat, an Arhat warrior's broadsword, weapons, the complete range of an Arhat's movements, and mnemonic rhymes to help with instruction. *Shaolin Legacy*, written under the name of "Sheng Xiao Dao Ren", remains controversial as to whether Kungfu was actually handed down by the Shaolin Temple. However, the publication of the book named after Shaolin Legacy reflects Shaolin Kungfu's deep influence. Additionally, Wu Shu's *Arms Record* of the early Qing dynasty records the Shaolin monk Hong Zhuan's spear techniques and Cheng Zongyou's Shaolin staff techniques. In the late Qing dynasty, more books on Shaolin Kungfu were published, such as Wang Zuyuan's *Internal Power Illustrated Handbook* in the years of the reign of Xianfeng Emperor, and Jiang Peng's *Shaolin Broadsword Spectrum* in the late Xianfeng

始，视少林寺僧的传武为聚众反清性质，因而进行压制。由此，武僧习武由公开变成隐蔽。清后期，随着禁教的削弱及麟庆对寺僧习武的正名，寺僧又可以公开习武。社会上，民间反清教门、帮会等利用少林功夫反清，使少林功夫的传播规模更大，流传更加广泛，最终促使少林功夫成为社会上最具影响力的武术流派。

民国时期虽然少林寺已没落，但少林寺僧仍保持习武的传统。民国初年，少林寺最具影响力的两位武术大师是恒林和妙兴。恒林精通少林各种功法，曾任少林寺武僧教头和住持，武术弟子众多。民国初年，匪患严重，精于武功的恒林出任少林寺保卫团团总，曾率少林僧兵与土匪进行了大小数十次战斗，皆获胜。恒林弟子妙兴，为少林武僧之佼佼者。他精通少林拳械及点穴、卸骨、擒拿、气功等诸多少林功夫，在继恒林出任少林寺住持后，打破少林寺秘技不外传的旧俗，传授给了众多俗家弟子。民国十四年（1925年）段之善游少林寺，在其所著的《游少林寺琐记》中记述了妙兴及众弟子习武的情况："其初所练皆系单人拳法，功力严整，手眼身法，步步周密。演练时，全场肃静，中逢节段，莫不鼓掌如雷。复演双人对手，拳脚飞舞，纵横颠覆，犹令观者，警目夺神，为之叹赞。拳脚之后，表演单刀，入场后但见白练上下翻飞，寒光闪灼，更使观众注目，鼓掌不绝。最后方丈妙兴法师同得意弟子对练镇山棍。身法灵敏，神严功整，双棍盘旋，抽发矫捷，目睹耳闻，棍声呼呼，敏若惊蛇，疾若游龙。鼓掌之间，不禁为之喝彩，饱尝眼福，叹观止焉！"妙兴大师及众僧演武情况是民国时期武僧习武的写照。

民国时期，少林功夫弟子中还走出两位将军，这就是许世友和钱钧。许世友于1914年至1921年在少林寺当杂役，习武达8年之久，当他16岁走出少林寺时，已是掌握了多种高深少林功夫的大家。钱钧于1916年13岁时入少林寺做杂工，习武达5年，学得了少林绝技朱砂掌。后来二人利用在少林寺学到的武功，在战场上大显身手，屡立战功。1955年许世友被授予上将军衔，钱钧被授予中将军衔。

Emperor reign. Successively in the 3rd year of the Xuantong Emperor reign (1911 CE), *Tianduo Newspaper* of Shanghai published the *Shaolin Patriarchal Clan System Diagram*, which contained anti-Qing sentiments. However, although the content of the Diagram is not all about Shaolin Kungfu, the publication itself illustrates that Shaolin Kungfu was more widely integrated into the community.

To sum up, during the Qing dynasty, the prohibition against religion had a great impact on the spread and development of Shaolin Kungfu. In the early Qing dynasty, it was mainly against the folk secret anti-Qing fraternities without specific restrictions on the Shaolin monks' Kungfu practice. At that time, the Shaolin monks could still practice Kungfu publicly on a small scale. However, from the years of the Yongzheng Emperor, the Shaolin monks' Kungfu activities were regarded as anti-Qing movements and thus were suppressed by the Qing court. As a result, the Shaolin monks' Kungfu practice became covert. In the late Qing dynasty, with the weakening of the prohibition against religion and the redress of wrongs against the Shaolin Temple by Lin Qing, the Shaolin monks could publicly practice Kungfu. Thus, Shaolin Kungfu became the most influential school of martial arts on an even larger scale and greater proliferation than before because of the use of Shaolin Kungfu by the anti-Qing ecclesial organizations and groups.

Despite the decline of the Shaolin Temple in the Republic of China era, Shaolin monks still maintained the tradition of Kungfu practice. In the early years of the Republic of China era, the two most influential Kungfu masters at the Shaolin Temple were Heng Lin and Miao Xing. Heng Lin, who was proficient in all forms of Shaolin Kungfu, once served as the head and abbot of the Shaolin Temple, recruiting many Kungfu disciples. Because of serious banditry, Heng Lin was appointed as the head of the Shaolin Temple Guard Corps for his superb Kungfu. He ever led Shaolin monks and warriors to win many battles with bandits. Among all the Shaolin monks, Heng Lin's disciple Miao Xing was one of the best for his mastery in Shaolin boxing and weapon, acupoints hitting, unlock bones, catch and hold, qi gong, etc. After Miao Xing became the abbot of Shaolin Temple, he broke the old customs that the secret skills of Shaolin Temple were forbidden to hand down to the secular disciples, but impart these secret skills to many of them. In the 14th year of the Republic of China era (1925 CE), when

1928年，国民军北伐，建国豫军樊钟秀以少林寺为司令部，袭其后方，旋被国民军石友三部击败，后石友三攻入少林寺，一把大火将少林重要殿堂焚毁，寺内所存少林功夫资料被焚殆尽，寺内武僧四处逃散，少林寺走入历史低谷。在少林寺被焚后，鉴于少林功夫奄奄一息的状况，当家武僧贞绪与素典、德禅等谋划重振少林功夫，并召回著名还俗武僧寂勤俗子吴三林大师，训练少林武僧，培养了德根、行章等四十余名武僧，同时还在由少林寺创办的少林中学中开设少林功夫课，广传武术。海灯法师也于1946年应住持德意之请，出任少林寺武术教师。贞绪、德根等武僧的演武、传武活动维系了民国时期少林寺武术的传承。

民国时期少林功夫在社会上进一步广传，尤其是少林寺周围的登封、偃师等地，少林功夫已根植民间，当地人民成为少林功夫的重要传播者。如登封的少林寺村、塔沟村、南照沟村、磨沟村、骆驼院、雷村、阮村、文村、大金店等处村民，习少林功夫者甚多，形成少林功夫村。1937年抗日战争爆发后，豫西九县成立"少林武术救国会"，登封、偃师、临汝、巩县数县有上万人参加，可见少林功夫的普及程度。就全国来说，民国时演练少林功夫者及各种少林功夫组织更多，不可胜计。中央国术馆刚成立时所设的课程就分为少林门和武当门两大类。

民国时期，随着少林功夫在全国的广泛传播，经民间不断演练、融会、综合、整理，形成了许多门派。从形式和内容上看，融会了民间武艺而形成的少林功夫已与少林寺历史上传承的少林功夫有了很大的区别。寺院传统的"拳打一条线""拳打卧牛之地"等特点，除少林地区还保留着这些特征外，其他地方已经不是很明显了，有的差别还相当大。

民国时期，社会上出现了空前的少林功夫整理出版热潮。从1911年至1945年，出版的少林功夫书籍，据不完全统计有四十余种。如尊我斋主人的《少林拳术秘诀》、赵连和的《达摩剑》、吴志清的《少林正宗练步拳》、金恩忠的《少林七十二艺练法》、姜容樵的《少林棍法》、

Duan Zhishan visited the Shaolin Temple, he wrote in his book *Humble Notes from Touring the Shaolin Temple*, which described the Kungfu practice of Miao Xing and his disciples. "The sole performance of the boxing techniques began first. The performance, full of controlled power with his hands and eyes in complete and thorough order, brought the whole audience into silence during practice and thunderous applause after each segment. When two opponents came onto the stage, their performance was so fast with palms and feet hardly recognized, which attracted the audience's rapt attention and won prolonged applause. When it came to the single-broadsword performance, we only saw the white silk waving up and down, gleaming in cold light, which brought the whole audience into exciting enjoyment. Finally, Abbot Miao Xing practiced Zhenshan staff techniques with his proud disciples. The twin staffs spiraled with brisk drawing and launching, with whirring sound like an agile snake and a brisk dragon. The audience couldn't help cheering for the marvelous performance with big applause, feasting their eyes on the performance and having socks knocked off." This is the portrayal of Kungfu practice at the Shaolin Temple during the Republic of China era.

During the era of the Republic of China, Xu Shiyou and Qian Jun stood out above all the disciples of Shaolin Kungfu as Generals. From 1914 to 1921, Xu Shiyou was a handyman at the Shaolin Temple and practiced Kungfu for eight years. After he left the temple at the age of 16, he had already mastered many forms of profound Shaolin Kungfu. Qian Jun entered the Shaolin Temple as a handyman in 1916 at the age of 13, and practiced Kungfu for five years with a mastery of the unique technique Zhusha Palm (Zhusha Zhang). Later on, the two disciples made outstanding military merits with their superb Shaolin Kungfu on the battlefield. In 1955, Xu Shiyou and Qian Jun were separately awarded the rank of General and Lieutenant General.

In 1928 the Northern Expedition of the National Army started. The Henan Army led by the General Fan Zhongxiu, occupying the Shaolin Temple as the headquarter, attacked the rear of the National Army. But shortly, it was defeated by the National Army led by Shi Yousan, who invaded the Shaolin Temple and burnt the primary palaces into ashes. The disastrous fire burnt thousands of Kungfu books, and the Shaolin monks fled like birds. Thus, the Shaolin Temple came to the lowest ebb in its history. Afterwards, in view of the dying state of

图1–16 少林稀有兵器虎头双钩
Rare Shaolin Weapons-- Shaolin Hu Tou Shuang Gou (Shaolin Tiger Head Double Hook)

朱霞天的《少林护山子门罗汉拳》，等等。民国时期出版的少林功夫书籍，除《少林七十二艺练法》《少林护山子门罗汉拳》等个别为少林寺传统的武术外，其余基本上都是流入民间的少林功夫，并已经过大量的加工整理，含有大量民间武术的成分，有的甚至为附会。比如《少林寺拳术秘诀》，就是把民间南派武术附会成少林功夫。随着社会上对少林功夫附会的增加，考证少林功夫历史及真伪的书籍也在这时出现，比如唐豪的《少林武当考》、《少林拳秘诀考证》、徐震的《少林宗法图说考证》等为少林功夫的正本清源起到了巨大作用。

四、现代少林功夫

中华人民共和国成立后，少林功夫被列为宝贵的文化遗产而得到了国家和社会的重视，少林功夫的功能也发生了巨大变化，由过去的用于

Shaolin Kungfu, the monk masters Zhen Xu, Su Dian, De Chan and other monks endeavored to seek out ways to revive Shaolin Kungfu. Master Wu Sanlin, an eminent monk who had resumed secular life, was invited back to the temple in an effort to restore it to former glory. Wu Sanlin, a secular disciple of Ji Qin, coached more than 40 Shaolin monks, including De Gen and Xing Zhang. Meanwhile, Shaolin Kungfu courses were opened at the Shaolin middle schools founded by the Shaolin Temple to widely disseminate Kungfu. The Master Hai Deng was also invited as a Shaolin Kungfu coach by Abbot De Yi in 1946. These activities by Zhen Xu and De Gen, etc. promoted the development of Shaolin Kungfu in the period of the Republic of China.

From 1912 to 1949, Shaolin Kungfu widely spread throughout the country, especially in areas around the Shaolin Temple such as Dengfeng county and Yanshi county. Shaolin Kungfu was deeply rooted among the people, who were the important communicators of Shaolin Kungfu. The villagers of Dengfeng county, including Shaolin Temple Village, Tagou Village, Nanzhaogou Village, Mogou Village, Camel Yard, Lei Village, Ruan Village, Wen Village, Dajindian Village and so on, were keen on Shaolin Kungfu and thus formed Villages of Shaolin Kungfu. In 1937, when the War of Resistance against Japan (1937—1945) broke out, nine counties in the west of Henan province set up the "Shaolin Wushu Salvation Association", enrolling tens of thousands of folks from Dengfeng, Yanshi, Linru and Gongxian counties, which indicated the popularity of Shaolin Kungfu. For the whole country, Shaolin Kungfu practisers and various Shaolin Kungfu organizations were increasing during the Republic of China era. Only two categories of courses, the Shaolin school and the Wudang school, were opened when the National Wushu Academy was established.

Meanwhile, with the nationwide spread, many schools of Shaolin Kungfu took shape throughout the whole country by means of continuous Kungfu drills, integration and combination and systematization. Because the Shaolin Kungfu of these schools are combined with folk techniques in forms and contents, they are quite different from the traditional Kungfu. The traditional Kungfu techniques, such as the "boxing of the Crow-fly Movement" and also "to box in a place as small as where an ox lies down", can only be seen and appreciated in the Shaolin areas. It is rare to find these traditional Kungfu techniques in other places and

格斗、搏击为主，转变成了强身健体的体育运动，并得到了广泛的普及和推广。

现代少林功夫的传播以社会为主，少林寺所在地登封，在1954年就将少林功夫列为全县民间艺术会演的重要项目。1959年，少林功夫作为体育项目参加了在郑州举办的体育运动会。在少林功夫的推广方面，1958年登封成立了"登封县业余武术体校"，专修少林功夫，并特聘少林寺著名武僧释德根担任武术教练。其任教后，培养了一大批少林功夫人才。"文革"开始后，业余体校停办，1970年县体委重新组建"登封县业余武术体校"，并调还俗武僧杨聚才出任少林功夫教练，之后又请少林功夫世家出身的梁以荃出任教练。少林功夫业余体校自创办起所培养的少林功夫人才，为后来少林功夫的复兴起到了重要作用。

1978年改革开放以后，少林功夫迎来了前所未有的发展机遇。1979年，登封十五中在学校首先成立了少林功夫专业队。1980年，第一所少林功夫学校在十五中创立，并由著名少林拳师王朝凡、吕学礼、郑书基、王宗仁任教。武校创办后得到了社会各界的广泛支持。1980年11月

图1-17 少林武术学校学员习武
Shaolin Kungfu School Students Practicing Wushù

some are of great difference with the traditional ones.

Also during this period, Shaolin Kungfu stirred up an unprecedented craze of collecting and publishing Kungfu materials. From 1911 to 1945, according to incomplete statistics, there were more than 40 published books of Shaolin Kungfu, such as the Master Zunwo Lodge's *The Secret of Shaolin Fist Techniques*, Zhao Lianhe's *Dharma Sword*, Wu Zhiqing's *Shaolin Traditional Lianbu Quan*, Jin Enzhong's *Shaolin 72 Techniques*, Jiang Rongqiao's *Shaolin Cudgel Techniques*, Zhu Xiatian's *Shaolin Gateguard Luohan Quan*, etc. The books of Shaolin Kungfu published in the Republic of China era, except for the books such as the *Shaolin Seventy-two Arts Practice Method*, *Shaolin Gateguard Luohan Quan* and others which record traditional Shaolin Kungfu, were basically folk Shaolin Kungfu, which, after being processed and sorted out, were found to contain a large number of elements of folk Wushu. Some books were even not related to the authentic Shaolin Kungfu at all. For example, *The Secret of Shaolin Fist Techniques* made a strained interpretation claiming that the folk Wushu of the Southern school was the authentic Shaolin Kungfu. With more and more far-fetched interpretations of Shaolin Kungfu, books on authenticity and verification of historicity came into being, such as Tang Hao's *Shaolin Wudang Textual Criticism* and *Textual Criticism for the Secret of Shaolin Fist Techniques*, Xu Zhen's *Textual Criticism for Shaolin Patriarchal Clan System Diagram*, etc, which played a vital role in the clarification of Shaolin Kungfu.

IV. Modern Shaolin Kungfu

Since the founding of the People's Republic of China, Shaolin Kungfu, has attracted great attention from the whole country as a precious cultural heritage. The function of Shaolin Kungfu has also undergone immense changes from grappling and fighting into a form of physical exercise with wide popularity and promotion.

Chinese community has acted as a vehicle for the spread of modern Chinese Kungfu. Dengfeng, where the Shaolin Temple is located, has already listed Shaolin Kungfu as an important sort of folk art performances since 1954. In 1959, Shaolin Kungfu was introduced into the Zhengzhou Sports Meeting as a sporting event.

13日,《中国青年报》以"路在名山异水间"为题报道了登封十五中少林功夫学校成长和发展的经过,河南省体委、省教育厅、团省委于当年正式命名该校为"武术传统体育项目重点学校"。1981年,有二十多年历史的"登封县业余武术体校"更名为"登封县少林功夫体校",是年该校也被省体委、教育厅、团省委列为"武术传统体育项目重点学校"。1980年后,少林功夫之乡登封民间自发成立的少林寺塔沟武术学校、少林寺武术学校等相继创办,由此揭开了民间办武校的序幕。1979年,香港中原电影公司依据唐代"十三和尚救唐王"的故事,在少林寺实地拍摄电影《十三和尚救唐王》。由于初次拍摄的演员均为香港演员及河南省京剧团的演员,拍摄近一半时,由于缺乏真正的武术及戏剧化太严重而被推翻重拍,并将电影更名为《少林寺》。同时邀请全国著名武术运动员李连杰、于承惠、于海、刘怀良、胡坚强、孙建魁等出演。1980年剧组再次到少林寺实地拍摄,1981年年底完成。1982年,《少林寺》电影先后在香港、内地及世界公演之后,由于电影拍摄为真功夫、真武术,立即在世界上引起了史无前例的强烈反响,开创了功夫片前所

图1-18 《少林寺》电影海报
Film Posters of the *Shaolin Temple*

In order to promote Shaolin Kungfu, in 1958, Dengfeng county established the "Dengfeng Amateur Wushu Sports School" specializing in Shaolin Kungfu, and employed the famous monk Shi Degen of Shaolin Temple as a Kungfu coach. He later coached a large number of Shaolin Kungfu students with skillful techniques. During the Cultural Revolution, the amateur sports schools were not reopened until, in 1970, the county Sports Committee reorganized the "Dengfeng county Amateur Wushu Sports School". The school designated Yang Jucai, a secularized Shaolin monk, and Liang Yiquan, a Kungfu master born into a Shaolin Kungfu family, as Shaolin Kungfu coaches. The skillful trainees from the Amateur Wushu Sports Schools played a significant role in the boom of Shaolin Kungfu.

Since the Reform and Opening-up in 1978, Shaolin Kungfu has ushered in unprecedented opportunities for development. In 1979, Dengfeng No. Fifteen Middle School first organized a Shaolin Kungfu professional team, and in the following year, it founded the first Shaolin Kungfu School, recruiting the famous Shaolin boxing masters as coaches, such as Wang Zhaofan, Lv Xueli, Zheng Shuji and Wang Zongren. The founding of the first Shaolin Kungfu School received cordial support from the community. On November 13, 1980, *China Youth Daily* reported the growth and development of this Shaolin Kungfu school with the title Path to the Famous Mountains and Waters. The Henan Provincial Sports Committee, the Provincial Education Department and the Youth League Provincial Committee officially appointed the school as a Key School of Wushu Traditional Sports Project. In 1981, "Dengfeng Amateur Wushu Sports School", with a history of over 20 years, was renamed as "Dengfeng Shaolin Kungfu Sports School", which was also identified as a "Key School of Wushu Traditional Sports Project" by provincial authorities. Since 1980, Shaolin Temple Tagou Wushu School and Shaolin Temple Wushu School were successively established by folks of Dengfeng county, which is the hometown of Shaolin Kungfu. This revealed the prelude of a non-government mode for opening Kungfu schools. In 1979, Hong Kong Zhongyuan Film Company shot the film *Thirteen Monks Saving Emperor Taizong* at the Shaolin Temple based on the real story of Tang dynasty. However the film shot had to stop halfway as the Hong Kong actors and local actors from Henan Peking Opera Troupe had no genuine Kungfu skills. The film producer then decided to shoot the film once again at the Shaolin Temple in 1980

未有的上座率。电影《少林寺》的成功,在全国乃至世界引起了空前的少林功夫热,到少林寺习武者不可胜数,少林功夫学校也成了热门。到1985年,登封的各类武术学校已发展到53所之多,来自国内各地的学员超过4000人。由于武术热的影响,各种少林功夫学校良莠不齐,许多不具备办学条件,有的甚至是滥竽充数。不仅如此,社会上各种假冒少林武僧的现象也层出不穷,严重影响了少林功夫的健康发展。少林功夫发祥地的登封县政府,针对本县乱办武校的现状命体育部门对少林功夫学校进行整顿,取缔47所,保留6所。之后登封县又批准了几所少林功夫学校,到1999年,登封少林功夫学校经批准的已达34所(未经批准,拳师自行收徒传武的还有30多家),学员来自全国所有省、自治区、直辖市,人数在万人以上。登封少林功夫学校的创办和发展,培养了大批少林功夫人才。1982年以后登封少林功夫学校毕业的学员,回去后大量创办少林功夫学校。据不完全统计,这些学员在全国已开办了百余所少林功夫学校,其学员不可胜数。

作为少林功夫发祥地的少林寺,自改革开放以后也很重视少林功夫的继承和发展,少林寺武僧素喜、素云、永祥等广泛收徒传艺。1986年,少林寺成立了"少林拳法研究会",由行正任会长,永信、印松任副会长,开始对少林功夫进行系统挖掘和整理,并出版了多期《少林拳》杂志。之后,少林寺还成立了武僧团,并多次到国内外进行交流表演,传授少林功夫。

为使少林功夫走向世界,1986年国家投资700多万元,在少林寺西700米处,创建了占地面积2.9万平方米,面向国内外招生、培养少林功夫人才的大型现代化综合性的嵩山少林寺武术馆。该馆自1988年9月开馆以来,先后为三十多个国家的十余万名国外来宾表演少林功夫,同时还招收了来自美国、新加坡、澳大利亚、瑞典、比利时、法国、德国、瑞士、西班牙等二十几个国家和地区的两千多名武术爱好者到此习武练功。

with a new name—*Shaolin Temple*. Many national famous wushu athletes, such as Li Lianjie, Yu Chenghui, Yu Hai, Liu Huailiang, Hu Jianqiang, Sun Jiankui, were invited to star in the film. In 1982, the film was first released in Hong Kong, the mainland of China and other countries, which immediately aroused an unprecedented and striking positive reaction throughout the world and created a hitherto record of seat occupancy rate of Kungfu films. The success of *Shaolin Temple* caused a record-breaking craze of Shaolin Kungfu at home and abroad. Under such a situation, Shaolin Kungfu attracted countless Kungfu practisers to the Shaolin Temple, which made the Shaolin Kungfu schools much more popular than ever. By 1985, the total number of the Wushu school in Dengfeng county had grown to 53, with more than 4,000 students nationwide. Consequently, the Kungfu craze had also caused bad effects on the development of Shaolin Kungfu, such as the unqualified schools and the fake Shaolin monks. The government of Dengfeng county, as the birthplace of Shaolin Kungfu, then took measures to rectify those Shaolin Kungfu schools. Only 6 schools were approved for running and 47 schools were banned. By 1999, the number of Shaolin Kungfu Schools approved by the government of Dengfeng county reached 34 (there were also more than 30 schools without authorization) with over 10,000 students from different provinces, autonomous regions and municipalities of China. The Shaolin Kungfu schools in Dengfeng have cultivated a large number of Shaolin Kungfu practitioners with proficient Kungfu skills. Furthermore, there are over 100 Shaolin Kungfu schools all over the world set up by alumni from Dengfeng Kungfu schools with countless trainees.

As the birthplace of Shaolin Kungfu, the Shaolin Temple highlights the legacy and development of Shaolin Kungfu since the Reform and Opening-up. The Shaolin monks, Su Xi, Su Yun and Yong Xiang, widely enrolled new Kungfu disciples. In 1986, the Shaolin Temple set up the "Shaolin Boxing Techniques Research Association", with Xing Zheng as Director, Yong Xin and Yin Song as Associate Directors, to systematically excavate and collate Shaolin Kungfu materials. A number of *Shaolin Boxing* journals were published by the association. Moreover, the Shaolin Temple also set up the Kungfu Monks Troupe, which often exchanged and performed Shaolin Kungfu at home and abroad.

In 1986, with the goal of going global, the Chinese government invested over

图1-19 少林武术图书
Bibliography of Shaolin Kungfu

新中国成立后,少林功夫的挖掘整理工作从20世纪50年代就开始了,1958年和1959年,河南省体委和国家体委先后几次派人到少林寺和登封县收集、挖掘、整理少林功夫,河南人民出版社在1958年还出版了《简易少林拳》一书,作为少林功夫推广书目。1963年,登封县文教局为了更好地继承少林功夫这一宝贵的文化遗产,请释德根大师口述,王欣淼记录整理,编印了新中国成立后第一本比较完整而系统记述少林功夫历史、主要内容及特点的《少林功夫概要》一书,并由登封县体委内部印行,这是新中国成立后的一本极为重要的少林功夫资料。1980年后,少林功夫的挖掘整理工作进入高潮,登封县体委专门成立了少林功夫挖掘整理小组,对少林功夫进行了系统的收集整理。之后,各种有特色的少林功夫书籍相继出版,梁以荃的《嵩山少林拳法》、张国臣、吕江水、马青海等人的《少林武术》、蔡龙云的《少林寺拳棒阐宗》、河南省武协的《少林武术》、梁宝贵的《少林寺内外传真功》等较为优秀的少林功夫书籍相继出版。这期间出版的书,尤以1982年由电影《少林寺》上映而引发的少林功夫热后出版的少林书籍为最多。在少林功夫出

7 million yuan in building the large-scale, modern and comprehensive Wushu Hall of Songshan Shaolin, which is located 700 meters west of the Shaolin Temple, covering an area of 2.9 hectares. The Hall is dedicated to students' recruitment from all over the world and the cultivation of Kungfu talents. Since its open in September 1988, the Shaolin monks have performed Shaolin Kungfu there for more than 100,000 foreign visitors from over 30 countries. Meanwhile, more than 2,000 wushu fans from over 20 countries and regions have been recruited to learn Kungfu here, such as the United States, Singapore, Australia, Sweden, Belgium, France, Germany, Switzerland and Spain,

Since the founding of the People's Republic of China, excavation and data collating of Shaolin Kungfu materials commenced in the 1950s. In 1958 and 1959, the Henan Sports Commission and the State Sports Commission successively sent staff to collect and sort out the historical documents at the Shaolin Temple and Dengfeng county. In 1958, Henan People's Publishing House also published a book *Basic Shaolin Boxing* to promote Shaolin Kungfu. In 1963, in order to better carry forward the precious cultural heritage of Shaolin Kungfu, the Cultural and Educational Bureau of Dengfeng county compiled *Brief of Shaolin Kungfu* according to the dictation by Master Shi Degen and the record by Wang Xinmiao. Internally distributed by the Dengfeng county Sports Committee, this book systematically describes the history, main contents and characteristics of Shaolin Kungfu, which is the most important Shaolin Kungfu materials since the founding of People's Republic of China. It was just after 1980 that the data excavating and organizing of Shaolin Kungfu came to such a peak era. The Dengfeng county Sports Committee specially set up a working group for it. Ever since then, all varieties of featured books on Shaolin Kungfu successively sprung up, such as Liang Yiquan's *Songshan Shaolin Fist Techniques*, *Shaolin Wushu* by Zhang Guochen, Lv Jiangshui and Ma Qinghai, Cai Longyun's *Introduction to Fist and Cudgel of Shaolin Temple*, the Henan Provincial Martial Arts Association's *Shaolin Martial Arts*, Liang Baogui's *Genuine Shaolin Kungfu*, etc. During this period, the film *Shaolin Temple* in 1982 contributed much to the boom of Shaolin Kungfu and to the publishing of books on Shaolin Kungfu. Many valuable Shaolin Kungfu historical materials have been collected and sorted out. Generally, the Shaolin Kungfu publishing upsurge has played an extremely

版热潮中，许多珍贵的少林功夫得到挖掘和整理。总的来说，现代少林功夫出版热的形成，为继承少林功夫这一优秀的文化遗产，推动少林功夫向前迈进还是起到了极为重要的作用。

五、海外的少林功夫

少林功夫作为中国优秀的传统文化，不仅在国内广为流传，而且在国外也已生根、开花、结果。

少林功夫在国外的传播历史悠久。据少林寺碑刻记载：元至正年间（1347年），日僧劭元和尚长期居住在少林寺，他精通汉文，擅长书法，初任书记，后任首座僧，并得到少林武术之传授。于1379年回国，将少林武术带到日本，广为传播，深受日本人民的尊敬，称之"国魂"。

在劭元之前，相传大智和尚于元泰年间（1312年）由日本来少林寺，苦行修炼十三年之久，学到了少林拳和少林棍。1324年回国，广收门徒，传授武技，使中国少林功夫传入日本。

明代，少林功夫体系形成。明末万历时俗家弟子陈元赟于万历四十一年（1613年）入少林寺习武，万历四十七年（1619年），精于少林功夫的陈元赟东渡日本，1635年居于江户（今东京）国昌寺，开始传授少林功夫。他在日本有众多门徒，被日本武术界称为少林功夫祖师，至今日本爱宕山残存的石碑上还刻有："拳法之有传也，自投化人陈元赟而始。"

清朝之后，随着华人向东南亚一带的迁移，许多精于少林功夫者进入该地区传授武术，新加坡、马来西亚、印度尼西亚、泰国等国家成为少林功夫比较集中的流传地。进入20世纪30年代，日本人宗道臣来到中国，在东北拜北少林义和门拳师文太宗为师习练少林拳法。1936年，宗道臣前往中国学习少林功夫，1946年归国后于次年在日本香川县创立

important role in carrying forward the excellent cultural heritage of Shaolin Kungfu.

V. Overseas Shaolin Kungfu

Shaolin Kungfu, as an excellent traditional Chinese heritage, not only enjoys nationwide popularity but also took root, blossomed and came to fruition abroad.

Shaolin Kungfu has a long history of spreading abroad. The inscription on the Shaolin Temple's tablet records that during the years of the Zhizheng Emperor reign (1347 CE) of the Yuan dynasty, the Japanese monk Shaoyuan, who resided at the Shaolin Temple for a long time, was proficient in Chinese and calligraphy. After he was nominated as the general secretary and assistant to the Abbot of the Shaolin Temple successively, he learned Wushu skills with the Shaolin monks, In 1379 CE, Shaoyuan returned to Japan and widely spread Shaolin Kungfu. Due to the high respect of the Japanese people, Shaolin Kungfu was regarded as the "National Soul".

It is said that, prior to Shaoyuan, the monk Dazhi came to the Shaolin Temple from Japan in the year of the reign of the Yuantai Emperor (1312 CE) and mastered Shaolin boxing and staff techniques after 13 years of ascetic practice. In 1324 CE, he returned to Japan, widely recruiting disciples and teaching Shaolin Kungfu. This is how the Chinese Shaolin Kungfu was introduced into Japan.

During the Ming dynasty, the Shaolin Kungfu system had already been formed. In the 41st year of the Wanli Emperor reign (1613 CE) of the Ming dynasty, Chen Yuanyun, a secular disciple, practiced Kungfu at the Shaolin Temple. Six years later, as a Shaolin Kungfu master, he traveled overseas to Japan. In 1635 CE, residing in the Guochang Temple of Edo (now Tokyo), he commenced to coach Shaolin Kungfu. Coaching a large number of disciples in Japan, Chen was regarded as a Shaolin Kungfu Master in the wushu circle of Japan. Till now, there are still remains of inscriptions on the stone tablets at Mount Atago-yama in Japan, "It was Chen Yuanyun who started the boxing technique coaching here."

After the Qing dynasty, with the migration of Chinese to Southeast Asia,

了"日本少林寺拳法联盟"。该组织发展迅速，目前拥有少林拳士140多万，2700多个支部，在世界的10多个国家还设有分支机构。在1979年4月，宗道臣回到了阔别四十多年的祖庭少林寺，受到了僧众及少林功夫同行的热烈欢迎，两国拳师还在一起交流了少林功夫。在这次访问中，中日友协会长廖承志会见宗道臣时还亲笔题写："少林豪杰，横眉前领；中日友好，前程似锦。"1980年4月，宗道臣再次率团访问少林寺，少林寺特立"日本少林寺拳法开祖宗道臣大和尚归山纪念碑"一通于寺院。其文如下：

少林武术，缘起中州，名冠天下。日本国僧人宗道臣入嵩山禅林，修得少林拳，归国后开创日本少林寺拳法，饬兴三法，二十五系，六百数十技。使中国之传统文化得以在日本生根、开花、结果。法师在日本传授少林寺拳法，同时弘扬中日友好之要义，并率先实践。1979年4月，法师于下山四十余年后，重访此地，使日本百万少林拳士对中日友好事业怀抱之热忱空前高涨。为纪念法师重访嵩山，并祝中日友好前程如锦，特立此碑。1980年5月吉日，日本少林寺拳法联盟成立。

自1980年后，日本少林寺拳法联盟几乎每年都要派团到少林寺归山朝圣，交流少林功夫。该组织从1979年起出版有《少林拳法》报纸及月

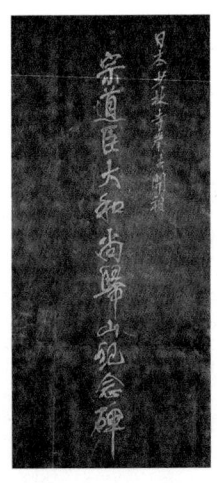

图1-20 宗道臣归山纪念碑
Zong Daochen's Return to the Mountain Monument

many Shaolin Kungfu masters began to teach wushu in various countries, mainly in Singapore, Malaysia, Indonesia and Thailand. In 1936, Zong Daochen came to Northeast of China to practice Shaolin boxing as a disciple of Wen Taizong, a boxing master of Northern Shaolin Yihemen School. Eleven years later, he went back to Japan and founded the "Japanese Shaolin Boxing Techniques League" in Xiangchuan county. Experiencing a fast growth, the League now has over 1.4 million Shaolin boxers, with more than 2,700 branches in Janpan and other over 10 countries all over the world. In April 1979, when Zong Daochen returned to the Shaolin Temple, where he had been apart for more than 40 years, he was warmly welcomed by the Shaolin monks and fellow Shaolin Kungfu practisers. The boxers from both countries had a deep exchange of Shaolin Kungfu. During the visit, Liao Chengzhi, the President of the China-Japan Friendship Association, wrote to him, "Shaolin boxers are brave pioneers for Sino-Japanese's friendship, to the bright future of which I sincerely wish." In April 1980, during the second visit of the League led by Zong Daochen, the League had a monument erected to commemorate their return to Shaolin Temple. It reads as follows:

Shaolin wushu, enjoying worldwide fame, originated in Zhongzhou. The Japanese Buddhist monk Zong Daochen mastered Shaolin boxing techniques at the Shaolin Temple and initiated Japanese boxing techniques of the Shaolin Temple in Japan. He summarized 3 principles, 25 systems and 600 techniques of Shaolin Kungfu, which thus allowed Chinese traditional culture to take root, blossom and come to fruition in Japan. He not only taught Shaolin Kungfu, but also made contributions to promote the Sino-Japanese friendship in practice. After more than forty years, he visited the Shaolin Temple again in April 1979, raising an unprecedented enthusiasm for Sino-Japanese friendship among millions of Japanese Shaolin boxers. This monument was to commemorate the master Zong's revisit to Mount Song, and convey the wish to the friendship of Sino-Japan. In May 1980, "Japanese Shaolin Temple Boxing Techniques League" was established.

Ever since the 1980s, the "Japanese Shaolin Temple Boxing Techniques League" has dispatched annual pilgrimage delegations to the Shaolin temple for exchange. From 1979, the League began to publish a newspaper called *Shaolin Boxing Techniques* and a monthly journal called *The Boxing Techniques of*

刊《少林寺拳法》。

自1978年改革开放后,特别是1982年电影《少林寺》在世界各国上映之后,世界上演习少林功夫形成空前高潮。据不完全统计,世界上不仅有四十多个国家数十万名武术爱好者到少林寺及少林寺武术馆观武,同时还有二十多个国家和地区的数千名武术爱好者先后到少林寺及少林寺武术馆、少林寺武术学校研修少林功夫。海外少林弟子也纷纷立碑于祖庭少林寺。其中,新加坡的少众山国术体育会于1984年在少林寺立了"归山朝圣"碑,美国的华林寺武术社于1984年在少林寺立了"归宗朝圣"碑,瑞士的少林太极拳协会于1988年在少林寺立了"归宗朝圣"碑,美国少林武艺中心于1992年在少林寺立了"少林朝圣"碑。在国外,据不完全统计,已有新加坡、日本、泰国、马来西亚、印度尼西亚、韩国、澳大利亚、美国、加拿大、墨西哥、巴西、法国、荷兰、保加利亚、西班牙、葡萄牙等上百个国家和地区成立了传授和学习少林功夫的组织。

在国外不断派团到少林寺学习少林功夫的同时,中国的少林功夫代表团到国外进行表演、交流和传艺。1980年,应日本少林寺拳法联盟

图1-21 新加坡"归山朝圣"碑
Monument of Pilgrimage to the Mountains in Singapore

Shaolin Temple.

Since China's Reform and Opening-up in 1978, and especially since the film *Shaolin Temple* was released in 1982, the world has witnessed an unprecedented upsurge in the spread of Shaolin Kungfu. According to estimates, there are hundreds of thousands of wushu fans from over 40 countries visiting the Shaolin Temple and the Shaolin Wushu Clubs to appreciate the Kungfu performance; besides, there are also thousands of wushu fans from more than 20 countries and regions coming for Shaolin Kungfu practice. Overseas Shaolin disciples worship the Shaolin Temple, the birthplace of Shaolin Kungfu, by setting up monument tablets in it. The monuments of "Pilgrimage to Shaolin Temple" were separately set up by Singapore"Shaozhong Shan National Martial Arts Sports Association" in 1984, by American "Hualin Temple Wushu Association" in 1984, by Swiss "Shaolin Taiji Boxing Association" in 1988, and by the American "Shaolin Wushu Center" in 1992. Furthermore, hundreds of countries and regions have established communities to teach and study Shaolin Kungfu, such as Singapore, Japan, Thailand, Malaysia, Indonesia, South Korea, Australia, the United States, Canada, Mexico, Brazil, France, the Netherlands, Bulgaria, Spain, Portugal, etc.

Along with frequent visits of foreign delegations to the Shaolin Temple for Kungfu study, Chinese Shaolin Kungfu delegations also went to the world for Kungfu performance, exchanges and teaching. In 1980, at the invitation of the "Japanese Shaolin Temple Boxing Techniques League", the Chinese Shaolin Kungfu delegations went to Japan for the first exchange in history, which unveiled the prelude of modern Shaolin Kungfu performance and dissemination. Since 1982, Shaolin Kungfu delegations dispatched by the Shaolin Temple and the Shaolin Kungfu Schools have made dozens of trips to foreign countries and regions, such as Japan, Singapore, Malaysia, Italy, the United States, Thailand, the Netherlands, Germany, France, Britain, Austria, Portugal, South Korea, Belgium, Hungary, Australia and New Zealand, for Shaolin Kungfu performances and skills exchange.

When the Shaolin Temple Wushu Hall first opened in September 1988, people from 8 countries and regions in the world participated in the "International Shaolin Wushu Performance Invitational Tournament". The tournament was successively held twice in 1989 and 1990, and each time Shaolin Kungfu fans from more than 10 countries and regions took part in the competition. Since

的邀请，少林功夫首次出国交流，揭开了现代少林功夫到国外表演、传武的序幕。1982年之后，由少林寺、少林功夫学校派遣的少林功夫团，先后几十次到日本、新加坡、马来西亚、意大利、美国、泰国、荷兰、德国、法国、英国、奥地利、葡萄牙，韩国、比利时、匈牙利、澳大利亚、新西兰等几十个国家和地区进行表演并传授少林功夫。

1988年9月，嵩山少林寺武术馆开馆时，世界上有8个国家和地区派人参加了在此举行的"国际少林武术表演邀请赛"。此项赛事在1989年、1990年又连续举行了两次，每次都有10余个国家和地区的少林武术爱好者参加比赛。从1991年起，规模更大的国际少林武术盛会"中国郑州国际少林武术节"在郑州和登封举行。首届有23个国家和地区的武术组织参加了比赛，至2018年已举办了12届。从第二届起，每届都有三十多个国家和地区的武术组织的近千名武术爱好者参加表演和比赛。国际少林武术节的举办，标志着少林功夫以更大的规模走向世界，并成为世界上重要的体育运动。

图1-22 国际少林武术节
International Shaolin Wushu Festival

1991, a big event called the "Zhengzhou International Shaolin Wushu Festival" has been held in Zhengzhou and Dengfeng. There were 23 national and regional wushu organizations from all over the world participating in the first session in 1991. By 2018, 12 sessions have been held. By the second session, there are nearly 1,000 participants from over 30 countries and regions. This Festival symbolizes that Shaolin Kungfu is striding into the world on a larger scale and has become a substantial sport game in the world.

第二章

博大精深的少林功夫

Chapter II

The Profound Shaolin Kungfu

少林功夫是一个博大精深的武术体系，内容极为丰富。按类别可分为徒手和器械两大类，器械又可分为长兵器、短兵器、软兵器等。按技法又可分为拳术、棍术、刀术、枪术、剑术、技击、气功等几十种。少林功夫最早出现的多是实战的格斗技法，从明代后期开始逐渐向套路化方向演化，并被固定下来，形成众多的套路。由此，体系完整的少林功夫体系形成。

一、拳术

拳是少林功夫的基础，也是少林功夫的基石。拳法的历史十分久远，它是在吸收中华传统武术的基础上而形成的。早在少林功夫的初创时期，寺僧首先开始练习的就是拳法。北魏时期僧稠禅师的"拳捷骁武"，就是少林武僧练习拳法的真实反映。另据少林寺留传的古代拳谱记载，少林寺出现最早的也是拳法。

当北魏时期达摩的禅宗在少林寺流传后，由于寺僧长期静坐，身体困倦，于是寺僧根据山林中鸟兽鱼虫的腾跃姿态，编出了十八个动作，供寺僧演练，后来这十八个动作被称为"罗汉十八手"。

从寺僧演练十八手开始，之后逐渐发展出了许多拳法。然而，早期的少林拳法是以实战搏击为主的，直到明代时仍是以搏击为主。明代金忠士看到寺僧的"角艺"、王士性看到的"拳棍搏击如飞"、袁宏道看到的"手搏"等都是少林拳以搏击为主的写照。

到明代后期，少林拳开始出现固定的套路，明末拳法大师玄机和尚留下来的《拳经》是少林拳法最早的套路。入清之后，由于寺僧不再参与战争，以搏击为主的拳法，开始以更大的规模向套路上转化，并形成众多的拳法套路，少林拳法练起来威武勇猛，变化多端，运行起来"拳打一条线"，手法上则曲而不曲，直而不直。少林拳还有"拳打卧牛之地"之说，就是说拳术运动区域很小，不受场地限制。少林拳法是少

Shaolin Kungfu is a profound martial art system with extremely rich content. It can be divided into two categories: bare hand forms and weapon forms. The weapon forms can be divided into long weapon forms, short weapon forms, and soft weapon forms, etc. According to the techniques or application, it can be divided into dozens of style of boxing, staff, broadsword, spear, sword, combat techniques, and qi gong, etc. The earliest styles of Shaolin Kungfu were actual combat techniques. From the late Ming dynasty, they gradually evolved toward the direction of the routine (tao lu), and were fixed and formed numerous routines (tao lu). Thus, the complete Shaolin Kungfu system was formed.

I. Fist and Palm Techniques

Fist and Palm Techniques are the foundation of Shaolin Kungfu and the cornerstone of Shaolin Kungfu. With the long history of the Fist and Palm Techniques, they are based on and have developed from the traditional Chinese Kungfu. As early as the beginning of Shaolin Kungfu, the monks in the temple began to practice the Fist and Palm techniques. In the Northern Wei dynasty, the "Master of Combat" of the Chan Master, Sengchou's swift and fierce combat techniques were the true examples of Shaolin Kungfu's Fist and Palm Techniques. Moreover, according to the ancient Fist and Palm Techniques books recorded by the the Shaolin Temple, the earliest combat techniques of the Shaolin Temple are also the Fist and Palm Techniques.

When the Chan of Bodhidharma in the Northern Wei dynasty was spread in the Shaolin Temple, the monks, squatting for a long time, were tired and sleepy, so the eighteen movements according to the prancing posture of the birds, beasts, fish, and insects in the forest were created by themselves for training themselves. The eighteen movements are called "Lohan 18 Forms (luo han shi ba shou)".

Since the practice of the Lohan 18 Forms of the monks, it gradually developed into a lot of other forms. However, the early Shaolin Fist and Palm Techniques were based on real combat until the Ming dynasty. In the Ming dynasty, the "monks' wrestling (jue yi)" recorded by Jin Zhongshi, the "Fast moving of the boxing and staffing" recorded by Wang Shixing, and the "boxing by hands (shou bo)" recorded by Yuan Hongdao, are all the portrayal on real combat

林功夫体系中内容最为广泛，套路最多的一种，少林拳法的套路总数有500多套，现在有名可查的也有近200套。

少林拳术套路的种类有：小洪拳、大洪拳、心意拳、梅花拳等。对练有三合拳、咬手六合拳、盖手六合拳等。

少林拳法的每个套路的功能各不相同，有练力的、有练气的、有练技击格斗的。而少林拳法的众多套路实际上就是拳法技艺的总结。

图2-1 吴南方拳师演练少林拳法
A Master of Kungfu, Wu Nanfang is Practicing Shaolin Boxing.

二、棍术

棍是少林功夫中最负盛名的兵器。棍术历史悠久，源远流长。相传，当年少林十三武僧助唐王打败王世充时，用的就是棍，故有"十三棍僧救唐王"之美名流传。在少林功夫形成的早期，最先使用的兵器就是棍，寺僧之所以先用棍，这里有两个方面的原因：其一，早期的少林

by which Shaolin Kungfu was based.

In the late Ming dynasty, the fixed routine of Shaolin Kungfu appeared. *The Boxing Scripture* created by the Grand Master Monk Xuanji in the late Ming dynasty is the earliest routine of Shaolin Kungfu. In the Qing dynasty, because the monks were no longer involved in the war, the Shaolin Kungfu which had based on combat mostly began to transform to routines, and formed a lot of Fist and Palm Techniques routines. The Shaolin Kungfu is powerful and varied, and it works in "boxing of the Crow-fly Movement", and the technique of "straightening in bending and bending in strengthening". The technique of Shaolin Kungfu also has the idea of "to box in a place as small as where an ox lies down", which means that the training area of Shaolin Kungfu can be very small and the training is not restricted by the training space. The Shaolin Fist and Palm Techniques are the most widely used in the Shaolin Kungfu system. The total numbers of routines in the Shaolin Fist and Palm Techniques are more than 500 sets, and among which there are nearly 200 sets of well-known cases even to now.

The categories of Shaolin Fist and Palm Techniques routines are:Xiao Hong Quan, Da Hong Quan, Xin Yi quan, Mei Hua Quan, etc. For Pair Training, there are San He Quan, Yao Shou Liu He Quan,Gai Shou Liu He Quan, etc.

Each of the routines of Shaolin Fist and Palm Techniques has different functions, such as power training, energy practicing, and combat training. The numerous routines of Shaolin Fist and Palm Techniques are actually a summary of the techniques and arts of combat.

II. Staff Techniques

The staff is the most famous weapon in Shaolin Kungfu and the Staff techniques have a long history. The legend goes that, when Shaolin Thirteen Kungfu monks helped the prince of the Tang dynasty defeat his enemy Wang Shichong, they used the staffs, and then the reputation of "Thirteen staff Monks rescuing the Prince of the Tang dynasty" was spread. In the early days of the formation of Shaolin Kungfu, the first weapon used was the staff. There are two reasons about why the monks in the temple first used staffs as the weapon. First, in the very beginning the Shaolin Temple is a Buddhist's holy place, and its

图2-2 少林棍术
Shaolin Cudgel Techniques

寺作为佛教圣地,寺僧以"慈悲为怀",所以寺僧是不可手持刀、枪、剑、戟这类铁制兵器,而棍则作为寺僧的生产和劳动工具,是经常使用的。其二,古时的少林寺地处深山密林,群兽出没,少林寺僧以棍作为防身的工具。由此,寺僧在手持棍棒作为劳动工具和防身的同时,把它当作一种兵器进行演练,逐渐形成套路。少林棍术套路体系形成比拳术套路体系形成还早。远在元末明初之时,少林棍就开始出现套路的倾向。相传,元末少林寺烧火和尚紧那罗持棍曾与红巾军进行作战。现在少林寺所传的风火棍、烧火棍等等据说都是紧那罗传下来的。到了明代中期,完整的棍法体系形成。僧兵也曾持棍参加了抗倭、保卫边关等众多战役,并由此而名扬天下,使其成为最出名的少林功夫。少林棍法在明代就以固定的形式传承下来,程冲斗的《少林棍法阐宗》是明代少林棍法的经典。清朝之后,寺僧习棍仍很盛行,创编的套路也很多,并一直成为少林功夫的旗帜。

少林棍术的套路种类有:少林棍、猿猴棍、眉齐棍、单盘龙棍等。

图2-3 少林六合棍对练
Pair Practicing Shaolin Liu He Gun

monks take leniency as the discipline. Therefore, they are not allowed to hold iron weapons such as broadswords, spears, swords, and halberds, and the staffs are often used as production and labor tools for the temple. Secondly, in ancient times, the the Shaolin Temple was located in the dense forests of the mountains, with beasts infested. The monks in the Shaolin Temple used staffs as tools for self-defense. Thus, while holding the staffs as labor tools and self-defense, the monks used it to practice as weapon and gradually formed into routines. The formation of the Shaolin staff routines system was earlier than the formation of the Fist and Palm Routine System. In the end of the Yuan dynasty and the beginning of the Ming dynasty, Shaolin staff forms began to appear as routines. According to the legend, at the end of the Yuan dynasty, the monk Kinnara, a fire monk at the Shaolin Temple, fought against the Red Turban Army with his staff. Now the Fenghuo Staff Techniques and Shaohuo Staff Techniques, etc. of the Shaolin Temple are said to have been handed down by Kinnara. By the middle of the Ming dynasty, a complete system of staff had been formed. Monk warriors also took part in numerous battles such as anti-Wokou and defending border crossings with staffs, which made staff techniques and Shaolin Kungfu famous all over the world. The

少林棍术的套路各具特色,是少林棍术的代表。少林棍术的套路也是棍法技艺的总结。

三、刀术

刀原本是民间武术和军事上最常使用的兵器。随着少林功夫的发展及僧兵参战的需要,刀也成了少林武僧经常使用的兵器之一。少林刀法体系形成于明代中后期。明代程绍的"金戈铁棍技层层"中就包含着刀法。在明末的时候,少林寺刀法广泛应用于战场。登封地方武装首领郜如城曾从少林寺练习拳棍和大刀,并运用大刀在战场上大显身手。清代之后少林刀术套路逐渐增多,技法也不断提高。少林刀法有"刀如猛虎"之说,就是刀练起来威武勇猛。少林刀多为缠头裹脑、翻转劈扫,再加上刺、撩、砍、拦、抛等构成完整的刀法系统。少林刀法出刀时气要运在两臂中,并随刀而出。少林单刀、双刀和大刀有"单刀看手、双

图2-4 少林单刀
Shaolin Single Broadsword

Shaolin staff techniques were passed down in the Ming dynasty in fixed forms and *Introduction to Shaolin Cudgel Technigues (Shaolin Gunfa Chanzong)* by Cheng Chongdou became the classic techniques. After the Qing dynasty, the monks kept practicing staff techniques more often, and many routines were created and compiled, which became the banner of Shaolin Kungfu.

The routines of Shaolin staff include: Shaolin Gun, Yuan Hou Gun, Mei Qi Gun, Dan Pan Long Gun, etc.

III. Broadsword Techniques

Originally, Broadsword was the most commonly used weapon in civil martial arts and military affairs. With the development of Shaolin Kungfu and the need for monk warriors to fight in the war, the broadsword has become one of the weapons frequently used by Shaolin Kungfu monks. Shaolin broadsword techniques system was formed in the mid-late Ming dynasty. In the Ming dynasty, Cheng Shao's proverb"The Golden Broadsword Techniques and the Iron Staff Techniques include many skills and techniques"gave a clue to its use. In the late Ming dynasty, the broadsword techniques of the Shaolin Temple were widely used in the battle. Gao Rucheng, the local armed chief in Dengfeng City, had practiced fist and palm techniques and staff techniques and broadsword techniques at the Shaolin Temple, and later on in battles his excellent broadsword techniques helped him very much in fighting. After the Qing dynasty, the routine of Shaolin broadsword techniques gradually increased and the techniques were constantly improved. Shaolin broadsword techniques have the saying of "tiger-like moving by broadsword", that is to say, broadsword practice has to be swift with power. Shaolin broadsword techniques mostly attack head and neck, with flipped and cleave and sweep skills, plus thrust, lift, chop, block, throw techniques and so on to form a complete broadsword techniques system. When practicing Shaolin broadsword techniques, the energy should be concentrated on both arms and come out with the movements. There is a common saying about"Single Broadsword depends on the hands techniques, Double Broadsword depends on the footwork, and Grand Broadsword depends on the body works".

The routines of Shaolin broadsword techniques include: Shaolin Dan Dao,

刀看走、大刀定手"之说。

少林刀术的套路有：少林单刀、少林双刀、梅花单刀、奋勇单刀等。

少林刀术的套路也是各具特色，是少林兵器的重要代表。

四、剑术

剑是少林武僧最常使用的兵器之一，也是少林十八般兵器中非常有代表性的一种。明代文翔凤在游少林寺时看到60名武僧练武时不仅有拳法而且有剑术。公鼎在少林寺观武后也看到的是"复有戈剑光陆离"的场面。这就是明代少林武僧练剑的写照。这也证明少林剑术形成于明代。进入清朝之后剑术套路不断增多。少林剑练起来优美豪放，故有"剑若游龙"之说。少林剑练起来行如飞燕，起落时如停风，刺剑时如钢钉，收剑时如花絮。

少林剑术的套路种类有：二堂剑、五堂剑、龙形剑、青龙剑等。

图2-5 少林剑术

Shaolin Sword Forms

Shaolin Shuang Dao, Mei Hua Dan Dao, Fen Yong Dan Dao,etc.

The routines of Shaolin broadsword techniques have their own characteristics and are important representative of Shaolin weapons.

IV. Sword Techniques

Sword is one of the most commonly used weapons of Shaolin Kungfu monks and one representative of the 18 classic weapons of Shaolin. In the Ming dynasty, Wen Xiangfeng visited the Shaolin Temple and saw 60 Kungfu monks practicing martial arts with not only Fist and Palm Techniques but also sword techniques. Gong Ding also saw the scene of "The fighting with dagger-axe and sword is shining" after watching Kungfu performance at the Shaolin Temple. This is the portrayal of Shaolin Kungfu monks practicing sword in the Ming dynasty. This also proves that Shaolin sword techniques were formed in the Ming dynasty. In the Qing dynasty, the number of sword techniques routines increased. It is beautiful and unrestrained to practice Shaolin sword, so it is called "Moving Shaolin sword is like a dragon swimming". Shaolin sword techniques are featured by "moving as the swallow flying, rising and falling as the wind stopping, stabbing as the steel nails drilling, and closing as the catkin falling".

The routines of Shaolin sword techniques include: Er Tang Jian, Wu Tang Jian, Long Xing Jian, Qing Long Jian,etc.

The routines of Shaolin sword techniques have their own characteristics and are important representative of Shaolin weapons.

V. Other Weapons

The weapons of Shaolin are said to be "the Eighteen Weapons". Besides staff (gun), broadsword (dao) and sword (jian), there are also trident (san gu cha), multifunction shovel (fang bian chan), single crutch (dan guai), nine-section whip (jiu jie bian), three-section stick (san jie gun) and so on. Shaolin weapons, although rarely used except staff, existed from the beginning of Shaolin Kungfu. The Eighteen Weapons system of Shaolin was also established in the Ming dynasty. Cheng Shao's proverb "The Golden Broadsword Techniques and the

少林剑术的套路也是各具特色，也是少林兵器的重要代表。

五、其他兵器

少林的器械有"十八般兵器"之说。除了棍、刀、剑外，还有三股叉、方便铲、单拐、九节鞭、三节棍等等。少林兵器械在少林功夫孕育时期已有，但使用不多，而运用较多的是棍。少林十八般兵器体系也是在明代确立的。程绍的"金戈铁棍技层层"、文翔凤看到少林寺60名武僧在演"掌搏者、剑者、鞭者、戟者……"这就是少林武僧练习十八般兵器的真实写照。自明末开始，少林武僧使用的兵器种类大大增加，远远超过了十八种，而且套路不断增多，这些兵器成为少林功夫体系的重要组成部分。

六、其他功法

少林功夫是一个博大精深的武术体系。除了拳法和器械外，少林武僧在长期的练功实践中，形成了众多独特的功法，如坐禅、童子功、轻功、硬功、梅花桩功等都是少林寺非常有名的功法。据记载，少林独特的功法形成的历史比较悠久。远在少林寺初创时期，著名武僧稠禅师能"跃至梁首"和"横踏壁行"，这显然就是在练少林轻功。唐代圆净的硬功也是非常过硬的，80岁时数名官兵"使巨力奋捶"都不能折其胫。明代是少林独特功法发展和确立的一个重要时期，这些功法寺僧不仅经常演练，而且形成套路。少林功法每个都有自己独特一面，并成为少林功夫精华之一。

Iron Staff Techniques include many skills and techniques" and "The combat of boxing, sword, whip and halberd and so on by 60 Kungfu monks in the Shaolin Temple" seen by Wen Xiangfeng are the real portrayal of Shaolin Kungfu monks practicing Eighteen Weapons. In the end of the Ming dynasty, the types of weapons used by Shaolin Kungfu monks have greatly increased, much more than eighteen types, and the number of routines has been increasing, and has become an important part of the Shaolin Kungfu system.

VI. Other Kungfu Forms

Shaolin Kungfu is a profound martial arts system. In addition to the Fist and Palm techniques and the weapons, the Shaolin Kungfu monks have formed many unique Kungfu techniques in the long-term practice and training, such as Zuo Chan Gong (Meditation), Tong Zi Gong, Qing Gong (Acrobatic Jumping Kungfu), Ying Gong (Hard Qi Gong), and Mei Hua Zhuang Gong (Plum Blossom Standing Kungfu). These are very famous Kungfu skills of the Shaolin Temple. According to historical records, those forms of Shaolin Kungfu were formed in a long history. Tracing back to the founding of the Shaolin Temple, the illustration of "leaping to the beam of rooftop and crossing walking on the wall" by the famous Chan Master Sengchou, is obviously the evidence of Shaolin qing gong. The Ying Gong (Hard Qi Gong) by the monk Yuanjing in the Tang dynasty was also very skillful. At the age of 80, when some warrior officers hit him by giant hammer, they could not even break his leg. The Ming dynasty is an important period for the development and establishment of the special Shaolin Kungfu forms. These special forms are not only often practiced by the monks, but also were formed as routines. Each form has its own unique characters and has become one of the essences of Shaolin Kungfu.

第三章

独具特色的少林功夫

Chapter III

The Unique Style of Shaolin Kungfu

少林功夫作为中国独具特色的武术流派，不仅是中国宝贵的非物质文化遗产，也是中华武林中一颗璀璨的明珠。少林功夫独具特色主要表现在这两个方面，一是功夫影响最为深远，二是技法特点最为鲜明。

一、影响深远的功夫

从中国的角度来说，少林功夫是中国功夫的一个流派，但它是历史最悠久、内容最广博、流传最广泛、影响最大的一派功夫，因而有"天下功夫出少林"之称。在国际上，少林功夫同样是声誉最为卓著、流传最为广泛的一派功夫，被认为是中国功夫的代名词。少林功夫之所以影响深远，主要有以下几个方面的因素。

1.少林功夫历史最为久远

中国功夫的种类非常繁多，除少林功夫外，还有武当拳、太极拳、峨眉拳、八卦掌、南拳、查拳等等。但就中国这众多的功夫历史源流而

图3-1 武僧少林寺山门前演武
Shaolin Warrior Monks Practicing Martial Arts in Front of the Gate of Shaolin Temple

Shaolin Kungfu, a unique style of Chinese Wushu schools, is not only one of the golden intangible cultural heritage of China, but also a brilliant pearl of Chinese Wushu. The unique style of Shaolin Kungfu lies in two features: the most profound influence and the most distinctive techniques.

Ⅰ. Kungfu with Profound Influence

In China, Shaolin Kungfu is one of the Chinese Kungfu schools with the longest history, the richest connotation, the widest spread and the greatest influence among all the schools. Thus there goes a saying that "All Kungfu under Heaven Originated from Shaolin". Internationally, Shaolin Kungfu is also known as the most famous and popular school of Kungfu, and has become the equivalent to Chinese Kungfu. The reason that it has such a profound influence lies in its following outstanding features.

1. The Longest History of Shaolin Kungfu

Besides Shaolin Kungfu, there are still a large variety of Kungfu styles, including Wudang Boxing, Taiji Boxing (tai ji quan), Emei Boxing (e mei quan), Eight Diagram Palm Boxing (ba gua zhang), Southern Style Boxing (nan quan), Cha Boxing (cha quan), etc. In terms of history and origination, Shaolin Kungfu emerged first and outlived other schools. Based on the existing historical records, the emergence of Shaolin Kungfu could be traced back to the 5th century (the Northern Wei dynasty). Along with the establishment of the Shaolin Temple in the Northern Wei dynasty, Shaolin Kungfu arose and flourished, which indicates that it has a history of more than 1,500 years. In the Sui and Tang dynasties, 13 Kungfu monks of the Shaolin Temple helped the authority of the Tang Empire defeat Wang Shichong, which made Shaolin Kungfu known across the country. The 14th and 15th century of the Ming dynasty witnessed the profound influence of Shaolin Kungfu on the formation of many schools of Kungfu. For instance, Wudang Boxing (wu dang quan), Mind-and-Will Boxing (xin yi quan), and even Taiji Boxing (tai ji quan) came into being based on extensively adopting practice method and skill strategies from Shaolin Kungfu. Therefore, the long history of Shaolin Kungfu is one of the chief reasons why it enjoys such enormous popularity throughout the world.

言,少林功夫是所有功夫流派中发源最早、历史最为久远的一派功夫。从现存的史料看,少林功夫的形成历史可以追溯到五世纪的中国北魏时期。远在北魏少林寺创建之初,少林功夫已开始孕育,并形成了雏形,也就是说少林功夫已有1500多年的历史。而隋唐时因少林寺十三武僧助唐王朝平定王世充,使少林功夫开始闻名于世。十四、十五世纪中国的明朝,是中国各种功夫门派的确立之时。而少林功夫是中国所有功夫门派中最先得到确立的一个功夫门派,而且对中国其他功夫门派的形成产生了深远的影响。比如武当拳、心意拳,甚至太极拳等都是在广泛吸收了少林功法的基础上而产生的。由此,少林功夫源远流长的历史是少林功夫闻名天下的一个重要原因。

2.少林功夫出自佛门

关于佛教,其教义是非常繁多的,但归纳起来,佛教的"不杀生""慈悲为怀"可以说是其最根本的主张和宗旨。由此,从佛教的角度来说,其与格斗搏击的杀生是格格不入的,或者说二者是截然相反的。然而,当佛教禅宗在中国形成之时,禅宗吸收了大量中国的传统文化,所以禅宗的世俗化最为明显,世俗的思想也对禅宗影响最为深远。因而,禅宗在形成之后,世俗所主张的"禁人为恶"思想也被禅宗所接受。受"禁人为恶"理论的影响,禅宗认为僧人所开的杀戒实际上是除恶扬善、匡扶正义。也就是说,禅宗是许可僧人以必要的武力手段来制止邪恶。由此,少林寺有了习武活动,其后少林寺武僧也不断演武参战,并且得到了历代帝王和社会的充分肯定和赞誉。不杀生的佛门产生武术其本身就是一件极为罕见的现象,也是最为吸引人们眼球的事,自然也倍受世人的关注并成为一个热点,进而推动少林功夫成为最有影响力的一派功夫。

3.少林功夫因僧兵参战而扬威

佛教主张"不杀生",自然也是反对战争的。对于战争而言,应该是世俗之间的争斗,与佛门并无关系。但是,从少林功夫的发展历程

2. Deeply rooted in Buddhism

In terms of Buddhism, there are numbers of doctrines. Generally, the complicated principles of Buddhism could be boiled down to ahimsa and leniency as its fundamental principle and advocacy. Therefore, they are religiously against or opposite to killing or fighting. Chan Buddhism, however, assimilated a lot of Chinese traditional culture when it came into being and was largely secularized. As a result, these secular thoughts exerted a profound influence on Chan itself. Thus, the secular proposition of prohibiting evil-doings was accepted by Chan. With the influence of such notions, Chan believes that monks can divert from ahimsa for the purpose of protecting virtues, to eliminate vices and uphold justice. In other words, Chan allows monks to stop evildoings by force. Kungfu was developed in the Shaolin Temple from this purpose. Kungfu monks frequently involved themselves in wars and were awarded and commended by emperors of successive dynasties and the community. The development of Kungfu in Buddhism of ahimsa is unprecedented. This attracted attention, gained recognition, and thus promoted Shaolin Kungfu to the most influential school of Kungfu.

3. Renowned for Using by the Warrior Monks in Wars

Buddhism advocates ahimsa, and in turn it's anti-war. War consists in fights in the secular world, and has nothing to do with Buddhism. Nevertheless, the fame of Shaolin Kungfu has been closely related with its war involvement. At the end of the Sui dynasty and the beginning of the Tang dynasty, discontented with Wang Shichong, the prince of Zheng, who seized the farmland of the Shaolin Temple, the Kungfu monks assisted the Tang dynasty to suppress Wang Shichong. The monks' loyal deeds were appreciated by the authority of the Tang dynasty. Not only were the monks rewarded, but also about 40-qing (266 hectares) land was granted to the Shaolin Temple. From then on, both Kungfu monks and Kungfu of the Shaolin Temple became known across the country, and the temple gained the fame of the Best-known Buddhist Temple in the World. Afterwards, Shaolin Kungfu monks were engaged in anti-Jurchen war at the end of the Northern Song dynasty and helped crack down the Red Turban Army at the end of the Yuan dynasty. During the Ming dynasty, the Kungfu monks served almost all the wars in border defense, the suppression of peasant uprising, and fighting against Wokou. Their outstanding performances promoted the spread and

上看，此功夫闻名于世与参与战争有着密切的关系。隋末唐初，少林寺僧因不满郑国王世充抢占其耕地，于是派僧兵助唐王朝平定王世充。战后，李唐王朝对少林寺僧的义举大加封赏，并赐地四十顷，参战僧也得到了封赏。从此，少林僧兵名扬天下，少林功夫也传扬于四方，少林寺由此也博得"天下第一名刹"之称。其后，少林僧兵又参加了当时的北宋末的抗金战争、元末与红巾军的战争。到了明朝，少林僧兵几乎参加了所有的战争，保卫边关、镇压农民起义、抗击倭寇等都留下了少林僧兵英武的身影。少林僧兵在战场上的大显神威，极大促进了少林功夫的传播，也极大扬名了少林功夫。由此，社会上便有了"少林寺名震人寰，不是禅宗是武拳"之说。此足见少林功夫因参战而闻名的事实。

4.少林功夫博大精深

少林功夫作为中国的一个功夫流派，在其漫长的发展过程中，率先成为内容广博、种类繁多、技法精湛的一派功夫。少林功夫从北魏开始发端之后，经唐宋金元几个朝代的发展，到了明朝时，少林功夫最先形成了完备的武术体系。在明朝时，少林功夫不仅包含有拳法，而且十八般兵器也是样样俱全。不仅如此，少林功夫在明朝时其技法也达到了空前的水准。拳术的出神入化，枪、刀、剑、戟的威武勇猛，在历次僧兵的参战之中得到了验证。由于明代少林拳法的精妙，故当时的人有了"今人谈武艺，天下其不让少林"之说。另外，少林功夫的套路也是各个功夫流派中最多的。据不完全统计，仅少林寺拳法流传下来的套路就有500余套。可以说少林功夫是一个内容广博的功夫库，几乎涵盖了中国功夫的方方面面。由于少林功夫内容广泛、技法精湛，这为人们从不同角度、不同方面学习和传播少林功夫起到了重要的作用，为少林功夫的扬名起到了重要推动作用。

5.少林功夫流传最广

少林功夫不仅是中国诞生时间最长、历史最久的一种功夫，而且流传也最为广泛的。早在中国的明朝时，由于少林僧兵的四方参战，少林

popularity of Shaolin Kungfu. Then came the saying that "The Shaolin Temple is renowned throughout the world for its Kungfu rather than Chan Buddhism." All these historical facts illustrated the link between the popularity of Shaolin Kungfu and its war involvement.

4. Profound connotations

Shaolin Kungfu was the first school which evolved comprehensive, multifaceted, and skillful movements during its long-period development. Starting from the Northern Wei dynasty, and further developed in the dynasties of the Tang, Song, Jin and Yuan, Shaolin Kungfu was the first to mature into a complete Kungfu system during the Ming dynasty. By this time, Shaolin Kungfu had established a complete system that included not only all types of boxing, but also the methods of the Eighteen Weapons. In addition, the skills of Shaolin Kungfu developed to an unprecedented level. The miracle of boxing and the power of such weapons as spear, saber, sword, and halberd were tested in the performance of Kungfu monks in the wars during the Ming dynasty. Because of its subtlety in that period, Shaolin Kungfu earned the reputation that *Shaolin goes to the first whenever Kungfu is mentioned*. Moreover, the number of routine types in Shaolin Kungfu also ranked the first place. The available documentation indicates that there are over 500 routines of boxing handed down in Shaolin Kungfu. So, we can see that Shaolin Kungfu is a treasure house that contains every aspect of Chinese Kungfu. Its comprehensive contents and excellent skills helped practitioners in learning from different angles and aspects, which promoted its spread and popularity.

5. The widest spread

Shaolin Kungfu is not only the one that emerged first with the longest history, but also the most wide-spreading one. During the Ming dynasty, with the involvement of martial monks in wars, Shaolin Kungfu in great measure was spread nationally. At the same time, people competed to learn Shaolin Kunfu because of its unparallel popularity. During the Ming dynasty people went to the Shaolin Temple to learn Kungfu and spread it all over the country. And in the Qing dynasty, the high-profile and superb skills of Shaolin Kungfu contributed to its large-scale expansion into the society. From the Kangxi Period in the Qing dynasty people began saying that "All Kungfu under Heaven Originated from

功夫就开始大规模的传向神州。同时，少林功夫无与伦比的知名度，也使少林功夫成为人们争相学习的一种功夫。明朝时，就不断有世俗之人入少林寺习武，并促使少林功夫传向四方。进入清朝之后，少林功夫极高的知名度和高超的技艺，使其以更大的规模开始向社会上传播，至迟在清朝康熙年间就产生了"天下功夫出少林"之说。少林功夫在国际上的传播同样是规模最大，而且也是最早的。因而，国际上以少林功夫为中国功夫的代名词，这也反映了少林功夫在国际上的流传也是极为广泛的。

二、特点鲜明的功夫

少林功夫作为一种武术流派，有其独特的风格和特点。长期以来，少林功夫在广泛传入社会之后，由于与民间武术的融合，形成了众多的少林功夫门派，比如以北方为主要流传地的称北派少林功夫，以南方为主要流传地的称南派少林功夫。各派少林功夫的特点也有所不同。少林寺所传的武术，在其发展过程中特点也不断地演化，明代程冲斗的《少林棍法阐宗》及清代张孔昭的《拳经》中所载的少林棍法与拳术的诀语，与今天诀语已有变化，尤其是当前套路化的少林功夫与原先以格斗为主的少林功夫差异更大。现根据流传于少林寺一带传统的少林功夫，将其特点综述如下。

1.短而精

少林功夫套路以短小精悍而著称。拳术套路大部分在三十六个动作以内。套路短，组合招式严密紧凑。整个套路练习所用时间短，目的是练习者在练功中能集中全身之能量，一气呵成，利于每个招式功夫的增长（包括手、眼、身法、步、精神、气、力、功等）。避免套路太长而使其因体力不足勉强敷衍的缺陷。

2.拳打一条线

少林功夫套路的起、落、进、退、闪、展、腾、挪等尽在一条线上

图3-2 武校学员演武
Trainees of Shaolin Kungfu School Practicing Martial Arts

Shaolin". Shaolin Kungfu was also the first to be introduced abroad and became the largest scope of Kungfu. Therefore, Shaolin Kungfu is also known as the synonym of Chinese Kungfu, which also evidences its international reputation.

II. Kungfu with Distinctive Features

As one of many Kungfu schools, Shaolin Kungfu has its unique style and features. Over a long period of time, Shaolin Kungfu has infiltrated into society, integrated with the folk martial arts, and as a result formed various sects of Shaolin Kungfu, including Northern Shaolin Kungfu practiced in Northern China and Southern Shaolin Kungfu practiced in Southern China. Each sect has its different features. These features of Shaolin Kungfu also improved in development. The formula in rhyme （Jue Yu） in *Introduction to Shaolin Cudgel Technigues (Shaolin Gunfa Chanzong)* by Cheng Chongdou in the Ming dynasty and Fundamentals of *Shaolin Boxing* by Zhang Kongzhao in the Qing dynasty is different from those of the present. The current routines of Shaolin Kungfu, in particular, differ greatly from those in the past that focused on combats. Based on the sects of Shaolin Kungfu around the Shaolin Temple, its features are summarized as follows:

1. Succinct but Concentrated Routines

The routine of Shaolin Kungfu is known for its succinctness and concentration. Most of the routines consist of no more than 36 movements, which are coherent and impenetrable. It takes very short time to complete each

运动。"死学活用",练功时把自己身形固定在一条线上,用时放开,犹如出笼之虎。另外,直线的运动,极有利于进退速度(战时速度为第一要素)。

3.步法随便

少林功夫为实战之需要,步法要求"随便"。《释家捶把十要诀》之"拳法妙术在移闪,动静呼吸一气连,来来去去须随便,惟在接取玄妙间"。第三句的"来来去去须随便"之意,为步法定下了基调。第四句的"接取"为守攻之意。如国家武术比赛规定的弓步为自己脚长度的五倍,马步为三倍,其身势必然犯"老"。因势"老"而使其身形进退困难,不能自如,另外也不利于下盘的稳固。少林拳最重要的特点是"拳打卧牛之地"。练功不分场地大小,对步法要求随便,大小以自己能发挥最大能量为宜,以利于"接取"为目的。

4.滚出滚入

分两层含义:一为身形的滚出滚入,二为手形的滚出滚入。身形的滚出滚入,起横落顺。进退之起势以横身(正身)为先,横进横退,利于进退速度。落势以顺身(侧身)为后。起势展其身形,落势闭其门户,顺身落势,对"敌人"来说,攻击目标为"线"形而非"面"形,攻击面积缩小,有利于防守。身形的起横落顺,形成了拧身滚动的滚出滚入运动身形的滚动,使其身形如泥鳅般的光滑,让对方难以捕捉。其次为手形的滚出滚入,少林拳的出拳特点为出阴(阴拳)回阳(阳拳),这样就形成了手法的滚出滚入。一方面增加杀伤力,另一方面有利于手臂的自我保护。在出招攻击时,手形滚出滚入,使其拳掌如钻,如弹头的旋拧,而非穿钉之力,谓之巧力。同时在实战中,"沾"法尤为重要。若我被敌所沾,其身势已死,拳、掌无效。手法的滚动圆滑,其形不定,又使对方难以截沾,增加我拳掌攻击的力度。《释家捶把十要诀》"第一要诀·明三节"云:"身以滚而起,手以滚而出,身进脚手随,三节身可齐"。因此可见"滚出滚入"在少林功夫中的重要性,

routine, thus enabling the practitioner to concentrate all his energy to complete in one attempt. This helps to improve each movement including hands, eyes, body techniques, foot work, spirit, Qi, power and Gong etc. Short and succinct routines consume less energy and help avoid the physical exhaustion than those tiresome long and complicated routines.

2. "Crow-fly Movement" Movements

One moves as crow flies when practicing each form of Shaolin Kungfu, whether rising, falling, advancing, retreating, swaying, stretching, jumping, or dodging. Being accurate in learning and flexible in application contributes to keeping movements in a straight line when practicing; quick and fierce as a tiger when attacking. In addition, this helps to speed up advancing and retreating (speed is of supreme importance in a fight).

3. Flexible Footwork

Shaolin Kungfu grew out of combat that requires free footwork. It is recorded in *The Ten Principles of Buddhist Boxing* that "The essence of boxing lies in the moving of body and footwork. Breath rhythms are supposed to be coordinating in both quiescence and moving. Free footwork is required in both attacking and retreating. And the key rests with the succession". The third sentence set the tone for the flexibility of footwork, and the word succession in the last sentence refers to transition between attack and defense. For instance, it is standardized in the national Kungfu competitions that the bow stance is fixed with the feet spaced five times length of one's own foot, and horse-riding stance fixed three times. However, too wide of a stance leads to difficulties and disjointedness for both advancing and retreating, and unsteadiness of the stance. One of the chief features of Shaolin Kungfu is to box in a place as small as where an ox lies down. So, the practice of Kungfu has fewer requirements to space, but expects flexible footwork in order to exert ultimate power, which serves transition.

4. Rolling Attack and Withdrawal

Rolling attack and withdrawal consists of two implications that cover both body and hand forms. Rolling attack and withdrawal of body requires frontal rising and sideways falling. Frontal rising adopted in both advancing and retreating for speediness while ends with sideways falling. Stretching body

图3-3 少林拳法
Shaolin Boxing

并形成了少林拳这一显著特点。

5.神形一体

少林古德云：练功时无敌如有敌，遇敌时有敌如无敌。要求学习少林功夫者必须"神形一体"。少林功夫的每一招每一式，都包含极其深奥的战略战术思想。战略上不可重敌亦不可轻敌，战术上虚实并用、指上指下、照前顾后、看左打右、对方体形高于我则攻其中下盘、对方体形低于我则攻其中上盘、避实就虚、借对方之势之力四两拨千斤等。每个招式都有其独到用法。在练功中，每一招每一式都以假想敌人进行攻防。于一招一式中，意、气、力同时到达，方可习之长功。

6.曲而不曲，直而不直

少林功夫的招法运用上，有"老嫩"之分。老者指招式太过，嫩者指招式不及。招式的"老嫩"影响出招发力。因此，少林拳法为避免老嫩之弊，采用非曲非直之法。发一拳一掌，其力量最大之瞬间在非曲非直之间。若将拳掌发"老"（伸直），成了强弩之末，只剩余力罢了；

in rising and crouching in falling minimize the attacked area of the enemy to a line in contrast to a plane, which contributes to defense. Frontal arising and sideways falling form rolling attack and withdrawal, which help one escape the enemy's capture like a slippery eel. Rolling attack and withdrawal of hand form requires palm of the fist turning downward (Yin Quan) in punching and upward (Yang Quan) in drawing back. On one hand, it enhances the lethality; on the other hand, it provides self-protection of the arm. Rolling attack of hand form helps the fist or palm punch drilling and twisting like a bullet instead of pegging, which is called knack force. In the practical combat, the application of sticky force skill is very important. The body movement losses flexibility and the palm or fist fails in attack if the enemy's sticky force works. To keep hand forms rolling and unpredictable increases attacking force and avoids enemy's interruption and sticky force. In Understanding of three-joints (Ming Sanjie), the first chapter of *The Ten Principles of Buddhist Boxing*, it says that "Keep rolling of body in rising and hand in punching. Hands and feet keep pace with body moving. Then the three-joints would be in place". It shows the importance of rolling attack and withdrawal as one of the distinctive features of Shaolin boxing.

5.Integration of Movements and Spirit

One eminent monk of the Shaolin Temple once said that one should take daily practice as serious as combats, and serious combats as easy as daily practice. It requires the integration of movements and intention in learning Shaolin Kungfu. Each movement of Shaolin Kungfu contains complicated strategies and tactics. Strategically, it is desirable to neither overestimate nor underestimate the enemy. Tactically, both feint and real movements should be applied through attacking up and down, defending front and back; diversionary tactics applied through making a feint left glance but attack right; and attacking the opponent's weaknesses and avoiding his strongholds applied through low blow to tall opponents and up to short ones; and skillful deflection through force borrowed from the opponent. Each movement functions for a distinct purpose. The practitioner is supposed to predict enemy's reaction to each of his movement in practice. Only through practice of integrating the explosion of mind, qi, and power simultaneously, one may make progress.

图3-4 少林传统拳法
Traditional Shaolin Boxing

若将拳掌发"嫩"（曲臂），乃发力之初,意、气、力,刚生之时，其力大部分仍被困在丹田内。嫩者不能近敌，老者则失重心，易被对方顺势制之。

7.起望高、束身而起，落望低、展身而落

起者招式之起势也，有"进"之意向；落者招式之落势也，有"退"之意向。起落进退为拳法中不可分割之一部分，分开则不可言不可用。有两层含义：一、起望高：指在进攻敌人的起势中，望敌之眼睛，以目注目，看敌之上盘。因为敌之上盘之手臂比下盘之腿脚灵活，故为我防守之重点部位。眼是心灵之窗，敌人的行动意向首先在眼神上表现出来。古拳谱云："手似流星眼似电，手为元帅眼为先行。"手未到眼先到，在敌之眼神里观察出敌之动向，进而选择我所"取"部位及选用招法。所以在起势时应望高，束身而进。束身指缩我之身形，闭我之门户。缩我之身形使之目标缩小，利于近敌，闭我之门户利于防守。二、落望低：落者落势，身形之落已近敌身，在起势近招架敌人上盘的

6.Bending in Straightening and Straightening in Bending

The improper application of Shaolin Kungfu movements can be compared to over-maturity or immaturity. Over-maturatity refers to the excess and immaturity the deficiency of movement application, which affect the generation of force. Therefore, the skill of bending in straightening and straightening in bending in Shaolin Kungfu is advocated to avoid excess or deficiency. This skill guarantees the optimal power generation. Over-maturity (full extension) leads to the power being exhausted like an arrow at the end of its flight. And immaturity (over bending) results in the besiegement of the mind, qi, and power in abdomen (Dantian) of one's body. Committing immaturity, one fails to access the enemy, while committing over-maturity, he losses balance and the opponent will take this advantage to dominate the combat.

7.Contract When Rising and Stretch When Falling

Practitioners are supposed to look up in preparation and contract body before rising, and look down in approaching and stretch body when falling. Rising refers to the start of the movement for advancing, while falling implies withdrawal after attack. Rising and falling are inseparable from advancing and retreating in boxing. If so, there is no way to interpret and apply them separately. It falls into two meanings. Firstly, looking up refers to focusing on the opponent's eyes in the rising for attack. One needs to observe the opponent's upper body through gazing at his eyes, because the arms and hands of the opponent move faster than his legs and feet, which are the foremost parts one needs to defend against. Eyes are the windows of the mind and one may predict the opponent's potential movement through his eye-sight. The ancient record of boxing says that hands are the marshal of the body and are supposed to move as fast as shooting stars, while eyes are spearheading as quickly as lightening. So before one moves his hands, he should watch the eyes of his opponent to predict the opponent's potential movement, so as to decide the opponent's target area of attack and to apply proper reaction. That's the reason for looking up in preparation and contracting body before rising. And contracting one's body is to reduce his body from exposure to attack, which contributes to defense. Secondly, looking down implies paying attention to opponent's legs and feet in the falling that approaches his opponent, in the same time of defending himself from attacking by the opponent's hands.

图3-5 少林拳术
Shaolin Boxing Techniques

同时,望敌之下盘足腿部。敌之形动必先动其足腿。足腿的运动方向也就是敌人身势变化方向,注其足腿,封其下盘,使敌不能近我,还有刨其根节之意图。展身而落,展其身形利于力量的发挥。

8.禅拳合一

修习少林功夫者有三层境界,初步境界为习其外表,练其外形,对自己外部形体的锻炼。中层境界为"神拳合一",化有形为无形,变有法于无法,无法可依,无招可循,制敌于无形中。古拳谱云:"打人不见形,见形不为能。"最高境界用心法指导一切,所斗之术为"心"法之争,非"形"法之战。由武入禅,由定生慧。此慧已是禅武合一的般若慧,非是常人之智慧。少林功夫是在禅定状态下用般若慧观照下的人体运动方式。少林功夫孕育在佛教圣地禅宗祖庭,在少林功夫中到处洋溢着佛光禅影,"禅拳合一"为少林寺功夫独具的重要特点。

9.以防为主

少林功夫产生在佛教圣地少林寺,是用来护寺、防身、健体之用。

The opponent's legs and feet move prior to his body moving, and their movements direct his change of body forms. The attention should be paid to the opponent's legs and feet so as to restrain his lower body movement to keep the opponent from approaching, and allow attacking his lower part to break his balance. To stretch one's body when falling contributes to force generation.

8. Unity of Chan and Quan (Boxing)

The practice of Shaolin Kungfu falls into three stages. In the primary stage, one does exercise for physical fitness. In the intermediate stage, one integrates spirit with boxing and conforms to no forms, or principles, which render the enemy unable to estimate and predict, so as to defeat him before he perceives. The ancient record of boxing says that defeat enemy before he perceives, or your Kungfu is inferior. In the ultimate stage fighting is guided with citta (Xinfa), which is far superior to combat skills. This is the stage one achieves the wisdom of Chan through Kungfu , and gains prajna (Hui) from jana (Ding). Prajna, integrating both Chan and Kungfu , is the ultimate wisdom superior to the one of common sense. Shaolin Kungfu is a physical exercise with schauen (Guanzhao) in the state of prajna. Shaolin Kungfu born in the ancestral court of Chan Buddhism, has absorbed the quintessence of Chan and Buddhism. The unification of Chan and boxing is one of its unique features.

9. Defense Outweighs Attack

Shaolin Kungfu, born in the Buddhist shrine, the Shaolin Temple, was for self-defense, self-toning and temple safeguarding. Same as other temples, it is Shaolin monks' primary obligations to practice Chan and Buddhism, and violence is their last resort. As far as mara (Mo) is concerned, force is also the last among thousands of methods to subdue and tame it. Such Buddhist disciplines place defense as the priority in Shaolin Kungfu. Its offensive movements also contain defensive ones for self-protection in combat. The difference between novices and masters is that novices tend to apply more attacks and are more liable to be beaten for their deficiency of defense, which lead to lose-lose situation. Speed, rather than skill, dominates in combat. However, masters tend to defeat opponents free of injury, which is especially true in Shaolin Kungfu.

少林寺亦与其他寺院无异，参禅学佛为僧人之本分，怖魔者万不得已而为之。对于"魔"，佛门用八万四千法门渡之，只有在万不得已的情况下，才用武力威慑，使之诚服而渡之。佛教戒律决定了少林功夫的招式结构以守、防为主。少林功夫的招式，即使进攻动作结构里面，也包含了许多防守招式。在实用中，这些动作亦最大限度地起了保护自己的作用。会功夫与不会功夫表现在：不会功夫的人是死打硬拼，攻多防少，完全把自己之体型暴露给敌人，这样两方交战之结果只能是两败俱伤，胜负在其速度的较量，而非技巧的较量。而会功夫的人是在使自己不受敌人伤害的情况下出手制敌，这一点在少林功夫中体现得更突出。

10.攻防合一

在少林功夫的招式结构上，不存在完全的进攻或完全的防守招式，攻中有守，守中有攻，只不过是攻防成分比例变化。在进攻动作中防守成分少些，在防守动作中进攻成分少些。

11.小手花众多

经过一千五百多年来少林寺历代僧人的研练，少林功夫结构紧凑严密，几乎每个动作中都有小手花。小手花所起作用相当大，截、沾、刁、扣、封、搅、扳、收等招法，这些小手花可称为少林功夫的精髓，使少林功夫达到滴水不漏的程度，让对方无空可钻。

12.朴实无华

少林寺历代僧人之生活方式是非常朴素的，不讲究吃穿，不着华丽外衣。这种朴素的生活方式和志趣也融进了少林功夫里面。少林功夫的作用在于防身、护寺、健身、入禅，所以它的招式结构完全在实用的基础上。每招每式甚至小手花，甚至意念，都为上述四项服务，不掺杂任何华丽、哗众取宠、拖泥带水内容，形成了朴实无华的特点。

13.刚健有力

在中国众多的武术流派中，少林功夫被称为外家。少林功夫之区别在于由外入内，由动入静，由刚入柔，与内家由柔入刚，到刚柔并济起

10. Attack in Defense and Defense in Attack

In the structure of forms and movements of Shaolin Kungfu, there is no exclusive attack or defense. There is attack in defense and defense in attack, nothing but changes in proportions of the two. Defending always hides in attacking and vice versa.

11. Various Hand Forms

Through the progress in the past 1,500 years, Shaolin monks have developed Kungfu to a complete and concentrated structure, which includes subtle but powerful hand forms in each movement. The skills of hand movements as intercepting (jie), unloading (zhan), hooking (diao), locking (kou), blocking (feng), stirring (jiao), twisting (ban), retracting (shou) are the essence of Shaolin Kungfu, which leaves no loophole for the opponent to exploit.

12. Simple and Plain

Shaolin monks have lived simple lives for ages and never fussed over food and clothing. Such simple life style also characterizes Shaolin Kungfu for self-defense, temple safeguarding, self-toning and Chan meditation. The design of movements and form structures is all based on practicability, and each of the movements, hand forms, and even the mind serve the above purposes. Thus, Shaolin Kungfu is simple and plain.

13. Vigorous and Powerful

Shaolin Kungfu is classified into the external (wai jia) among various schools of Kungfu. It is characterized by the progress from external to internal, dynamic to static, and hard to soft, in contrast with the internal (nei jia) featuring advancing from soft to hard, and coupling the two. The different origination leads to vigorous and powerful Shaolin Kungfu. In *The Ten Principles of Buddhist Boxing* the lockstep of the four ends is emphasized. The four ends include hair as the end of blood, nails as the end of tendons, teeth as the end of bones, and tongue as the end of muscles. It requires force generated powerfully from each body part to the four ends simultaneously following the instruction of mind. Sometimes roars are applied to strengthen the explosion of power in order to enhance the attacking force.

14. Inclination of Body Contraction

Body contraction serves three purposes. Firstly, it contributes to defense through minimizing the body that stultifies the enemy's attack. And the progress

步不同。由于起步的不同，形成了少林功夫的刚健有力。《释家捶把十要诀》阐述了齐四梢。四梢者，发为血梢，甲为筋梢，牙为骨梢，舌为肉梢。要求练功者发欲冲冠，甲欲透骨，牙欲咬金，舌欲摧齿。心一颤四者皆至，四梢齐内劲出矣。甚至用发声助之，目的是为了力量功夫的增进，增加其攻击力。

14.缩身动作多

缩身作用有三：一者利于防守，身形的束缩，目标缩小，使敌不宜取之。自闭门户，使敌不宜进入。展身而缩，以形体增加截封力量，使之有效。二者利于进攻，目标缩小利于闯入敌门。缩身后的展身，束身而展，以身形增加进攻部位力量。三者，闪、腾、挪灵活，看猴观猿，便知其妙。因以上诸多长处，所以少林功夫结合了许多束身动作，从而形成了这个特点。

15.腿法多

在少林传统腿法中，不存在高腿法。因高腿法之弊端有三：一是下盘不稳，宜被对方击倒或自倒。"倒"在拳法中被称为死势，交战中应尽可能避免死势。少林功夫虽有见死反活法解之，但还是避之为妙。二是展我身形，门户自开，无法顾及诸多空档，宜被对方进入。三是以根节攻击对方中节、梢节（上盘），使进攻距离拉长，降低进攻速度。古拳谱云：腿起望膝，膝起望怀，脚起撩阴，肘发护心，手似两扇门，全凭脚打人。少林腿法的特点主要为偷袭，在双手打开、封死、使敌成为死势的情况下，方可起用"撩阴脚"。由此可见少林腿法的特点及腿法在少林功夫中的重要性。因腿力量大，杀伤力强，少林功夫注重腿的利用。

16.发声多

少林僧人演练少林功夫套路，不时会发出"嗯、噫、哈、哼、威"等如虎啸般的怒吼。这在其他拳种中不多见。发音之作用众多，大致可分为以下几个方面：以发音带气、带力；以发音释放胸腹运动中之滞

of body contracting also accumulates the defending force to block the attack. Secondly, it facilitates counter-attack in moving with contracted body. The progress of body stretching out from contracted body increases the attacking force of the attaching body parts. Lastly, contracting makes one's body more flexible, to which one will understand its advantage through observing monkeys jumping. Actually, body contraction is frequently applied and combined in Shaolin Kungfu.

15. Diverse Leg Techniques

Shaolin Kungfu's leg techniques do not include high-kicks because of their three defects. First, they tend to cause unbalance of lower parts of the lower body and risks falling. Falling down is regarded as a death posture in boxing and should be avoided in combat. Although there are some solutions to reverse in Shaolin Kungfu, practitioners are supposed to avoid high-kicks. Second, they lead to body spreading and expose unprotected parts to the enemy's counterstroke. Third, they lengthen attacking distance and decreases speed when kicking the opponent's upper body. The ancient boxing record says that the one is supposed to use the shank of the lifting leg to cover the supporting knee, and the lifting knee to cover the stomach, to kick the enemy's crotch and keep the elbow protecting the chest. It is the kick that disables the enemy and hands stultifies the enemy's attack like a pair of swinging doors. The leg technique of Shaolin Kungfu is for sneak attacks, for example, to the enemy's crotch, when his hands respond to an attack. Such a feature is highlighted because of leg techniques' power and effectiveness. Therefore, the application of leg techniques is emphasized in Shaolin Kungfu.

16. Accompanied by Frequent Roars

Shaolin monks frequently make roars such as en, yi, ha, heng, wei when practicing Kungfu. This is rare in other schools of boxing. It helps to exert force, discharge qi in the stomach, boost force, and terrify or trap the opponents.

17. Repetitive Movements

Among the routines of Shaolin Kungfu, there are some repetitive movements, which have been regarded as redundant movements and removed by some layman practitioners. As a matter of fact, master monks designed these movements meticulously and accurately in each routine. Except for its differences in various routines, each repeated one has its own function. Take Shaolin Xiaohong Boxing as an example. It has repeated pushes and body contractions. As Xiaohong Boxing

图3-6 少林棍术
Shaolin Staff Techniques

气；以发音加重"狠"之音念，以助气力的增加；还有以发音镇敌；以发音诱敌等。

17.重复动作多

在少林功夫套路中，有一些动作反复出现，被不懂功夫的修炼者视为累赘，自作聪明，给以删除。岂不知古德们在对套路的编排上考虑得极其周密细致，每个套路除了其招法差异外，均有其不同的用处。如少林小洪拳的反复推掌，缩身。小洪拳是少林功夫的入门基础拳，有修身收心作用。因是入门之拳种，故其动作力求简单易懂。习少林功夫与其他技术相同，均是由易到难。武术入门先收其心，每天反复习练小洪拳，坚持三年，其法自悟，其功自成。其动作反复地重复，套路又长。少林拳每个套路各有其不同的作用。古德们在编排套路时，要对某个招式加重其训练力度，故加以重复。往往这个招式为这个套路的绝招，为了让修习者重点掌握而加以重复，这是主要目的之一。如耀肘在基础拳

is a primary boxing with the function of body-toning and mind concentration, it takes simplicity and lucidity as its objective. Learning Shaolin Kungfu, as that of other skills, is a pilgrimage from easy to difficulty. In the primary stage, one needs to concentrate his mind and keeps on practicing for three years, only after then may he understand and master it. Some actions are repetitive in long routines and function differently from one another. Master monks design repetitive movements to increase its practice intensity. One of their chief objectives is that they are the crucial movements to be mastered through repetitive practice. For instance, the movement Elbow Attack (Bazhou) not only exists in Xiaohong Boxing, but also repeated in other routines such as Arhat Boxing (luo han quan), Dahong Boxing, Dai Boxing, Short Boxing (Duan Boxing), Plum-blossom Boxing (mei hua quan), etc. It is the same for Tiger's Head in Claws (Dahu Baotou), Rest Head on One Arm (Wo Zhen), Tiger Leaps Across Ravine (Menghu Tiaojian), Sparrow Hawk Crosses Mountain (Yaozi Fanshan), etc. Some other movements are repetitive in one routine, for example, Push Hand (Tui Zhang) and Crouch Body (Suoshen) in Xiaohong Boxing, Embrace Moon (Huaizhong Baoyue) in Hong Boxing, Twist

图3-7 少林武僧千佛殿练武
Shaolin Warrior Monks Practicing Martial Arts in the Hall of One Thousand Buddhas of the Shaolin Temple

小洪拳里有，在罗汉拳，大洪拳，代拳，短拳，梅花拳等套路里均反复出现。大虎抱头，卧枕，猛虎跳涧，鹞子翻山等均是如此，这是在不同套路里的重复。在同一个套路里动作亦时常重复，如小洪拳里的推掌、缩身，洪拳的怀中抱月、撅手、单鞭、七星、云顶，罗汉拳里的反扑身、硬崩实砸、左右摔掠等等。

18.内外合一

这里所讲的内外谓内功和外功，内功亦可称为气功，外为外部形体的功夫。真正的气功是意念，是"心"境。练武需要气功，气为力之辅助、力之基础。意、气、力本为一体，不可分割而论之。《释家捶把十要诀》第十章节"纳气分路法"："捶打十分力，力从气中出，运气贵呼缓，用气贵呼急。"由此可看出力、气的关系。练气功者，通过意念的训练，达到养气之目的，设万念为一念。其功夫的深浅在于所设程度，所"定"之时间长短。怎么设，由动入静，由外形的动而入静境。意念的高度专注使身体之潜力聚集在一念上，其力自出。平时通过对意念（气）的专项训练，用时专注于手脚，其力自现。

Hand (Jueshou), Single Whip (Danbian), Seven Star (Qixing), and Cloud Hand (Yunding) in Hongquan, and Dive Back (Fanpushen), Punch Hard (Yingbeng Shiza), Left and Right Wrestling (Zuoyou Shuailüe) in Arhat Boxing (luo hanquan), etc.

18. Unity of Internal and External Exercises

In terms of internal Kungfu and external Kungfu, the former is also known as qi gong, and the latter physical exercise. The authentic qi gong is psychic force or a state of mind. Qi gong is necessary in Kungfu, because qi is the assistance and base of force. Mind, qi, and force form a trinity. As for Acceleration and Operation of Qi, the tenth chapter in *Ten Principles of Buddhist Boxing* says that Full force stemming from qi is required in boxing and qi is supposed to be slow in accumulation and fast in application, which explains the relationship between force and qi. The qi gong practitioner cultivates qi through exercising psychic force and then in turn concentrates his mind. The assessment of one's Kungfu depends on the extent he foresees and duration of jana he experienced. The method is from cesta (Dong) to santa (Jing). The extreme concentration of psychic force inspires one's potential and generates power. If one has done specialized exercise of psychic force (qi), power will be generated automatically when he concentrates on hands and feet in combats.

第四章

内涵丰厚的少林功夫

Chapter IV

The Rich Connotation of Shaolin Kungfu

一、兼容并蓄的少林功夫

每当人们来到少林寺千佛殿，总会被眼前几十个深浅不一的脚坑所震惊，这些脚坑是少林僧人们练功形成的"站桩坑"，亦称"练功脚坑"，是武僧习武时跺脚踏地再加上年长日久和功夫高深而留下的。每一个脚坑都渗透着少林武僧的辛勤汗水，都凝聚着少林功夫的深刻底蕴。

少林功夫从起源到现在已经有1500年的历史，在发展过程中，不断丰富，吸收各家流派之所长，逐渐形成了自己的技术体系和理论。

自北魏孝文帝拓跋宏在太和十九年建寺至北周宇文阐当政的80年间，就先后换了20个皇帝。社会一直动荡不安，统治者极度腐败，你争我夺，战火四起，民不聊生。有很多名人高士逃到嵩山少林寺，更名换姓，削发为僧。这些隐士，在来寺之前往往都身怀绝技，皈依沙门后，也将自己的武功传给少林。

图4-1 拳法对练
Shaolin Boxing Pair Practicing

I. Inclusive Shaolin Kungfu

Whenever people visit the Thousand Buddhas Hall in the Shaolin Temple, they will always be shocked by dozens of footpits of varied depth there. These footpits, also known as "practice footpits", have been left by the Kungfu monks through ages of Kungfu practice. Every footpit is infiltrated with the hard work of Shaolin Kungfu monks.

Shaolin Kungfu has a history of 1500 years from its birth till today. In the course of its development, Shaolin Kungfu has been enriched constantly. It has absorbed the strengths of various Kungfu schools and gradually formed its own technical system and theory.

During the 80 years since the temple was built in the 19th year of the Taihe Emperor's reign (personal name Tuoba Hong, posthumous name Xiaowen) (495 CE) of the Northern Wei dynasty to the reign of Emperor Jing (personal name Yuwen Chan, 573 CE—581 CE) of the Northern Zhou dynasty, twenty emperors had been successively replaced. During this period, the whole country was caught in turmoil, and the rulers were extremely corrupt. Incessant fighting among the warlords made it hard for ordinary folks to make an honest living. Many celebrities fled to the Shaolin Temple at Mount Song, changed their names, and became ordained as Buddhist monks. These hermits, before going to the temple, were often armed with superb Kungfu skills. They converted to the Buddhism and passed on their Kungfu to Shaolin monks.

Among them there were the following extraordinary examples. Sun Xi (Buddhist name Sengchou), a famous Buddhist monk in the Northern Wei dynasty, had been practicing Kungfu for four years with his grandfather Sun Cai before he became a monk. He was good at boxing and qigong. According to *Anecdotes in Court and Commonalty*, the monk could leap to the beam of rooftop, lift heavy weight of over 500 kilograms. His fist was swift and fierce, and his movements shocked the audience...

In the Sui dynasty, Ma Shantong (Buddhist name Zisheng) from Taihe county, Jiangxi province, started to practice Kungfu since his childhood and acquired superior Kungfu skills. In the 7th year of the Kaihuang Emperor's reign

北魏的孙溪，法名僧稠，出家前跟祖父孙才习武四年，擅长拳术和气功。《朝野佥载》记载：僧稠能跃至梁首，引重千钧，拳捷骁勇，动骇物听……

隋代马善通，法号子升，江西泰和人，自幼习武，功夫超群，隋文帝开皇七年（587年），因好打抱不平，挥拳打死知府父子，为躲避追捕，也逃奔少林寺。

唐代的圆净和尚，自幼习武，善练刀、枪、鞭术，尤擅气功，后皈依少林，号称铁和尚。

宋代是少林功夫发展的兴旺时期，据《少林拳谱》记载："宋末，少林寺高僧福居曾邀请全国十八家武术师到少林寺演练三年，各取其长，汇集成少林拳谱。"少林拳术增加至170余套，马籍的短打，孙垣的猴拳，刘兴的勾搂探手，谭方的滚臂贯耳，燕青的粘拿跌法，林冲的鸳鸯脚，孟苏的七势边拳，崔连的窝里炮捶，杨滚的捆掳，王郎的螳螂，高怀德的摔掠等。据说宋太祖赵匡胤也向少林寺传了拳法，《历代祖师传》说宋太祖曾来寺，还调遣诸州名将轮驻少林寺，一来授艺于僧，二来取僧之长。《北拳汇编》云："少林派亦称外家，赵匡胤为开山祖师也。"《纪效新书》曰：宋太祖有三十二式长拳，又有六步拳、猴拳、华拳名世。

除了拳术外，十八般武艺也频传少林，如杨家枪、罗家枪、梅花枪、燕青刀、春秋刀、猿猴棒、龙泉剑、八仙剑、九节鞭、叉、钩、戟、镖、斧、箭、镰、锏、槊、圈、锤、铲、匕首等一百三十余套。

金元时期李叟和白玉峰是闻名全国的武林高手，先后入寺授技，李叟传大、小洪拳，棍术和擒拿，白玉峰传龙、虎、蛇、豹、鹤五拳及气功，把少林寺的罗汉十八手发展到一百七十多手，又编著了《五拳精要》，阐述龙拳、虎拳、蛇拳、豹拳、鹤拳的练习和用法，为少林功夫的发展起到了推动作用。

明代的董瑞，法号了华，原在明军任督粮官，身怀绝技，擅长飞

of the Sui dynasty (587 CE), Ma took up the staff for others, and threw fists to kill the magistrate of a prefecture together with his son. To escape the pursuit Ma fled to the Shaolin Temple.

A monk of the Tang dynasty named Yuanjing practiced Kungfu since his childhood. He practiced sword, spear, and whip techniques, especially good at qigong. Later he converted to Shaolin and became known as the Iron Monk.

Shaolin Kungfu prospered in the Song dynasty (960—1279 CE). According to the *Shaolin Boxing Manual* (*Shao Lin Quan Pu*), "At the end of the Song dynasty, an eminent Shaolin monk Fuju invited 18 Kungfu masters from across the country to practice in the Shaolin Temple for three years, each contributing their own strengths to compose the Shaolin Boxing Manual." Shaolin Boxing techniques expanded to more than 170 sets, including Ma Ji's Close Combat (duan da), Sun Yuan's Monkey Boxing (hou quan), Liu Xing's Hook-and-hug-explore Hand (gou lou tan shou), Tan Fang's Rolling Arm (gun bi guan er), Yan Qing's Smashing Method (nian na die fa), Lin Chong's Mandarin Duck Leg (yuan yang jiao), Meng Su's Seven-Style Side Boxing (qi shi bian quan), Cui Lian's Nest Cannon Boxing (wo li pao chui), Yang Gun's Bundling Arrest (kun lu), Wang Lang's Mantis Boxing (tang lang quan), Gao Huaide's Wrestling (shuai lue) and so on. It is said that Emperor Taizu of Song (personal name Zhao Kuangyin) also passed boxing methods to the Shaolin Temple. *The Biography of the Masters of the Past Dynasties* (*Li Dai Zu Shi Zhuan*) states that Zhao Kuangyin had not only come to the temple in person, but also dispatched the famous generals of multiple states to the temple to teach Kungfu to the monks, while learning from the monks' strengths. *The Compodium of Northern Boxing* (*Bei Quan Hui Bian*) states, "The Shaolin School is also known as the external (wai jia quan), and Zhao Kuangyin is its founder." According to the *New Book on Military Efficiency* (*Ji Xiao Xin Shu*): Emperor Taizu of Song practiced 32-form long boxing (chang quan), also well-known for his Six-Step Boxing, Monkey Boxing, and Hua-Mountain Boxing (hua quan).

Besides boxing skills, routines involving 18 weapons have also been transmitted in the Shaolin Temple, consisting of more than 130 sets of Kungfu involving Yang's Spear, Luo's Spear, Plum Flower Spear, Yanqing Sabre, Chunqiu Sabre, Monkey Staff, Longquan Sword, Baxian Sword, and methods on 9-section

镖、技击，外号飞侠。王庆，法号平明，自幼好武擅文，武艺超群，曾在天水打擂获胜，名震全国。周太和，法号可明，河南固始人，幼年随祖父习武，练得一身好武艺，为谋生计，在永城一带卖艺，受地痞欺负，一气之下，劈死地痞逃到少林。生在四川的全文中，自幼好武，苦练十年，考中武举，后任巴山县令。万历二十七年皇太子朱恒温游览巴山，强抢民女，被全文中斥责。皇太子回京后陷害全文中，削其官职。全文中亦出家为僧。

清代的蔡林，辽东人，自幼随祖父习武，功夫不凡，18岁从军，后升为戍边副将，因为闲谈中说了不利于朝廷的话，被人诬告后逃到少林寺。

近代的王文斌，原籍长春，幼年习武，立有为国争光之志，卖地筹款，四方拜师，精通洪拳、通臂拳、螳螂拳、八卦拳、黑虎拳和技击等，在东北三省颇有名气。为了提高武技，于1920年出家少林寺。

带着绝技到少林的名士不胜枚举，少林功夫也因此吸收了众家之长。同时，少林功夫也流传于民间各地，形成众多武术流派和拳种，如南少林、北少林、少林长拳、少林大战拳、少林武拳、罗汉拳、六合拳、梅花拳、红家拳、咏春拳等。

明末清初，太极拳和形意拳的创立，都与少林拳有一定的渊源。

传说张三丰虽然创立了内家拳，但是他本人出自少林，精通少林拳，在此基础上修正、发展才形成了内家拳。据唐豪先生多方考证，太极拳为明末清初河南省温县陈家沟陈王廷所创编。陈王廷创编太极拳，间接吸收了少林寺拳法。众所周知，陈王廷将戚继光著的《纪效新书·拳经捷要篇》中拳法三十二式里的二十九式，并收到他的一百单八式长拳中，其中有懒扎衣、金鸡独立、探马拳、七星拳、倒骑龙、悬脚虚、丘列势、抛架子、拈肘势、一霎步、擒拿势、下插势、埋伏势、井栏直入、鬼蹴脚、指挡势、兽头、伏虎势、高四平、倒插势、小神拳、雀地龙、一条鞭、朝阳手、雁翅势、拗鸾肘、当头炮、顺鸾肘等。而

whip, trident, hook sword, halberd, dart, axe, arrow, sickle, maces, long spear, arm ring, hammer, shovel, dagger, etc.

During the Jin dynasty and the Yuan dynasty, Li Sou and Bai Yufeng were famous Kungfu masters in the country. They successively joined the Shaolin Temple to teach Kungfu, where Li Sou taught Da, Xiao Hong Quan, staff techniques and arrest techniques, while Bai Yufeng taught Dragon boxing, Tiger boxing, Snake boxing, Leopard boxing and Crane boxing. They expanded the 18 styles of Shaolin Kungfu to more than 170 styles, and compiled the *Five Boxing Essentials*. They expounded on the practice and usage of Dragon Boxing, Tiger Boxing, Snake Boxing, Leopard Boxing and Crane Boxing. These achievements further contributed to the development of Shaolin Kungfu.

Dong Rui (Buddhist name Liaohua) of the Ming dynasty, used to be a government official in charge of food supply. He had brilliant Kungfu expertise, particularly with excellent skills in close combat and darting, which earned him a nickname of Flying Knight. Wang Qing (Buddhist name Pingming) who excelled in both Kungfu and liberal arts once won the championship of an open contest in Tianshui and became known across the whole country. Zhou Taihe (Buddhist name Keming), native to Gushi county of Henan province, made a living on street performance around Yongcheng county. Once he was bullied by a local street thug. He could not restrain his anger but to kill the bully and fled to the Shaolin Temple. Further, Quan Wenzhong of Sichuan province had been fond of Kungfu since his childhood. He won the candidacy in the imperial examinations at the provincial level and was appointed the magistrate of Bashan county. In the 27th year of Wanli Emperor's reign (1599 CE), the Crown Prince Zhu Hengwen visited Bashan and took a civilian girl by force. Quan Wenzhong scolded him. After returning to Beijing, Zhu framed Quan Wenzhong and removed him from his post. Quan Wenzhong turned to become a monk.

Cai Lin, native to eastern Liaoning province in the Qing dynasty, learned Kungfu from his grandfather when he was young. He joined the army at the age of 18 and then rose to the rank of deputy general of a garrison. Being falsely accused of saying something unfavorable to the royal court he fled to the Shaolin Temple to avoid persecution.

Wang Wenbin, a contemporary man of Changchun origin, started to practice

图4-2 张三丰
Zhang Sanfeng

戚继光在他著的《拳经》中讲，他吸收了民间16家著名拳种，其中包括少林拳法。陈氏太极拳中的一些名称和动作，如金刚捣碓、单鞭、斜行、七星、高探马、白鹤亮翅、野马分鬃、金鸡独立等与少林拳法相同。

对于形意拳的来源，黄铭新在《形意拳起源考》一文中，通过几个方面比较后得出结论，形意拳来源于少林五拳。

以拳术和棍术为核心体系的少林功夫，来源于民间，流传于民间，不仅具有较高的技术层次，而且较好地解决了武术在封建社会环境下适应性与实用性相统一的问题，因而能够在民间获得广泛的流传和极高声誉，形成其他武术门派和拳种不能望其项背的武术地位。

Kungfu at an early age. With an ambition to win glory for his country, he raised funds from land sales, and went around to learn Kungfu. Finally, he became well versed in Hong Boxing (also known as Hung Ga), Penetrating-Arms style (tong bi quan), Mantis Boxing (tang lang quan), Bagua Boxing (Eight-Diagram boxing, ba gua quan), Black Tiger Boxing (hei hu quan) and other forms of attack and defense in Kungfu. He became well known in Northeast China. In order to improve his skills of Kungfu, in 1920 Wang became a monk at the Shaolin Temple.

Because of the contribution of the above-mentioned Kungfu masters and countless others, Shaolin Kungfu has absorbed the strengths of all kungfu schools. At the same time, Shaolin Kungfu has also spread among the folks, forming a number of Kungfu schools and boxing styles, such as Southern Shaolin, Northern Shaolin, Shaolin Long Style (shao lin chang quan), Shaolin Dazhan Style (shaolin da zhan quan), Shaolin Wuquan Style (shao lin wu quan), Arhat Style (luo han quan), 6-match Style (liu he quan), Plum Blossom Style, Hung Ga Style (hong jia quan), Wing Chun Style (yong chun quan) and so on.

Both Taichi (tai ji quan) and Shape and Intention Boxing (xing yi quan), which were established in the late Ming and early Qing dynasty, somewhat originated from Shaolin Boxing.

Legend has it that Zhang Sanfeng founded Internal Boxing (nei jia quan), but he himself came from Shaolin and was proficient in Shaolin Quan. On this basis, he revised and developed Neijiaquan. According to Tang Hao's research findings, Taijiquan was created by Chen Wangting, a native of Chen Jiagou village, Wenxian county, Henan province in the late Ming and the early Qing dynasty. It indirectly absorbed the Shaolin boxing techniques. As is known to all, Chen Wangting incorporated 29 forms out of 32 forms created by Qi Jiguang, into his Long Boxing of 108 styles. It was recorded in the Chapter on the *Fist Canon and the Essentials of Nimbleness* (*Quan Jing Jie Yao Pian*) *in Qi Jiguang's New Treatise on Military Efficiency* (*Ji Xiao Xin Shu*). These 29 forms include: Casually Hitch-up your Clothes (lan zha yi), Golden Rooster Standing on One leg (jin ji du li), Scouting Horse Strike (tan ma quan), Seven Star Strike (qi xing quan), Mount the Dragon Backwards (dao qi long), Suspend the Leg as Empty Bait False Prey Posture (xuan jiao xu), the Qiulie Posture (qiu

二、少林禅武医的完美结合

嵩山少林寺是中国佛教禅宗的祖庭和少林武术的发祥地，有"天下第一名刹"之称。自北魏创建以来，1500多年的历史积淀，使少林寺形成了底蕴丰厚的文化。少林的文化有禅宗、武术、医学、古塔、金石、壁画、古建、书法等等。在少林寺众多的文化当中，禅宗、武术和医学是少林文化的代表，而将禅武医有机结合起来则成为少林寺最有特色的文化，因而被世人称为"少林三宝"。

北魏太和十九年（公元495年），居于洛阳的印度高僧跋陀，因"性爱幽栖，林谷是托，屡往嵩岳，高谢世人"（唐道宣《续高僧传》），于是孝文帝在少室山北麓为之建造寺院让其落迹传法，因寺院坐落于少室山阴的丛林之中，故名少林寺。跋陀在少林寺所传的为小乘禅法，但不久即失传。

北魏时，印度又一位高僧菩提达摩航海来到中国，刘宋末年抵达宋境，北魏孝昌时（公元525—527年）到达魏都洛阳，后达摩来到嵩山少

图4-3 菩提达摩浮雕
The Relief of Bodhidharma

lie shi), Cast Body Forward (pao jia zi), Take the Elbow in Hand Posture(nian zhou shi), One Instant Step (yi sha bu) , Capture and Grab Stance (qin na shi), Downward Stabbing Stance (xia cha shi), Ambushing Posture (mai fu shi), Well-railing Four-wise Balanced (jing lan zhi ru), Ghost Kick (gui cu jiao), Finger Opposition Posture (zhi dang shi), Beast Head Position (shou tou), Prone Tiger Posture (fu hu shi), High Four levels Posture (gao si ping), Reverse Stabbing Position (dao cha shi), Spirit Fist (xiao shen quan), cross-leg method (que di long), Single Whip Posture (yi tiao bian), Facing-sun Hand (chao yang shou), Wild Goose Wings (yan chi shi), Joining Together the Luan Elbows (niu luan zhou), Cannonball against the Head (dang tou pao), Synchronize the Luan Elbows (shun luan zhou) etc. Qi's *Fist Canon* claims that he absorbed 16 folks boxing methods, including Shaolin Boxing. The names and movements of some stances in Chen's Taijiquan (Taiji Boxing) are the same as those in Shaolin Boxing, including Buddha's Warrior Attendant Pounds the Mortar (jin gang dao dui), Single Whip (dan bian), Walk Obliquely (xie xing), Seven Star Strike (qi xing), White Crane Spreading Wings (bai he liang chi), Parting the Wild Horse's Mane (ye ma fen zong), Golden Rooster Standing on One Leg (jin ji du li) and so on.

As for the origination of Shape and Intention Boxing (Xing yi quan), in an article entitled *The Origin of Xing yi quan*, Huang Mingxin, through multiple comparisons, came to the conclusion that Xing yi quan came from the Five Styles of Shaolin Kungfu (i.e., Dragon Styles, Tiger Styles, Leopard Styles, Snake Styles, and Crane Styles).

Shaolin Kungfu, with boxing and staff techniques as its core system, has come from and disseminated among the folk. It not only has a high level of techniques, but also better solves the problem of harmonizing adaptability and practicability of Wushu in the feudal society. Therefore, it was able to gain a wide dissemination and high reputation among the people, earning a position hardly equaled by any other styles of boxing or other Kungfu schools.

II. Combination of Shaolin Chan, Kungfu and Medicine

The Shaolin Temple in Songshan Mountain is the ancestral court of Chinese

林寺一带传法。相传达摩在少林寺北五乳峰的天然石洞中面壁九年，在其面壁的过程中，达摩感到传承已久的小乘禅法已走向没落，于是他根据佛教大乘的基本理论，结合北魏时期中国的国情及佛教的发展状况，创立了以"静坐修身、直指人心、见性成佛"为基本宗旨的佛教禅宗。达摩所传之禅自称"教外别传"，主张"不立文字"，仅以"壁观"作为修行之法，而传法的经典仅为四卷《楞伽经》。达摩的修行主要为"入道四行"：一曰"报怨行"，即要有甘心忍辱的品行；二曰"随缘行"，即命运随缘而定；三曰"无所求行"，即不可贪求欲望；四曰"称法行"，即事情要应理而行。

达摩在少林寺传法于慧可之后离开嵩山，梁大同二年（536年）遇毒而卒，葬于熊耳山，起塔定林寺。达摩所创的禅宗，摒弃了小乘佛教烦琐的教义和冗长的经典，给苦苦修行者带来了"成正果"简捷而便利的渠道。禅宗经二祖慧可、三祖僧璨、四祖道信、五祖弘忍、六祖慧能的充实和发展，尤其是慧能对禅宗的变革而成的"顿悟"学说，主张

图4-4 少林寺十方禅院
Courtyard of Chan in the Shaolin Temple

Chan Buddhism and the birthplace of Shaolin Wushu, known as "the Best Temple under Heaven". Since its establishment in the Northern Wei dynasty, a rich culture of the Shaolin Temple has been formed through more than 1500 years' historical and cultural accumulation. The Shaolin culture consists of Chan, Kungfu, medicine, ancient pagodas, stone carvings, murals, ancient architecture, calligraphy, and so on. Among the numerous sub-cultures of the Shaolin Temple, Chan, Wushu and medicine are their representatives. And the integration of Chan, Wushu and medicine has distinguished the culture of the Shaolin Temple from others. Therefore, they are called the "Three Treasures of Shaolin".

In the 19th year of the Taihe Emperor's reign (495 CE) in the Northern Wei dynasty, an eminent monk from India named Batuo lived in Luoyang. He was "seclusive by nature, enjoying the forest, valley, and repeatedly going to Songshan Mountain, and remaining isolated from the world" (*Continuation of Biographies of Eminent Monks*, by Daoxuan in the Tang dynasty). Emperor Xiaowen built a temple on the north side of Mount Shaoshi for him to teach Buddhism. The Temple was located in the jungle of Mount Shaoshi, so it was named Shaolin Temple (literally translated as the temple in the forest of Mount Shaoshi). Batuo taught Hinayana Buddhism in the Shaolin Temple, but it soon got lost.

During the Xiaochang Emperor's reign (525—527 CE) of the Northern Wei dynasty, another eminent Indian monk named Bodhidharma came to China from India. He arrived in the territory of the Song dynasty to preach Buddhism in the late Song dynasty of the Liu Monarchy. Bodhidharma came to the Shaolin Temple, where in a process of wall-gazing mediation for nine years, Bodhidharma realized that the long-standing Hinayana Buddhism had been on the decline. So, he, contemplating the reality of the Northern Wei dynasty and development of Buddhism, created the Chan Buddhism based on a fundamental principle–sitting for self-cultivation, pointing directly to human mind, and obtaining Buddhahood upon seeing into (one's own true) nature. The Bodhidharma's Chan claims that Chan should be "transmitted outside the scriptures" and "not based upon written words and letters". They simply apply the "wall-gazing" as the only practice method, and the classics for practice only include four volumes of the *Sangha Sutra*. Bodhidharma's practice is mainly to "follow the Four Practices": first, the "practice of retribution of enmity", that is, to have a willingness to be humiliated;

"放下屠刀",就可"立地成佛"。这种简单易行的修行方法由于容易被佛教徒所接受,后来迅速在中国流传起来。在中国其他佛教宗派相继走向衰落甚至消亡之时,出现了"禅宗独盛"的局面。

禅宗在中国的流传过程中,逐渐汉化,并成为中国文化的重要组成部分。在历史上,禅宗文化对中国的政治、经济、文化和哲学都产生了深远的影响,可以说是渗透到了中国社会的各个角落,也影响着中国人思想的许多方面。由此,禅宗文化,是中国文化中非常值得人们研究和探索的文化,尤其是其主张的平静、忍让等,许多至今还是我们应该吸取和借鉴的。作为禅宗祖庭的少林寺是禅宗文化的旗帜,是禅宗文化的代表。少林武术也称少林功夫、少林武功,是中国宝贵的文化遗产,是中华武术的重要组成部分。它内容广博,种类繁多,技法精湛,享誉中外。

少林武术,历史悠久,源远流长。它是在广泛吸纳中国传统武术基础上产生的。

唐代少林武僧因助唐平定王世充使少林武术名冠天下。唐代之后,历代少林寺僧不断对少林武术进行推演,逐渐形成特色突出,内容广博的少林武术体系。尤其是明代,是少林武术的一个大发展时期,这期间形成了博大精深的少林武术体系。

演练少林武术不仅可以强身健体,防身抗暴,还可以修身养性,陶冶性情。少林武术动作优美,演练起来还会给人以美的艺术享受。由此,少林武术是中华文化的重要组成部分,是中华武术文化的精华。少林寺作为少林武术的发祥地,武术文化独树一帜。

少林医学是少林文化的又一个杰出的代表,其历史也十分久远。少林医学是在中华医学的基础上形成的,它是少林寺僧人为了适应长期坐禅及治疗因习武练功和参战致伤而逐渐确立起来的。

早期少林医学是为僧人医病的。随着禅宗在少林寺的传播,少林僧徒由于长期打坐,身体的器官因此受到损伤,出现腰酸背痛、脊椎弯

second, the "practice of acceptance of circumstances", that is, destiny depends on the kharma; third, the "practice of the absence of craving", that is, no greed or desire; fourth, the "practice of accordance with the Dharma", that is, life should abide by reason.

Bodhidharma left Mount Song after passing the Buddhism creed to Huike in the Shaolin Temple. In the 2nd year of the Datong Emperor's reign (536 CE) of Liang dynasty, Bodhidharma died of poisoning. He was buried in Mount Xiong'er, where a memorial pagoda was built in the Dinglin Temple to commemorate Bodhidharma. Bodhidharma's Chan Buddhism abandoned the tedious teachings and lengthy classics of Hinayana Buddhism, and found a simple and convenient way for ascetic practitioners to achieve "fruitful results". It was further enriched and developed by Huike, Sencan, Daoxin, Hongren, and Huineng. Huineng's "sudden awakening" theory was transformed from Chan, which advocated "obtaining Buddhahood" immediately after "laying down the butcher's knife". This simple and easy way of practice was easily accepted by Buddhists and quickly spread across China. When other Buddhist sects in China declined or even disappeared one after another, there emerges the scene of "Chan Buddhism flourishing alone".

Chan has been gradually sinicized and become an important part of Chinese culture with its dissemination across China. In history, Chan culture has exerted profound influence on China's politics, economy, culture and philosophy. It can be said that it has virtually penetrated into every corner of the Chinese society and affected many aspects of Chinese thoughts. Therefore, Chan culture is worthy of research and exploration, particular its notion of serenity and tolerance, many of which are still worth learning today. As the ancestral home of Chan, the Shaolin Temple is the banner of Chan culture and the representative of Chan culture. The Shaolin Wushu, also known as Shaolin Martial Arts or Shaolin Kungfu, is a precious cultural heritage of China as well as an important component of Chinese Kungfu. It has a wide range of contents, with exquisite techniques of great varieties.

With a long history, Shaolin Kungfu has developed through extensively absorbing traditional Chinese Kungfu.

In the Tang dynasty, Shaolin Kungfu monks helped Prince Li Shimin (later

曲、骨质增生等。在这种情况下，僧人在坐禅时，通过呼吸吐纳来调节神经，疏通脉络，于是创立了以养生为主的内养功。

少林僧徒在习武时，不免会受伤，尤其是僧兵参战，造成的创伤更大，由此少林寺僧为了适应医伤的需要，在中华伤科的基础上又创立了具有少林特色的伤科疗法。此外，少林僧徒为了医病，在不断的实践过程中又创立了药物、素疗通窍等具有特色的医病方法。

嵩山少林禅武医文化作为中华优秀传统文化的一部分，具有非常重要的文化价值，代表着少林文化的内涵，体现着少林文化的精髓。少林禅武医文化还具有非常重要的学术价值，是研究和揭示少林文化奥妙的一个重要源泉。少林禅武医文化也具有重要的历史价值，包涵了丰厚的古代文明信息，是少林优秀传统文化的载体。少林禅武医文化同时也具有非常重要的实用价值，是人们修心、健身、养生的重要手段，也是人们生活中不可多得的养生资源。少林禅武医自诞生以来，不仅受到中国人的喜爱，也深受世界人民的喜爱，并被视为珍贵的人类非物质文化遗产。2015年，少林禅武医被列入河南省非物质文化遗产代表作名录，成为中华优秀的人类非物质文化的重要组成部分。

在少林寺禅武医文化的发展和形成过程中，明朝万历年间少林寺永化堂开山祖师无言正道起到了决定性的作用。就是无言正道把禅修引入医疗之中，使之形成具有少林特色的医术。无言正道执掌少林寺时，还使博大精深的少林武术形成完备的武术体系。而把禅宗、武术和医学融为一体形成的以禅修心、以武健体、以医养身为核心的禅武医文化，也是无言正道的首创。而由无言正道创立的少林禅武医现已成为少林文化的珍宝。

enthroned as Emperor Taizong of the Tang dynasty) defeat Wang Shichong, which made Shaolin Kungfu known across the country. After the Tang dynasty, the Shaolin Temple continued to develop Shaolin Kungfu in the following dynasties, and gradually formed a Shaolin Kungfu system with outstanding characteristics and extensive contents. The Ming dynasty in particular witnessed the great development of Shaolin Kungfu, in which a profound Shaolin Kungfu system was formed.

The practice of Shaolin Kungfu, not only strengthens the body and improves self-defense, but also maintains self-cultivation and edifies temperament. The Shaolin Kungfu is graceful in action, and practicing Shaolin Kungfu will give people a beautiful artistic enjoyment. Therefore, Shaolin Kungfu is an important part of Chinese culture as well as the essence of Chinese Kungfu culture. The Shaolin Temple, as the birthplace of unique Shaolin Kungfu, accordingly enjoys high reputation for its Kungfu culture.

Shaolin Medicine is another outstanding representative of Shaolin culture, which also has a very long history. Shaolin Medicine, developing on the basis of Chinese medicine, was gradually established by Shaolin Temple monks, in order to adapt to long meditation, and to treat injuries resulted from battles or Kungfu practice.

Early Shaolin medicine was developed to treat the monks' illness. As Chan was transmitted in the Shaolin Temple, the practice of lengthy meditation subjected the Shaolin monks to physical harms, such as back pain, spinal curvature, and bone hyperplasia. To cope with these problems, when the monks sit in meditation, they learned to adjust their nerves and dredge their veins through inhaling and exhaling, thus creating a kind of internal health-supporting practice.

When the Shaolin monks practise Kungfu, they may inevitably be injured. Particularly when the monk warriors participated in the war, they suffered more serious wounds. In order to treat their wounds, the Shaolin Temple established a traumatic therapy with Shaolin characteristics on the basis of Chinese Traumatology. In addition, Shaolin monks have created distinctive medical methods including drugs, vegetarian diet remedy, and other treatments in the process of continuous practice.

As a part of outstanding traditional Chinese culture, the Songshan Shaolin

三、少林功夫与军事

据《史记》载：轩辕黄帝在与蚩尤作战时，就开始对勇士进行持械格斗和角觚的训练。到商代后，出现了庞大的常备军，频繁的战争使人们认识到，要战胜对手，就要有高于对手的本领。为了提高战斗力，必须事先对战斗人员进行身体素质和散手等军事技能的训练。春秋战国时期，"相搏"在军队中相当普及，统治者为了提高战斗力，每至春秋两季都要沙场点兵，进行"角试"。到了唐宋以后，少林功夫对军事的作用越来越大。这里不能不提的是少林僧兵。

少林僧兵产生于隋末。隋炀帝时，由于连年的战争，加上荒旱，农民起义纷起，拥有百顷良田的少林寺成了农民军进攻的对象。隋大业末，农民军一举攻入少林寺，把寺院烧得只剩下一座孤塔。在此情况下，寺僧为了保护少林寺，于是开始组织武僧，与农民军对抗。此事载于裴漼《皇唐嵩岳少林寺碑》中："大业之末，九服分崩，群盗攻剽，

图4-5 少林武僧出山门
Shaolin Warrior Monks Going out of the Shaolin Mountain

Chanwuyi (three things in one with Chan meaning Zen or meditation, Wu meaning Wushu or Kungfu, and Yi meaning Medicine or Healing) Culture has very high cultural values, representing the connotation and essence of Shaolin culture. It also has high academic values, as an important source for studying and revealing the mystery of the Shaolin culture, high historical values, as a carrier of excellent traditional Shaolin culture containing abundant information, and high practical values as an important means for people to cultivate, exercise and maintain health. It is also a rare health-supporting resource. Since its birth, Shaolin Chanwuyi has been cherished not only by Chinese people, but also by people all over the world. It is regarded as a precious human intangible cultural heritage. In 2015, Shaolin Chanwuyi was listed as one of Henan province's representative intangible cultural heritages, becoming an important part of China's excellent human intangible culture.

During the formation and development of the Shaolin Chanwuyi Culture in the Shaolin Temple, Wuyan Zhengdao, the ancestral master of Yonghua Hall (Yonghua Tang) during the Wanli Emperor's reign (1573—1620 CE) of the Ming dynasty, played a decisive role. It is said that the Chan is introduced into the medical treatment by Wuyan Zhengdao, which helped form a medical technique with Shaolin characteristics. When he was in charge of the Shaolin Temple, he also made the profound Shaolin Kungfu a complete Kungfu system. The Shaolin Chanwuyi Culture, which was formed by integrating Chan, Kungfu and Medicine, is the first of its kind, with Chan to cultivate mind, Kungfu to strengthen body, and Medicine to maintain life. The Shaolin Chanwuyi Culture founded by Wuyan Zhengdao has become a treasure of Shaolin culture.

III. Shaolin Kungfu and Military

According to Records of the *Grand Historian*, when the Yellow Emperor fought against Chiyou (or the Yan Emperor), he began to train the warriors in armed fights. From the Shang dynasty onwards, each dynasty has maintained a massive standing army. Frequent wars made them realize that to defeat their enemies they must have superior fighting skills over their enemies. In order to improve combat effectiveness, the combatants must be trained in military skills

图4-6 《皇唐嵩岳少林寺碑》
The Shaolin Monastery Stele on Mount Song

无限僧俗。此寺为山贼所劫,僧徒拒之,贼遂纵火焚塔院,院中众宇,倏焉同灭。赡言灵塔,岿然独存。"

在与农民军进行的战争中,"寺僧拒之"仅仅是带有僧兵性质的武装组织出现的端倪。此后,由于战争的扩大,少林寺被迫大规模组织僧兵武装,来保护少林寺及庞大的田产,以避免重蹈寺院被焚的覆辙。唐武德二年(619年),原隋大将王世充废越王杨侗,拥兵东都洛阳,自立为皇帝,国号为郑。王世充占据嵩洛一带后,用其侄王仁则为将,率重兵驻守少林寺西北五十里的柏谷坞。这里原是隋文帝赐封少林寺百顷良田的所在地。王仁则到后,不仅侵占了少林寺的封地,而且在那里建了一座军事重镇,名为"辕州",打算"乘其地险"来对抗李唐王朝。

唐武德三年(620年)七月,高祖李渊发诏书,命其子陕东道行台、上柱国、秦王李世民总统诸路军马东征王世充。武德四年(621年)四月,李世民与王仁则在嵩洛一带激战正酣,在此关键时刻,驻守少林寺柏谷庄护卫封地的武僧志操、惠玚、昙宗等,因不满王仁则霸占

such as physical fitness and Sanshou. During the Spring and Autumn Period and the Warring States Period, "strike" was quite popular among the military troops. In order to improve combat effectiveness, the rulers had to go to the battlefields every spring and autumn to conduct a "fight test". After the Tang and the Song dynasty, Shaolin Kungfu played an increasingly important role in the military. What can't be ignored here are Shaolin monk warriors.

Shaolin monk warriors emerged at the end of the Sui dynasty. During the reign of Emperor Yang of the Sui dynasty, a number of years' wars and droughts led to peasant uprisings. And the Shaolin Temple, with 100 qing (around 667 hectares) fertile land, became the peasant army's attack target. At the end of the late Sui dynasty, the peasant army fought into and burnt the Shaolin Temple, leaving only a single tower unburned. This prompted the temple to strategically organize Kungfu monks both for defense and for resisting the peasant army. This is recorded in the inscription on the *Shaolin Monastery Stele on Mount Song* authored by Pei Cui, stating that "In the last years of the Daye Emperor's reign, the whole country disintegrated. Banditry launched indiscriminate assaults on the population, monks and laity alike. The Temple (Shaolin) was pillaged by roving bandits. When the monks resisted them, the bandits set fire and burned the stupas and courtyard. Within an instant all the buildings perished in the flames. Only the Spirit Stupa remained as lofty as ever."

In combating the peasant army, "the monks resisted them" (in the inscription) marked the beginning of forming armed teams of monk warriors. Since then, the expansion of the war forced the Shaolin Temple to organize large-scale armed monk warriors to protect the Shaolin Temple and its vast land, so as to avoid repeating the tragedy of the Temple being burned. In 2nd year of the Wude Emperor's reign (619 CE) of the Tang dynasty, Wang Shichong, a former general of the Sui dynasty, abolished Yang Dong, the king of Yue, and declared himself emperor of a new Zheng dynasty. Wang established his capital in Luoyang. After occupying the region of Songluo, Wang Shichong, together with his nephew Wang Renze, led a heavy force to garrison Baiguwu (Cypress Valley), about 25 kilometers northwest of the Shaolin Temple. This is the place where Emperor Wen of the Sui dynasty bestowed on the Shaolin Temple 100 qing (around 667 hectares) fertile farmland. When Wang Renze arrived, he not only seized the

其封地,于四月二十七日率领以十三武僧为主的少林僧兵,乘夜间攻入王仁则大营,一举生擒王仁则,并将其献于李世民。少林武僧的举动给唐军以极大的支持和鼓舞,不久李世民乘势击败王世充,平定了中原最大的割据势力。

在以昙宗等十三武僧为首的僧兵将王仁则献于李世民后,李即于四月三十日发布了《告柏谷坞少林寺上座书》,对少林僧兵的功劳大加赞誉:"法师等并能深悟机变,早识妙因,克建嘉猷,同归福地,廓兹净土,奉顺输忠。"李世民还对少林僧兵"赏物千段",同时还要给参战武僧封官加爵,但寺僧"只愿出家,行道礼拜,仰报国恩,不取官位"。其后李世民又对少林寺频降玺书宣慰,多有赏赐。参战有功的十三武僧虽不受官,但均受封赐,昙宗还被封为"大将军僧"。少林僧兵助李世民的举动,不仅使少林寺以武勇闻,而且使少林僧兵从此名扬于天下。正如明徐学谟诗云:"怪得僧徒偏好武,昙宗曾拜大将军。"据唐《赐田牒》碑所载,唐武德四年(621年)李世民敕授的少林寺立功僧如下:

上座僧:善护

寺主僧:志操

都维那僧:惠玚

大将军僧:昙宗

同立功僧:普惠、明嵩、灵宪、普胜、智守、道广、智兴、满、丰。

在少林僧兵得到李唐王朝的大力封赏后,少林寺院也被"兼承宠赐",成为天下名刹。由此,少林寺不仅有了僧兵,而且得到了众多优厚的待遇,这为以后少林僧兵龙跃于沙场奠定了基础。

在唐初少林僧兵助李世民平定王世充后的很长时间里,少林寺僧虽然习武,但未参与战争。到中唐元和时,僧圆净曾助李师道反唐;宋代宗印也曾组织少林僧兵武装助宋抗金;元末少林僧兵还参加了对红巾军

granted territory of the Shaolin Temple, but also built a military town named Yuanzhou, where he planned to "take advantage of the land with difficult access" to fight the Tang dynasty of Monarchy Li.

In July of the 3rd year of the Wude Emperor's reign (620 CE) of the Tang dynasty, Emperor Gaozu (personal name Li Yuan) issued an edict, ordering his son Li Shimin, then the Prince of Qin, to lead military troops to attack Wang Shichong. In April of the 4th year of of the Wude Emperor's reign (621CE), Li Shimin and Wang Renze fought bitterly in the region of Songluo. Kungfu monks Zhicao, Huiyang, and Tanzong, who were stationed at the Shaolin Temple in Baiguzhuang, were dissatisfied with Wang Renze. On April 27th, they led the Shaolin monk warriors, with thirteen Kungfu monks as the backbone to attack Wang Renze's battalion at night. They captured Wang Renze alive, and presented him to Li Shimin. The Shaolin monk's move gave great support and encouragement to Li's military troops. Soon Li Shimin defeated Wang Shichong and settled the largest separatist force in the Central Plains.

After Shaolin monk warriors, headed by 13 major Kungfu monks including Tanzong, captured and presented Wang Renze to Li Shimin. On April, 30th, Li immediately issued an edict (*Letter to serior Baiguwu Shaolin Temple*) addressing the Chief Monk of the Shaolin Temple, highly commending Shaolin monk warriors' meritorious deeds, "The masters of the Shaolin Temple deeply comprehended and adapted to the changing circumstances. They launched great strategies to capture the evil bastard, through which they cleansed the Land of purity and yielded Buddhist fruits. Together, they returned to the Early Paradise, to dedicate loyalty to the Tang dynasty through providing for Buddhism." Li Shimin was to bestow on the participating monks "thousands of properties" as well as official ranks, but the Shaolin monks "would rather remain reclusive and repay the state graciousness through worshiping Buddhas than take official posts." Afterwards, Li Shimin issued multiple edicts for condolence and gave them plenty of grants. Although the major 13 Kungfu monks declined official posts, they were still knighted and granted titles. Among them, Tanzong were rewarded with the title of General-in-chief. Li Shimin's acts not only made Shaolin Temple known for its bravery, but rendered Shaolin monk warriors known across the country, as versed by Xu Xuemo: "No wonder monks here much prefer martial art, their

的战争。但这三次僧兵参战的规模较小，影响不大，多不为世人所知。少林僧兵参战时间长、规模大、影响深远的要数明代少林僧兵。

明代少林僧兵首次参战在正德年间（1506—1521年）。据《明史》载，明朝中后期，远逃塞外的蒙古贵族鞑靼，不断侵扰北方边境。为此，明王朝在山西、陕西边关设立军事重镇，并不断调遣各地武装前往镇守，少林僧兵也应征前往。据少林寺塔林中建于明嘉靖二十七年（1548年）的《敕赐祖庭少林禅寺敕名天下对手教会武僧友公三奇和尚塔铭》载：正德时，武宗下令征调少林僧兵保卫边关，僧兵在周友（号三奇）的带领下，出征山西和陕西等边关镇守，并屡建战功。为表彰少林僧兵的功绩，武宗特赐封僧兵将领周友以"都提调言总"之职。后云南苗族上层贵族叛乱，受武宗之命，周友再次率领训练有素的少林僧兵前往云南平叛，所有参战的僧兵均受到"官赏"。又据塔铭知，三奇有"僧俗徒众千外余名"，分布于河南、山东及两直隶四省几十个州县。可见周友所率的以僧兵为骨干的武装是一个人数众多的武装组织。

周友之后，少林僧兵更加频繁地参与战争，据明万历九年（1581

图4-7 《豁免粮差碑》
The Grain Taxation Exemption Monument

master Tanzong was once honored as General for his part." The inscription on *the Stele to Farmland Granting Certificate* lists the following monks of meritorious deeds in the 4th year of the Wude Emperor's reign (621 CE).

Dean (shangzuo): Shanhu

Abbot (sizhu): Zhicao

Overseer (duweina): Huiyang

General-in-chief (da jiangjun): Tanzong

Other monks of meritorious service: Puhui, Mingsong, Lingxian, Pusheng, Zhishou, Daoguang, Zhixing, Man, Feng.

After Shaolin monk warriors received the generous grants and rewards from the Tang dynasty of Monarchy Li, the Shaolin Temple became known across the country. As a result, the Shaolin Temple not only possessed a squadron of monk warriors, but also received a great deal of favorable treatments, which laid the foundation for Shaolin monks warriors' active battle participation.

For a long period after Shaolin monk warriors helped Li Shimin defeat Wang Shichong in the early Tang dynasty, the Shaolin monks, though practicing Kungfu, did not participate in the war. During the Yuanhe Emperor's reign in the middle of the Tang dynasty, a Shaolin monk named Yuanjing helped Li Shidao rebel against the Tang dynasty; in the Song dynasty, another Shaolin monk named Zongyin organized Shaolin monk warriors to help the Song dynasty fight against the Jin dynasty; at the end of the Yuan dynasty Shaolin monk warriors also participated in battles against the Red Turban Army. Due to the minor scale of these three war participations, their impact was negligible, or not known to the public. However, the Shaolin monks' extensive war participation in the Ming dynasty was large in scale and far-reaching in influence.

In the Ming dynasty, the Shaolin monk warriors entered the war for the first time during the Zhengde Emperor's reign (1505 CE—1521 CE). According to the *History of the Ming Dynasty*, in the middle and late Ming dynasty, the Mongolian aristocrats who fled their country continuously invaded the northern border of the Ming dynasty. To this end, the Ming dynasty set up military fortifications along the border in Shanxi and Shaanxi provinces, and constantly dispatched armed forces to guard the fortifications, and Shaolin monk warriors were also recruited. The inscription on one Shaolin Temple pagoda built in

年)立的《豁免粮差碑》载:"先年,上司调遣寺僧,随征刘贼、王堂、师尚诏、倭寇,阵亡数僧。"由此可知,明朝正德时,少林僧兵还参与镇压了刘六、刘七领导的农民军。据《明史纪事本末》载,此次参战的少林僧兵三百余人,死七十余僧。嘉靖元年(1522年),山东青州爆发了王堂领导的矿工起义,少林僧兵应明王朝之征调前往镇压。明嘉靖三十二年(1553年),河南柘城人师尚诏率农民起义,拥众数万,并攻入归德(今河南商丘),少林僧兵应征在周参率领下前往镇压。明万历三年(1575年)《少林寺竺方参公塔铭》载周参率僧兵镇压师尚诏起义情况:"嘉靖三十二年,上司明文调用截杀,领僧兵五十名,征师尚诏。歼贼兵,运大智于杀场,战雄兵于顷刻,不过尽忠于国。"从镇压刘六、王堂、师尚诏农民军看,明王朝已将少林僧兵作为其统治的重要军事力量。在征战立功后,明官府还数次发文,豁免了少林寺的粮差。

明朝僧兵的参战,数抗倭战争最为世人称道。起于明初,盛于明代中叶的倭寇(日本海盗),经常在我沿海一带烧杀掠抢,成为明朝重要的外患。为此,明王朝不断调遣军队前往东南沿海一带御倭,少林僧兵也参加了这场战争。此事万历二十三年《豁免粮差碑》有载:"嘉靖间,刘贼、王堂及倭寇并师尚诏等倡乱。本寺武僧,屡经调遣,奋勇杀贼,多著死功。"《明史·兵志》:"倭乱,少林僧应募者四十余,战亦多胜。" 嘉靖四十年(1561年),抗倭名将俞大猷,也曾带少林武僧普从、宗擎赴沿海抗倭前线参战三年。又据《日知录》及《云间杂志》载:嘉靖中,少林僧兵三十余人,在接到都督万表的檄文后,在月空的率领下,持铁棒在战场上击杀大量倭寇,三十多名僧兵最后全部战死沙场。明代少林僧兵不仅参战,而且还大力帮助明朝训练官军。据万表《海寇议》载:"其后倭乱,表结少林僧,习格斗法,屡歼其众。"此外,《海寇议》《江南经略》《倭变志》等还载有众多少林派僧兵参战的情况。《上海掌故丛书·倭寇》载参加抗倭战争的少林派僧兵有88人,战死21人。明代少林僧兵参加的抗倭战争在少林僧兵史上写下壮丽

the 27th year of the Jiajing Emperor's reign (1548 CE) states that during the Zhengde Emperor's reign (1505 CE—1521 CE), with the order of Emperor Wuzong, the Shaolin monk warriors under the leadership of a Kungfu monk named Zhou You (nicknamed Sanqi, literally meaning three magics), went to defend the border of Shanxi and Shaanxi provinces, and repeatedly attained great achievements. In recognition of their achievements, Emperor Wuzong specially appointed Zhou You regiment chief commander. Later when the upper aristocrats of the Miao nationality in Yunnan rebelled, Zhou You, ordered by Emperor Wuzong, once again led the well-trained Shaolin monk warriors to go to Yunnan to settle the rebellion. All the monks who participated in the war were entitled to "official rewards". According to the inscription on the tower stele, Zhou You has "over a thousand disciples", scattered in dozens of counties across 4 provinces including Henan, Shandong, South Zhili and North Zhili. It can be speculated that the armed forces led by Zhou You with monk warriors as the backbone formed a considerable armed organization.

After Zhou You, Shaolin monk warriors participated in the war more frequently. According to the *Grain Taxation Exemption Monument* erected in the 9th year of the Wanli Emperor's reign, "over the past years, when the superior dispatched the temple monks to crack down Japanese pirates, as well as rebels led respectively by Liu brothers, Wang Tang, Shi Shangzhao, a number of monks deceased." In the Zhengde Emperor's reign (1506—1521 CE) of the Ming dynasty, Shaolin monk warriors also participated in the suppression of the peasant army led by Liu Liu and Liu Qi. According to the *Biographies Series of History of the Ming Dynasty*, more than 300 Shaolin monk warriors participated in the war, and more than 70 of them deceased. In the first year of the Jiajing Emperor's reign (1522 CE), when the miners uprising led by Wang Tang broke out in Qingzhou, Shandong province, the Shaolin monk warriors were sent to suppress them. In the 32nd year of the Jiajing Emperor's reign (1553 CE), Shi Shangzhao, native to Zhecheng, Henan province, led a squad of peasants to rise up. The troop recruited tens of thousands of people, and attacked Guide (currently Shangqiu city in Henan province). The Shaolin monk warriors were enlisted under the leadership of Zhou Can to crack down the rebellion. The inscription written in the 3rd year of the Wanli Emperor's reign (1575 CE) on the *Pagoda commemorating*

图4-8 《改公禅师塔铭》
The Inscription on the *Pagoda in memory of Chan Master Gaigong*

的一页。

在明末，少林僧兵还参与了同农民军进行的战争。据《明史·史记言传》等载，崇祯时，史记言曾聘少林武僧为之训练军队，并参与了对农民军的战争，后史在两武僧护卫下逃走时被农民军杀死。又据《登封县志》《中州杂俎》载，明末登封人李际遇率万余农民军驻扎于御寨山（少室山），因少林僧兵与之为敌，李际遇乘其不备，"率数百人，裹甲以入，徐至经堂，正挝鼓膜拜，贼各出刃砍僧，僧之不备，俱为贼歼"。又据清康熙十六年（1677年）立的《改公禅师塔铭》载，明崇祯年间，兵部尚书杨嗣昌奉旨在山西、湖广、河南等处与李自成农民军作战，调少林武僧守备道宗、道法、庆余、庆盘、同贺、玄清参战。从明代《豁免粮差碑》所载知，明代少林有常设僧兵武装，称为"武僧守备"，随时应明王朝之征调参战。

民国是少林寺历史上风云变幻最激烈的时期之一。这期间少林寺所发生的事，既有壮举也有悲剧。进入民国之后，随着清王朝对少林寺禁锢的终结及社会的动荡，沉寂了近三百年的少林僧兵在民国初期又重新

Monk Zhou Can describes the event. "In the 32nd year of the Jiajing Emperor's reign (1553 CE), the superior sent a written order to call for an interception. Zhou Can led a squadron of 50 monk warriors to help crack down the rebelling troops led by Shi Shangzhao. They, loyal to the country, fought skillfully and defeated the bandits instantly." The extensive involvement of Shaolin monk warriors in the suppression of Liu Liu, Wang Tang and Shi Shangzhao's peasant army suggests that the Ming dynasty had taken Shaolin's troops as an important military force under its rule. After the campaign, the Ming dynasty also issued multiple documents to exempt the Shaolin Temple from grain taxation.

Among all the wars involving Shaolin monk warriors in the Ming dynasty, the one against Wokou was the best known. Since the beginning of the Ming dynasty, the Japanese pirates, flourishing in the middle of the Ming dynasty, had often pillaged the coastal areas and became a serious concern of the Ming dynasty. Therefore, the Ming dynasty continually dispatched troops to the southeast coast, and the Shaolin monk warriors were also enlisted. In the *Stele to the Exemption from Grain Taxation*, it is inscribed that: "During the Jiajing Emperor's reign, when Liu brothers, Wang Tang, Japanese pirates, and Shi Shangzhao caused social chaos, Shaolin Kungfu monks, repeatedly dispatched, fought bravely. Many monks distinguished themselves at the risk of their lives. The chapter on Military Records in the *History of Ming dynasty* states that "Due to the invasion of Wokou, more than 40 Shaolin monks were enlisted, and they achieved multiple victories". In the 40th year of the Jiajing Emperor's reign (1561 CE), General Yu Dayou, a famous anti-Wokou hero, recruited two Shaolin Kungfu monks respectively named Pu Cong, Zongqing to fight at coastal anti-Wokou front for three years. According to Gu Yanwu's *Daily Reflection* and Hu Wenming's *Cloud Notes*: In the middle of the Jiajing Emperor's reign, after receiving Wan Biao's (then military governor) call to the battle, over 30 Shaolin monk warriors led by a monk named Yuekong went to the front and killed a large number of Wokou with iron staff. Eventually, all of them fought to death in the battlefield. The Shaolin monk warriors of the Ming dynasty not only participated in the war, but also vigorously helped the Ming dynasty to train the army. Wan Biao's *Proposal on Maritime Banditry* (*hai kou yi*) states, "In the ensuing turmoil caused by Wokou, Wan Biao invited Shaolin monks to participate in fighting against them. Thanks

出现，并参与了一系列战争。

民国元年（1912年），少林寺著名武僧恒林升任执掌嵩山佛教的登封县僧会司僧会（会长）。恒林少林功夫高超，胆识过人。民国初期，由于时局混乱，土匪横行，豫西尤为严重。少林地区也是匪患重灾区，这里常常是"伏莽出没"，甚至少林寺僧也曾被土匪掳去。民国八年（1919年），学者陈万里到少林寺游览，恒林问道："曾否带有手枪？有则藏诸身侧，备土匪。"众人听后皆呈"骇异之色"。对于匪患的严重程度，杨圻在《少室观雪图记》中云："匪亦入山中，洗劫净尽，至无鸡犬。"在此情况下，恒林被推为少林寺保卫团团总。恒林就任后即开始购置枪支并以武功训练僧人为主的武装，由此揭开了少林僧兵参战的序幕。

民国九年（1920年）秋，豫西遭荒灾，土匪蜂起，四处烧杀掠抢。身为少林寺保卫团团总的恒林，率领训练有素的少林僧兵，在登封县城、梯子沟、白玉沟、熬子坪等地与土匪进行了大小数十战，无不胜。是年，匪首朱保成、牛邦、孙天章、段洪涛等联合夜袭巩县鲁庄，因天明被人发现，土匪向西南逃窜，巩县九区民团追击，当他们经过偃师府店时，偃师十四区和十五区民团也参加追击。当恒林得报后，率少林寺保卫团僧兵在少林寺西南截击土匪。当土匪行至熬子坪时与恒林的少林寺保卫团发生激战，少林寺保卫团僧兵一举击溃土匪，土匪大部分被歼，其余瓦解远遁，少林寺保卫团此次获胜使少林寺缴获大量枪弹。从此，恒林及少林僧兵威震四方，远近土匪闻其名不敢犯其境。战后，河洛道尹阎伦如赠恒林"少林活佛"匾额以旌表其功。省长张凤台也给恒林颁发奖章和奖状。从此，拥有大量枪支且精通武功的少林僧兵，成了登封县一支重要的武装力量。其后，登封县城数度被土匪围攻，少林寺保卫团多次应招前往参战。

1923年秋，恒林圆寂后，其得意弟子妙兴继任少林寺住持和登封县僧会司僧会。妙兴精通武功，为近代最著名的武僧。妙兴上任后继续

to the monks' relentless fighting practice, they killed large numbers of Japanese pirates." In addition, other works including *Military Strategy and Tactics in South China* (*Jiangnan Jinglue*), *the Evolution of Wokou* (*wo bian zhi*) also describe Shaolin monks' participation in the anti-Wokou battles. The chapter on *Wokou in Shanghai Story Series* (*Shanghai zhang gu cong shu*) states that 88 Shaolin monk warriors participated in an anti-Wokou war and 21 monks sacrificed their lives in the battlefield. In short, Shaolin monk warriors' battle participation marked a magnificent chapter in the history of anti-Wokou war.

In the late Ming dynasty, Shaolin monk warriors also participated in battles against the peasant army. According to the *Biography of Shi Jiyan* in the History of the Ming dynasty, during the Emperor Chongzhen's reign, Shi Jiyan employed Shaolin Kungfu monks to train the army and participate in the war against the peasant army. Later, when he escaped under the guard of the two Kungfu monks, he was killed by the peasant army. In addition, according to *Dengfeng County Annals*, and *Anecdotes of Zhongzhou*, at the end of the Ming dynasty, tens of thousands of peasant troops, led by a Dengfeng native named Li Jiyu, were stationed in Yuzhai Mount (Mount Shaoshi). As the Shaolin monk warriors contended against them, Li Jiyu once took advantage of their lack of preparation. "Hundreds of armored soldiers led by Li Jiyu slowly approached the sultra recitation hall, when the monks were worshipping while drumming. Due to their lack of preparation, all the monks were killed by the bandits with knives." Furthermore, the inscription on the *Pagoda in memory of Chan Master Gaigong* erected in the 16th year of the Kangxi Emperor's reign (1677 CE) states that during the Chongzhen Emperor's reign of the Ming dynasty, when Yang Sichang followed the emperor's will to fight against peasant rebellion army led by Li Zicheng in Shanxi, Huguang region, and Henan provinces, he enlisted the assistance of Shaolin Kungfu monks including Daozong, Daofa, Qingyu, Qingpan, Tonghe and Xuanqing as assistance. According to the record on *Grain Taxation Exemption Monument*, Shaolin was furnished with permanent armed monk warriors during the Ming dynasty, who are called the Kungfu monk garrison, constantly ready for the governmental requisition to fight in wars.

The Republic of China witnessed one of the most turbulent periods in the history of the Shaolin Temple. During this period, what happened in the Shaolin

图4-9 恒林大和尚碑
The Stele to Master Henglin

训练少林僧兵武装。民国十一年（1922年），河南地方武装首领樊钟秀被吴佩孚收编为暂编第四团团长。是年，樊受吴佩孚之命到登封收抚任应岐、陈青云等地方武装，路过少林寺时，见大雄宝殿损坏，捐资400元作为修寺之资，并拜少林寺住持恒林为师。由此，樊与少林寺关系甚密。1923年吴佩孚命师长张玉山到登封收编湖北别动队，其第一旅旅长卢耀堂觊觎少林僧兵武装及枪弹，任命妙兴为一旅第一团团长，驻扎少林寺。

民国十四年（1925年），胡景翼与阚玉琨爆发"胡阚"战争。此时，因援助孙中山而被任命为"建国豫军"总司令的樊钟秀，从广东开赴河南协助胡景翼与阚玉琨作战，阚部崔继华从密县败退，樊请妙兴率少林僧兵第一团出战，妙兴遂指挥少林僧兵与阚部倒戈的李镇亚一起，共同击败崔继华部，樊军占领登封县城。

1927年3月，妙兴率领以少林僧兵为骨干的第一团，在少林寺誓师出征，随卢耀堂旅开驻郑州。后第一团与任应岐部在舞阳作战，妙兴阵亡，少林僧兵武装从此瓦解。1928年，冯玉祥部国民军北伐时，樊钟秀由于与少林寺关系密切，以少林寺为司令部攻其后方，寺僧暗助樊军，

Temple was both heroic and tragic. After entering the period of the Republic of China, the Qing dynasty's restraint on Shaolin Temple came to an end and social unrests prevailed. The Shaolin monk warriors who had been silent for nearly three hundred years reappeared in the early Republic of China and participated in a series of battles.

In the 1st year of the Republic of China (1912 CE), Henglin, a well-known Shaolin Kungfu monk chaired the Monk Association of Dengfeng county, which was in charge of the Songshan Buddhist affairs. He was both highly skillful in Kungfu and exceptionally visionary. In the beginning of the Republic of China, the whole country was chaotic with rampant banditry. This was particularly true in the west of Henan province. The shaolin area is seriously inflicted with banditry disturbances, for looting and robbery were common, and even Shaolin monks could fall victim to abduction. In the 8th year of the Republic of China (1920 CE), when a scholar named Chen Wanli came to visit the Shaolin Temple, Henglin asked, "Do you bring along handguns? If so, keep it around to prevent bandits." Upon hearing these words, all looked horrified. As to the seriousness of banditry, Yang Qi made the following remarks in his essay entitled *On the Appreciation of Snow in Mount Shaoshi*, "Bandits also invaded mountain settlements and looted everything. As a result, even chicken and dogs were hardly visible." Under such a circumstance, Henglin was selected as the chief of Shaolin Temple Defense Corps. After Henglin took office, he started to purchase ammunition and train an armed force equipped with Kungfu, the majority of which were shaolin monks. This unveiled a prelude to Shaolin Kungfu monks' war participation in the Republic of China.

In the autumn of the 9th year of the Republic of China (1920 CE), the western Henan province suffered from famine, and the bandits started robbery and looting. Heng Lin, the chief of the Shaolin Temple Defense Corps, leading his well-trained Shaolin monk warriors, launched dozens of battles against the bandits in the Dengfeng county town, Tizi Gou Village, Baiyugou Village and Aoziping village etc. and won all of them. In the same year, the head bandits including Zhu Baocheng, Niu Bang, Sun Tianzhang, Duan Hongtao and others jointly attacked Luzhuang village at night. They were discovered at dawn and fled to the southwest. The militia of the 9th district in Gongxian county

后冯部石友三率军攻入少林寺,一把大火焚烧了少林寺,千古名刹再遭浩劫。抗日战争时,少林寺永贵、素祥、志元、行香等多名武僧还参加了抗日战争。

新中国成立以后,少林僧兵虽然不再需要,但是少林功夫在军事训练和军队运动项目上得到了更广泛的开展。1953年中国人民解放军军事体育学校成立,把散手格斗列为重要训练科目。1965年,总参军训部编写了《步兵分队格斗教材》,作为部队训练的重要内容。1986年,全军体育训练内容改革,将少林拳列入训练内容,还增加了擒拿、散打等项目。

可以预言,少林功夫作为优秀的民族传统文化和良好的军队运动项目,必将被新生代的军队锻造出更大的辉煌。

四、少林功夫与艺术

1.碑刻

少林寺历代立有281通、304品古代碑刻,这些碑刻不仅反映了少林寺的兴衰,见证了少林功夫的发展,同时也是中国古代碑刻艺术的瑰宝,多为金石家、书法家所称道。

在少林寺山门后至天王殿中间有一大甬道,两侧有小马道,为寺院碑刻集中之地,由于碑多如林,故称"碑林"。这里原存放少林寺众多名碑,如唐代《大唐天后御制诗书碑》《灵运禅师功德塔铭碑》,宋代《三十六峰赋》,元代《息庵禅师碑》《珪公禅师碑》,明代《千崖万壑碑》《少林观武碑》《释迦双迹灵像碑》《淳拙禅师碑》等。1984年至1992年,这些重要碑刻均移至新建的碑廊内保存。如今碑林尚存有碑刻35通,其中明碑10通,清碑11通,现代碑刻13通,年代不详的1通。知名的有明代《豁免粮差碑》《月舟禅师碑》,清代《承修少林寺工程

Chapter IV The Rich Connotation of Shaolin Kungfu   149

pursued the bandits. When bandits passed Fudian village of Yanshi county, the militia of the 14th and 15th districts in the Yanshi county also participated in the pursuit. When this was reported to Henglin, the Shaolin Temple Defense Corps intercepted the bandits in the southwest to the Shaolin Temple. When the bandits went to Aoziping village, a fierce battle broke out between the bandits and Henglin's Shaolin Temple Defense Corps. The Shaolin Temple defenders defeated the bandits in one fell swoop. Most of the bandits were killed, and the rest collapsed and fled. The Shaolin Temple Defense Corps seized a large number of guns and other ammunition. Since then, Henglin and his Shaolin monk warriors became well known. Bandits, far or near, dared not offend them. After the war, the Mayor of Luoyang (he luo dao yi) awarded Henglin a reward plaque inscribed with the "Shaolin Living Buddha" to honor his merits. Zhang Fengtai, Governor of Henan province, also awarded medals and certificates to honor Henglin. Since then, the Shaolin monk warriors, who possessed a large number of guns and were proficient in Kungfu, had become an important armed force in Dengfeng county. Later, when Dengfeng county was besieged by the bandits several times, the Shaolin Temple Defense Corps were also recruited to participate in the battles.

In the autumn of 1923, Henglin deceased. His favorite disciple, Miaoxing, succeeded him to be seated as the Shaolin Temple abbot and the Chief of the Monk Association of Dengfeng county. Miaoxing was proficient in Kungfu, and was the most famous Kungfu monk in modern times. After he took office, he continued to train the Shaolin monk warriors. In the 11th year of the Republic of China (1922), Fan Zhongxiu, the local armed leader of Henan province, was incorporated into the Tentative Fourth Regiment by Wu Peifu and appointed the regiment commander. In the same year, Fan was sent to Dengfeng county to take in the local armed forces headed by Ren Yingqi and Chen Qingyun. When Fan passed by the Shaolin Temple, he saw that the Great Buddha Palace Hall was damaged. He donated ¥400 as a fund for temple renovation, and took Henglin, the abbot of the Shaolin Temple, as his Kungfu instructor. As a result, Fan forged a close relationship with the Shaolin Temple. In 1923, Wu Peifu ordered Zhang Yushan, a division commander, to join the Hubei Special Brigade in Dengfeng. Lu Yaotang, the commander of Zhang's first brigade, coveted the arms and guns of Shaolin monk warriors, and appointed Miaoxing as the commander of his first

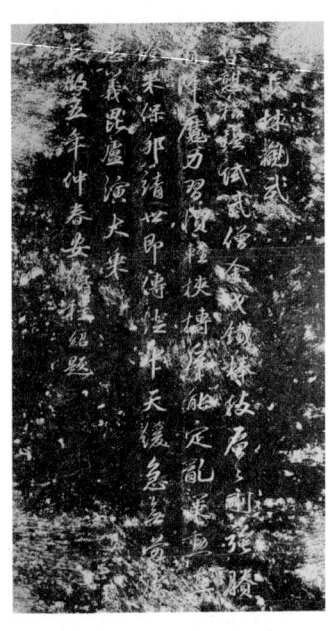

图4-10 明代少林观武碑
Shaolin Martial Arts Appreciation Monument of the Ming Dynasty

碑》《禁焚山林碑》，现代《日本宗道臣大和尚归山纪念碑》等。碑廊即少林寺慈云堂，旧时为千佛庵，在山门后碑林东侧，建于清康熙时。碑廊现存有古碑106通，其中北齐1通，唐碑6通，宋碑5通，金碑5通，元碑10通，明碑69通，清碑7通，年代不详的3通。

寺内所存的《太宗文武圣皇帝龙潜教书碑》是少林寺院现存最早的少林功夫实物资料。该碑现存于少林寺碑廊内，刻立于初唐。碑高1.07米，宽0.45米。碑文为八分隶书，刻唐武德四年（621年）四月三十日李世民颁发的《告柏谷坞少林寺上座书》。碑上第三行有草签的"世民"二字。

这通最早反映少林僧兵的碑刻为金石、书法家所争论不休。《金石录》认为此书为后人重书，碑额隶书"太宗文皇帝御书"七个字是开元神武皇帝的笔迹。《弇州山人稿》认为此碑刻的书法不是很工整，但也不俗，应该是出自幕僚之手。"世民"两个字，当是李世民亲书的行草。碑额的开元神武皇帝书是后人胡乱加上去的。《金石文字记》也同样认为"世民"两字为李世民亲笔所写。

battalion to station in the Shaolin Temple.

In the 14th year of the Republic of China (1925), a war broke out between Hu Jingyi and Kan Yukun, known as the "Hu Kan" war. Then, Fan Zhongxiu, who was appointed the commander-in-chief of the Henan Army for his assistance to Sun Yat-sen, went from Guangdong to Henan to assist Hu Jingyi to help him fight against Kan Yukun. Kan's army, led by Cui Jihua, retreated from Mixian county. Fan invited Miaoxing to lead the first regiment of Shaolin monk warriors to join in the fight. Then, Miaoxing ordered Shaolin monk warriors to fight together with Li Zhenya who revolted against Kan Yukun. As a result, Cui Jihua was defeated, and Fan's army occupied the Dengfeng county town.

In March of 1927, in the Shaolin Temple, Miaoxing, leading the first regiment with the Shaolin monk warriors as the backbone, took oath for expedition. They marched to Zhengzhou with Lu Yaotang's brigade. Later, Miaoxing's first regiment and Ren Yingqi's army fought in Wuyang, where Miaoxing fought to death in the battle, and the Shaolin's armed forces collapsed. In 1928, when Feng Yuxiang's National Army was on its Northern Expedition, Fan Zhongxiu, closely related to the Shaolin Temple, took Shaolin Temple as his headquarters to attack the rear of Feng's troops. The Shaolin Temple helped Fan's army secretly. Later, the army of Shi Yousan affiliated to Feng Yuxiang, attacked the Shaolin Temple, and burned it with a big fire. The ancient Temple was ravaged again. During the period of the Anti-Japanese War, Shaolin Kungfu monks including Yonggui, Suxiang, Zhiyuan, Xingxiang and others also participated in the war against Japanese invasion.

After the founding of the People's Republic of China, Shaolin monk warriors were no longer in need to participate in military actions, but Shaolin Kungfu was more widely practiced in military training and military sports. In 1953, the Chinese People's Liberation Army Military Sports School was established, and sanshou combat sport (san shou ge dou) was listed as an important training subject. In 1965, the General Staff Military Training Department compiled the *Infantry Division Fighting Textbook* as an important part of military training. In 1986, when the sports training contents of the whole army were reformed, the Shaolin boxing (Shaolin quan) was included as as a training subject, together with other items such as arrest (qin na) and sanda (san da).

在少林寺的钟楼前,还立有一通《皇唐嵩岳少林寺碑》,也是唐代少林僧兵和功夫的最早见证者。该碑刻立于唐朝开元十六年(728年),玄宗时光禄大夫、吏部尚书、上柱国裴漼撰文并书丹,碑刻宏大,高3.6米,宽1.32米。碑首雕盘龙,额刻唐玄宗亲书的"太宗文皇帝御书"隶书七个大字。

其碑文开始写唐太宗李世民兴起于山西太原,后住于广武,广开召贤之门,后率军攻王世充。少林寺武僧志操、惠玚、昙宗等,看到唐朝将取代天下的大势,于是率领僧兵,攻击郑军王仁则大营,生擒王仁则,并将其献于李世民。李世民对少林寺及武僧大加褒奖,频频降诏书慰问,并赐给少林寺良田四十顷,水碾一具。这通碑是继《太宗文武圣皇帝龙潜教书碑》之后,又一个比较明确反映少林功夫及僧兵的见证物。叶封《嵩阳石刻集记》认为此碑在少林寺嵩山诸碑行书中,当属第一。

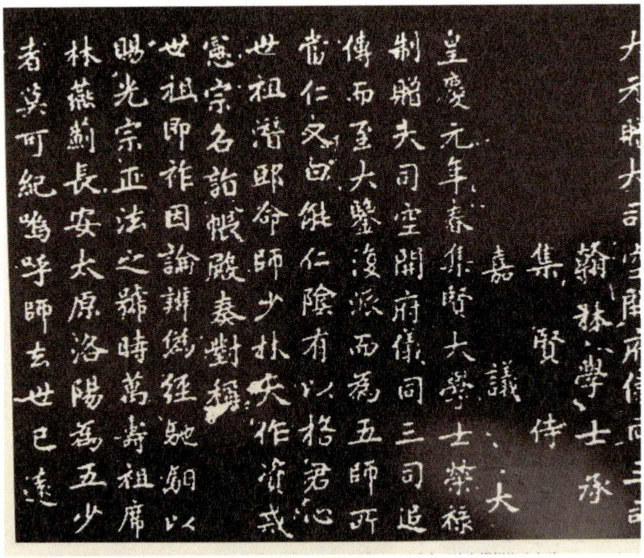

图4-11 裕公碑局部
Part of the Monument of Yu Gong

It can be predicted that Shaolin Kungfu, an excellent national traditional culture and a good military sport, will be forged into greater brilliance by the new generation of the army.

IV. Shaolin Kungfu and Arts

1. Steles

There are 281 steles bearing 304 ancient inscriptions in the Shaolin Temple in successive dynasties. These inscriptions not only have recorded the rise and fall of the Shaolin Temple, but also witnessed the development of Shaolin Kungfu. They are also treasures of ancient Chinese inscription art, which are widely hailed by sculptors and calligraphers.

A large collection of stone steles concentrate along a major road running from the Mountain Gate to the Heavenly Kings (Devaraja) Palace Hall, as well as along the paralleling minor bridleways. The large number of stone steles earns this place the name of Forest of Steles. Here also stand various renowned monuments of the Shaolin Temple, such as the *Monument in Memory of Empress Wu Zetian's Poetry*, the *Virtue Tower Monument to Chan Master Lingyun* from the Tang dynasty, *the Stele of Poems of Thirty-six Peaks* from the Song dynasty, *the Monument to Chan Master Xi'an*, the *Monument to Chan Master Guigong* from the Yuan dynasty, *the Monument to Thousand Cliffs and Abysses*, the *Shaolin Martial Arts Appreciation Monument*, the *Monument to Sakyamuni's Footprints*, *the Monument to Chan Master Chunzhuo* and so on from the Ming dynasty. From 1984 to 1992, these important steles were moved to and stored in the new monument corridor. To date there still stand 35 steles in the Forest of Steles. Among them, 10 are from the Ming dynasty, 11 from the Qing dynasty, 13 modern ones, and 1 from a time unidentified. The best-known steles include the *Grain Taxation Exemption Monument* and *the Monument to Chan Master Yuezhou* from the Ming dynasty, *the Shaolin Temple Construction Project Monument* and *the Monument to Forbidding Burning Mountain Forest* from the Qing dynasty, a modern monument to commemorate the return of Japanese monk Doshin So and so on. The monument corridor is the Ciyun Hall of the Shaolin Temple, which used to be called Thousand Buddhas Palace Hall, standing to the

《唐少林寺戒坛铭》《弇州续稿》认为：戒坛石为学生张杰书，当是时，杰年少且不以书名，而笔法老成及尔。又时未尽习帝书，故犹有瘦劲意。

在少林寺的碑刻中，刻立于唐贞元十四年（798年）的《嵩岳少林寺新造厨库记》碑，乃吏部侍郎顾少连所撰，崔溉正书，笔法近拙，而颇古穆。

宋《少林寺达摩颂》为黄庭坚题书，字径四寸余，挥洒自如，史称其楷法妍媚成一家，草书尤奇伟。

《面壁之塔》上的"面壁之塔"四字为蔡京所书，题云：太师鲁国公京属书，宣和壬寅八月资政殿学士河南尹范致虚立石。《嵩阳石刻记》说：京书严而不拘，逸而不外，规矩大字，冠绝古今，鲜有俦匹。

原存于《少林寺志》的庆公碑，是元初少林僧兵的见证者，由名儒薛友谅撰于延祐五年（1318年），笔势清劲。

《少林禅师裕公碑》为元代集贤侍讲学士、中奉大夫赵孟頫所书。

图4-12 明代金忠士诗碑
Memorial Monument of Jin Zhongshi's Poetry in the Ming Dynasty

east of Forest of Steles. It was built in the Qing dynasty. In the stele corridor there stand 106 ancient monuments, including 1 stele from the North Qi dynasty, 6 from the Tang dynasty, 5 from the Song dynasty, 5 from the Jin dynasty, 10 steles from the Yuan dynasty, 69 from the Ming dynasty, 7 from the Qing dynasty, and 3 from a date unidentified.

The Shaolin Monastery Stele on Mount Song in the temple is the earliest physical material related to Shaolin Kungfu. The stele, now stored in the Shaolin Corridor of Steles, was engraved in the early Tang dynasty. The monument, 107 centimeters high and 45 centimeters wide, was engraved in standard official scripts with the *Letter to the Dean of the Shaolin Temple at Cypress Valley*, issued by Li Shimin in the 4th year of the Wude Emperor's reign (621 CE). The third line of the scripts contains the autograph of Shimin (世民) in the cursive form of Chinese calligraphy.

This earliest inscription about Shaolin monk warriors caused continuous debates between epigraphers and calligraphers. *The Records of Epigraphy* purports that the edict was rewritten later, and the seven characters of the inscription ("太宗文皇帝御书" Taizong wen huang di yu shu, literally translated as: the royal edict written by Emperor Li Shimin) were the handwriting of the Emperor Xuanzong of Tang dynasty. *The Manuscripts of Yanzhou Shanren* argues that since the calligraphy of this inscription is not neat or orderly, but still remarkable, it should be written by the aides. The two Chinese characters "Shimin" must be Emperor Li Shimin's cursive calligraphy. The inscription of Kai Yuan Shen Wu Huang Di Shu (translated literally as: royal calligraphy by Emperor Xuan zong) on the top of the stele was added casually by the descendants. *The Records of Epigraphy* also argues that the two characters 世民, (Shimin, the personal given name of Emperor Li Shimin) were written by the emperor in person.

In front of the bell tower of the Shaolin Temple, there also stands the *Shaolin Monastery Stele on Mount Song*, which is also the earliest evidence of the Shaolin monk warriors and Kungfu in the Tang dynasty. The inscription was erected in the 16th year of the Kaiyuan Emperor's reign (728 CE), authored by Pei Cui. That is a grand inscription, measured 360cm high and 132cm wide. The head of the stele is engraved with a dragon, and inscribed with seven grand

赵之书法,为元朝第一。

刻立于明朝正德十二年(1517年)的《那罗延护法示迹碑》是明末少林僧兵与红巾军作战的实物资料,由正德时少林寺住持文载禅师所撰。

刻立于万历元年(1573年)十月的《豁免额外粮差碑》。现存于少林寺碑廊,高1.35米,宽0.62米。碑上为"河南等处承宣布政使司分守河南道、左参政"的批文。这些都是很好的书法作品。

另外,明代塔林中还有数块塔铭,也是记载了明代少林僧兵参战的情况,也是功夫与碑刻艺术的完美结合之作。

2.绘画

图4-13 清麟庆少林校拳
Linqing's Shaolin Xiao Fist in the Qing Dynasty

反映少林功夫的绘画以少林寺白衣殿内的练功壁画最为引人注目。少林寺白衣殿位于千佛殿东南,建于清初,是一座面阔五间,进深五架

Chinese characters ("太宗文皇帝御书") in official script, which are literally translated as the royal calligraphy by Emperor Taizong.

The inscription starts with statements that Emperor Taizong of Tang, named Li Shimin, who arose in Taiyuan, Shanxi province, and later encamped in Guangwu, Henan province, opened door wide to recruit talents. He led the army to attack Wang Shichong. Viewing that the Tang dynasty would take charge of the whole country, the Shaolin Kungfu monks such as Zhicao, Huiyang and Tanzong led monk warriors to attack the camp of Wang Renze. They captured Wang Renze alive and presented him to Li Shimin (later enthroned as the Emperor of the Tang dynasty). Li Shimin generously rewarded the Shaolin Temple and its Kungfu monks. He issued multiple edicts of condolences, and granted the Shaolin Temple 40 qing (266 hectares) of fertile farmland, and a water mill. This monument is another testimony of Shaolin Kungfu and its monk warriors, besides the *Stele of Emperor Li Shimin's Edict to Shaolin Temple*. Ye Feng, in *A Collection of Songyang Stone Carvings*, holds that this tablet ranks the first among the steles in the Shaolin Temple for its calligraphy of cursive style.

According to *The Continuation of Yanzhou Manuscripts*, *the Inscription on Ordination Altar from the Tang dynasty*, the Ordination Altar Inscription was written by Zhang Jie, a renowned calligrapher in Tang dynasty. At that time, he was still young, but his calligraphy was sophisticated, thin but strong.

Among the inscriptions in the Shaolin Temple there is one inscription *On Building the Kitchen Storehouse in Songyue Shaolin Temple*. It was inscribed in the 14th year of the Zhenyuan Emperor's reign (798 CE), composed by Assistant Minister of Personnel Gu Shaolian, handwritten by Cui Gaizheng with a hardy and solemn writing style.

The inscription of the *Ode to Dharma in the Shaolin Temple* was written by Huang Tingjian, a renowned calligrapher in the Song dynasty. It is recorded that his calligraphy cherished easy charm, illustrated by his unique regular scripts and grand cursive styles.

The four characters "面壁之塔"(mian bi zhi ta, literally translated as the *Tower of Wall-gazing Meditation*) on the *Wall-gazing Meditation Tablet* is written by Cai Jing, a famous calligrapher in Northern Song dynasty. According to *Records of Stone Carvings in Songyang*, Cai Jing's handwriting is rigorous but

的大硬山式建筑。在白衣殿内的南北墙壁上有清末绘制的《武僧演武图》，又称《罗汉手搏像》《少林锤谱》。其北壁绘的是少林武僧在大雄宝殿前格斗的场面，共16组，33位武僧。壁画中除一个是一对二进行格斗外，其余均是两两相对。此幅壁画场面绘的是清朝道光八年（1828年）三月二十五日，朝廷大员麟庆代巡抚杨海梁祭嵩山至少林寺，寺僧为之演武时的情景。大雄宝殿及周围的殿堂上张灯结彩，热闹非凡，大雄宝殿月台望柱中右侧留长辫、着清代官服者为麟庆及随从，中间左侧为组织演武的少林寺住持及其他执事。此幅壁画原载于麟庆的《鸿雪因

图4-14 紧那罗王御红巾（之二）
Mural of King Jin Na Luo Against the Red Turbans

缘图记》一书。当年麟庆游少林寺观武后在其所著的《鸿雪因缘图记》一书中绘了一幅《少林校拳图》，后寺僧将《少林校拳图》扩大后绘于白衣殿北壁。北墙壁画是清代少林武僧演功的真实写照，其招招式式都体现出了少林功夫的深邃及格斗技击性强、实战性强的特点。白衣殿的

unconstrained, free but not wanton, which made it unprecedentedly charming.

The Stele Commemorating Huiqing (qing gong bei) originally stored in the *Shaolin Temple Annals* is a testimony of the Shaolin Temple's monk warriors in the early Yuan dynasty. It was written in the 2nd year of the Yanyou Emperor's reign (1318 CE) by Xue Youjian, a renowned confucian scholar. His calligraphy is elegant and powerful.

The Stele to the *Shaolin Chan Master Yugong* was written by Zhao Mengfu, the top calligrapher of the Yuan dynasty.

The Narayana Protector Demonstration Monument, which was engraved in the 12th year of the Zhengde Emperor's reign (1517 CE) in the Ming dynasty, features the physical materials of the Shaolin monk warriors fighting against the Red Turban Army in the late Ming dynasty. It was written during the Zhengde Emperor's reign by the abbot of the Shaolin Temple, Chan Master Wenzai.

The Stele on Exemption of Additional Grain Taxation, measured 1.35 meters high and 0.62 meters wide, was engraved in October of the 1st year of the Wanli Empeor's reign (1573 CE). All these abovementioned monuments and steles made impressive calligraphy works.

In addition, there are several tower inscriptions in the Forest of Pagodas of the Ming dynasty. They also record the Shaolin monk warriors' war participations in the Ming dynasty, which present perfect combinations of Kungfu and the art of inscription.

2. Paintings in the Shaolin Temple

The most impressive paintings related to Shaolin Kungfu are those murals on Kungfu practice in the White Robe (Avalokitesvara) Palace Hall, located to the southeast of the Thousand Buddhas Palace Hall. It was built in the early Qing dynasty and is a large gable-roof building with five bays in width, and over five beams in depth. On the northern and the southern walls of the White Robe Palace Hall, there is a mural entitled *Kungfu monks Performing Martial Arts* painted in the late Qing dynasty, also known as *Arhats' Hand Fighting* or the *Shaolin Illustrated Chart of Boxing*. The painting on the northern wall depicts the scene of Kungfu monks fighting in front of the Great Buddha Palace Hall, including 16 groups or 33 Kungfu monks. All are fighting one on one, except for one monk fighting against two. This mural depicts a performance scene on

南壁上壁画为《少林器械图》。绘的是麟庆观看少林武僧演练刀、枪、剑、戟、袖圈等十八般兵器格斗的场面，共计有15组，30名武僧。这幅壁画再现了清代少林兵器的特点，是珍贵的少林兵器实物资料。

在白衣殿神龛北侧，绘有两幅《十三和尚救唐王》壁画，是用艺术的方法表现当年少林寺十三武僧助唐王李世民的情景。这两幅中，南一幅绘的是少林寺十三武僧将秦王李世民从古洛阳监牢中救出的场面，在高高的洛阳城门外，十三武僧奋力保护李世民冲出重围，后边是王世充的追兵，十三武僧手持枪、刀、剑、棍、圈与王世充军进行激烈搏斗。壁画的上方绘的是唐朝的援军，图中骑白马留长辫者，即是秦王李世民。此幅壁画非常传神，把十三武僧救李世民绘得栩栩如生。北一幅绘的是武功高强的少林寺武僧擒住王仁则的场面，图中被捆绑着，身着将帅服者为郑国大将王仁则，周围手持刀枪剑棍者为少林寺十三武僧。

在西壁神龛南侧也有两幅《紧那罗王御红巾》壁画。内容是元末少林武僧紧那罗王与红巾军进行大战的场面。这两幅壁画是根据元末少林武僧与红巾军作战的真实故事演化而成的。南侧一幅绘的场面是红巾军过少林寺，少林武僧紧那罗王一脚踏太室山，一脚踏少室山，高举烧火棍，大吼一声挡住红巾军的去路。北一幅绘的是紧那罗王率少林僧兵与红巾军激战并击败红巾军的场面。这两幅壁画反映了元末红巾军与少林武僧进行战争的历史事实。

另外，少林寺千佛殿的巨幅壁画《五百罗汉图》也充分反映了少林功夫的魅力，在艺术家的笔下，五百罗汉手里有的拿着棍子，不可否认，其中许多是作为兵器使用的。艺术家夸张地描绘了罗汉的外貌特征，令人望而生畏的老虎渲染了战斗的气氛，显然已经将少林功夫提高到大乘诸神的地位。

3.雕塑

少林寺锤谱堂中有一组反映少林功夫的雕塑。锤谱堂原名西来堂，又名西来庵，在山门后碑林西侧。据乾隆十三年《少林寺志》载，西来

March 25th, the 25th year of the Daoguang Emperor's reign (1828 CE) in the Qing dynasty. Then, when a senior official named Linqing (with a full name of Linqing Wanyan) visited the Shaolin Temple, on his way to pay homage to Songshan Mountain on behalf of Governor Yang Hailiang, Shaolin Kungfu monks performed for him. In the painting, the Great Buddha Palace Hall and the surrounding temples were lively, full of lights. To the right side of the platform there were Linqing wearing a long plaid and the official suit of the Qing dynasty, together with his followers. On the mid-left there were the Abbot of the Shaolin Temple and other deacons who organized the Kungfu performance. This mural originally appeared in Linqing's book (*Hong Xue Yin Yuan Tu Ji*). After appreciating the Kungfu monks' performance, Linqing painted a picture entitled *Shaolin Boxing Contest* and included it in his book *Hong Xue Yin Yuan Tu Ji*. Later the painting was enlarged and painted on the northern wall of the White Robe Palace Hall. This mural is a true portrayal of the Shaolin Kungfu monks' performance in the Qing dynasty, which reflects the profundity of Shaolin Kungfu and its strengths in fighting. The mural on the southern wall of the White Robe Palace Hall presents *the Chart of Weapons in the Shaolin Temple*. It depicts Lin Qing's appreciation of Shaolin Kungfu monks practicing 18 types of weapons such as sabres, spears, swords, trunks and armhole, involving 15 groups or 30 Kungfu monks. This mural reproduces the characteristics of the Shaolin weapons in the Qing dynasty and makes a precious material evidence related to the Shaolin weapons.

To the north of the shrine in the White Robe Palace Hall, there are two murals depicting *the thirteen monks' rescuing Li Shimin* (later enthroned as the Emperor of Tang). In an artistic way, the mural presents the scene of the 13 Kungfu monks rescuing Li Shimin (then the Prince of Qin) from a prison in ancient Luoyang. Among the two paintings, the painting on the south depicts the story. Outside the high Luoyang gate, the monks are struggling to safeguard Li Shimin getting out of the encirclement. The monks armed with spears, sabres, swords, staffs, and circles fought fiercely with Wang Shichong's army. On the top of the mural are the reinforcement troops of the Tang dynasty. On the bottom of the mural, the one wearing a long plaid riding a white horse is Li Shimin, the Prince of Qin. This mural is very expressive, vividly presenting the scene of the

堂为康熙时曾任登封县僧会司僧官的少林寺僧真喜创建，真喜徒孙、时任登封县僧会司僧官的海岱于乾隆初年重修，清道光时又重修。1985年，重修少林寺时，建42间850平方米的四合院式长廊，并将历代少林寺武僧习武的主要拳法及僧兵历史故事，分14组、215尊塑于长廊之中，由此名之"锤谱堂"。

4.古塔

古塔乃少林寺历代僧人包括武僧的墓地。少林寺僧圆寂火化后（亦有非火化者），将骨灰放入地宫，上面建塔以示纪念。塔前有塔额，标僧名及称谓，塔后多有塔铭，记述僧人生平。

少林寺西500米处的少溪河北岸，密布高低不一、大小不同的塔，占地面积约14000平方米，被称为"塔林"。塔林现存有唐、宋、金、元、明、清古塔229座，现代塔2座，计231座。古塔中，有朝代可考者，唐塔2座、宋塔2座、金塔8座、元塔43座、明塔140座、清塔10座、年代不详者24座。另外，少林寺周围尚存有古塔15座，其中唐塔4座、五代塔1座、元塔1座、明塔2座、清塔4座、年代不详的古塔3座。

图4-15 少林寺塔林
Shaolin Temple Pagoda

monks' rescuing Li Shimin. The painting on the north presents a scene of the highly skillful Shaolin Kungfu monks' capturing Wang Renze alive. The one in marshal suit and tied up is Wang Renze, a great general of State Zheng, who is surrounded by the 13 Shaolin Kungfu monks holding sabres, spears, swords and staffs.

There are also other two murals to the south of the shrine on the eastern wall, depicting a scene derived from a real battle between Shaolin warriors and the Red Turban Army at the end of the Yuan dynasty. In the painting on the south, a Shaolin Kungfu monk, the reincarnation of Kinnara, screamed to block the Red Turban Army, wielding a stove poker, standing atop the lofty peaks of Mount Taishi and Mount Shaoshi. In the painting to the North, Kinnara led the Shaolin monk warriors fighting and defeating the Red Turban Army. These two murals reflect the historical facts of a battle between the Red Turban Army and the Shaolin Kungfu monks at the end of the Yuan dynasty.

In addition, the giant mural in the Thousand Buddhas Palace Hall of the Shaolin Temple, entitled *Five Hundred Arhats* also fully reflects the charm of Shaolin Kungfu. In the artist's work, a part of the five hundred Arhats are holding staffs, many of which are undoubtedly used as weapons. The artist depicts the appearance of Arhats in an exaggerating manner, and the fearsome tiger intensifies the battle atmosphere, apparently raising Shaolin Kungfu to the status of Mahayana gods.

3. Sculptures

There are a group of sculptures in the Shaolin Temple demonstrating Shaolin Kungfu, stored in Kungfu Hall (chui pu tang). Kungfu Hall was originally named West Arrival Hall (xi lai tang), located on the west of the Forest of Steles after the Mountain Gate. According to the *Shaolin Temple Annals* composed in the 13th year of the Qianlong Emperor's reign, the West Arrival Hall was built during the reign of Emperor Kangxi by a Shaolin monk Zhenxi, then an official of the Monk Association of the Dengfeng county. It was renovated in the early years of the Qianlong Emperor's reign, and another renovation took place during the Daoguang Emperor's reign. In 1985, the Shaolin Temple was renovated again. Forty-two rooms were built along a quadrangle complex corridor surrounding a courtyard of 850 square meters. Along the corridor stand 215 sculptures grouped

图4-16 少林寺塔林裕公塔
The Pagoda in Memory of the Shaolin Chan Master Yugong, in the Shaolin Pagoda Forest

少林寺古塔千姿百态，是研究少林寺，研究少林功夫，研究中国古代建筑、雕刻、书法艺术的博物馆。少林古塔受世俗文化影响较深，塔的大小等级受封建等级制度的影响。塔有一、三、五、七级之分，等级最高者为七级，这表明佛教实际上也存在着等级制度。塔林中塔层为单数，是由世俗"单数为阳、双数为阴"的建筑阴阳思想影响所造成的。塔上的塔铭，与社会上俗人的"墓志铭"是完全相同的。刻着八卦的塔，是佛教禅宗吸纳诸家文化的表现；密宗的"喇嘛塔"，则是禅宗与各宗派之间相互融合的产物。

少林古塔总体分石制和砖制两种，形态有唐式、宋式、金式、元式、明清式，有长方形、四边形、六边形、柱形、锥形、圆形、瓶形、喇叭形等。塔林中的229座古塔，几乎没有完全相同的。这些造型各异的塔是古代建筑艺术的杰作。塔上的砖雕、石雕造型精美，独具匠心，

into 14 divisions featuring major boxing techniques and the stories of Kungfu monks. Thus, the West Arrival Hall is also called Kungfu Hall (chui pu tang).

4. Ancient Pagodas

Ancient Pagodas in the Shaolin Temple had been built in memory of the eminent monks (including Kungfu monks) through generations. After those monks deceased, their bodies were cremated and the ashes were buried in the underground palace, on which pagodas were built for commemoration. The fronts of these pagodas carry the Buddhists' names and the titles of deceased monks, while the inscriptions on the rear record their life experiences.

On the north bank of the Shaoxi River, about 500 meters west to the Shaolin Temple, there stand pagodas of varied shapes and sizes, covering an area of about 14,000 square meters, which is called the Forest of Pagodas. There remain 229 ancient pagodas from the Tang, Song, Jin, Yuan, Ming and Qing dynasties, and 2 built in modern times. Among the ancient pagodas with identified building time, there are 2 from the Tang dynasty, 2 from the Song dynasty, 8 from the Jin dynasty, 43 from the Yuan dynasty, 140 from the Ming dynasty, 10 from the Qing dynasty, and 24 with unidentified building time. In addition, there are 15 ancient pagodas located around the Shaolin Temple, including 4 from the Tang dynasty, 1 from the Five dynasties, 1 from the Yuan dynasty, 2 from the Ming dynasty, 4 from the Qing dynasty, and another 3 with unidentified construction date.

The ancient pagodas of the Shaolin Temple constitute a museum for studying the Shaolin Temple, Shaolin Kungfu and ancient Chinese architecture, sculpture and calligraphy. The pagoda styles in the Shaolin Temple have been deeply influenced by the secular culture. The size and the ranking of the pagodas bear the influence of the feudal hierarchy. The pagodas have one, three, five and seven stories, with the seven-story pagoda as the highest. This actually reflects the hierarchical system in Buddhism. The feature of the odd-number stories is influenced by the secular notion of architecture that "the odd numbers are associated with Yang, and even numbers with Yin". The inscription on the pagoda is exactly the same as those of the lay people in the secular society. The pagoda engraved with eight trigrams is the manifestation of Buddhist Chan's absorption of various schools of culture; and the "Lama Pagodas" of Esoteric Buddhism represent the integration of Chan Buddhism with various other sects.

为雕刻艺术珍品。塔上的塔铭、塔额、篆、行、草、隶、楷应有尽有，各具特色，为难得的书法艺术品。

反映元末少林僧兵与红巾军进行战争的古塔，见于明朝洪武六年（1373年）四月建的《训公提点之塔》的塔铭上。这座位于少林寺塔林中的四边形三级砖塔的塔身背面刻有一方塔铭。铭文全称为"嵩山少林寺松源训公提点塔铭并序"。据铭文载，元朝至正末，松源训公出任少林寺提点，时红巾军大举进攻少林寺，僧兵反击，最后僧兵战败，少林寺被攻陷，松源被迫逃出少林寺，避难于秦水。还有一个元末少林僧兵与红巾作战的见证物是位于少林寺塔林中的《嵩岩之塔》。这座建于明朝洪武六年（1373年）五月的四边形三级砖塔，在其塔身后部有一方"嵩山祖庭大少林禅寺宝应住持嵩岩俊公和尚塔铭并序"的铭文。铭文载，元朝末年，红巾军进攻少林寺，僧兵与之战，少林寺失守，嵩岩逃出避难于汶水。关于红巾军进攻少林寺后，少林寺的残状，明洪武初登

图4-17 少林寺塔林参公塔
Can Gong Pagoda in the Shaolin Temple

Most Shaolin ancient pagodas have brick or stone structures, featuring styles of the Tang, Song, Jin, Yuan, Ming and Qing dynasties. Their shapes vary from rectangular, quadrangular, hexagonal, cylindrical, conical, round, bottle-shaped and trumpet-shaped, etc., with virtually no identical ones among them. These pagodas of varied shapes are the masterpieces of ancient architectural art. They carry unique and exquisite brick and stone carvings, which are the treasures of carving art. The inscriptions on the pagoda feature all types of scripts including seal scripts, running scripts, cursive scripts, official scripts and regular scripts, making them rare works of calligraphy.

A battle between Shaolin monk warriors and the Red Turban Army at the end of the Yuan dynasty was narrated in the inscription on the rear of a *Pagoda commemorating the Chief Kungfu Monk Juexun*, which was built in the 6th year of the Hongwu Emperor's reign (1373 CE) of the Ming dynasty. It states that when Juexun was appointed the chief Kungfu monk late in the Zhizheng Emperor's reign of the Yuan dynasty, the Shaolin Temple was assaulted by the Red Turban Army. The defense monk warriors were defeated and the Shaolin Temple was seized by the Red Turban Army. Juexun was forced to flee from the Shaolin Temple and take refuge in Qinshui. Another pagoda titled *Songyan Pagoda* also evidences the battle between the Shaolin monk warriors and the Red Turban Army at the end of the Yuan dynasty. This quadrangular three-story pagoda was built in 6th year of Hongwu Emperor's reign (1373 CE) of the Ming dynasty, to commemorate Abbot Song Yanjun. The inscription on the pagoda records a similar story to the one mentioned above. A dilapidated Shaolin Temple after its fall was recorded on the Stele on *Remodeling Buddha Statue* written by Shan Xizhi, the sheriff of Dengfeng county. "The end of the Zhizheng Emperor's reign of the Yuan dynasty witnessed the country in turmoil. All the temples were damaged across the country, and only half of the Shaolin Temple was still in existence."

The earliest physical evidence of the Ming dynasty for the Shaolin Kungfu and monk warriors was found on the pagoda commemorating the Kungfu monk Zhouyou (nicknamed Sanqi) in the Forest of Steles. The quadrangular three-story pagoda was built in June, the 27th year of the Jiajing Emperor's reign (1548 CE) in the Ming dynasty. On the front of the pagoda, it is inscribed that during

封知县山锡之撰的《重装佛像碑》有载:"至正之末,天下板荡,海内名刹,焚毁殆尽,祖庭仅存其半。"

最早记载明代少林功夫及僧兵的实物资料是位于少林塔林中的《友公三奇和尚塔》。该塔建于明朝嘉靖二十七年(1548年)六月,为四边形三级砖塔。在塔身正前有一块正书塔额,额文刻"敕赐大少林禅寺名天下对手教会武僧友公三奇和尚之塔",额文下还刻有铭文。据额文及其下的铭文载:明正德时(1506年—1521年)统率着千余名僧兵的三奇和尚,受武宗之命镇守边关,立下大功,受到武宗嘉奖。后武宗又派三奇统兵征战云南,僧兵均又受到奖赏。这块不大的塔铭,见证了明代中期驰骋疆场,屡建战功的少林僧兵,也是明代最有价值的反映少林功夫的真实资料。

建于明朝万历三年(1575年)三月的《敕赐少林禅寺提点参公竺方和尚塔》,为五级密檐式砖塔,在塔身后有一方正书《少林寺竺方参公塔铭并序》铭文。文载嘉靖三十二年(1553年)周参受官府调遣,率50

图4-18 征战有功的少林僧兵万庵和尚塔铭

The Monument Inscription Motto of the Monk Wan'an with Merits in the War

the Zhengde Emperor's reign (1506—1521) in the Ming dynasty, Monk Sanqi who commanded more than a thousand monk warriors, was ordered by Emperor Wuzong to defend the border fortification. He made great achievements, and was thus awarded by Emperor Wuzong. Later Emperor Wuzong sent Sanqi and his troops to fight in Yunnan, and the monk warriors were rewarded again. This modest pagoda evidences the Shaolin monk warriors' war participation and their fierce fights in the wars in the middle of the Ming dynasty, making it the most valuable genuine material reflecting Shaolin Kungfu in the Ming dynasty.

Another five-story brick pagoda was built in March, the 3rd year of the Wanli Emperor's reign (1575 CE), to commemorate the chief Kungfu monk named Zhou Can. On the rear of the pagoda there was an inscription, which states that Zhou Can, dispatched by the government in the 32nd year of the Jiajing Emperor's reign (1553 CE), led 50 monk warriors to crack down the rebellion of Shi Shangzhao.

Another quadrangular 7-meter high five-story dense-eave quadrangular brick pagoda commemorating the chief Kungfu monk Guangshun (also known as Wan'an) was built in the 47th year of the Wanli Emperor's reign (1619 CE). The inscription states that Monk Wan'an, once serving as the chief Kungfu monk in the Shaolin Temple, made considerable military achievements.

A quadrangular three-story 5-meter high pagoda was built in the 5th year of the Tianqi Emperor's reign (1625 CE) of the Ming dynasty to commemorate ancestral monk Pushi (nicknamed Dacai, literally translated as a Great Talent), which also illustrates that Pushi was a renowned Kungfu monk for his meritous deeds in the war.

V. Shaolin Kungfu and Literature

The movement names of many routines in Shaolin Kungfu come from classical Chinese literature. For instance, some well-known characters in the *Romance of the Three Kingdoms* inspire the names for the routines in the Shaolin Kungfu, including Huang Zhong Shooting Arrows (Huang Zhong fang jian) in Shaolin Fierce Tiger Boxing (Shaolin Menghuquan), Huangzhong Pulling the Bow (Huang Zhong la gong) in Shaolin demon-conquering boxing(Shaolin

名僧兵镇压师尚诏起义的情况。

万历四十七年（1619年）立的《顺公万庵塔》，为四边形五级密檐式砖塔，水磨砖砌成，高7米。在塔身的前方有一方正书塔额。额文刻"敕赐少林寺都提举征战有功顺公万庵和尚塔"。从额文知，万庵和尚曾任少林寺武僧头领都提举，后征战而立功。

建于明朝天启五年（1625年）四月的《大才使公塔》，为四边形三级砖塔，高5米。塔身前刻塔额，额文刻"敕赐祖庭大少林禅寺恩祖征战有功大才使公寿筹八十三岁之本大和尚之灵塔"。从额文知，使公（普使）在明代也因征战沙场而立功，是著名武僧。

五、少林功夫与文学

少林功夫中许多套路动作名称都来自中国古典文学。如少林猛虎拳的"黄忠放箭"，少林降妖拳的"黄忠拉弓"，少林天罡劈水扇的"孔明挥扇""关公撩袍""赵云闯关""张飞骗马"等动作招式来源于《三国演义》的典型人物。

二路少林五合拳的"哪吒搅海"，一路二路少林猛虎拳的"八戒翻耙""天王托塔"，少林草镰的"悟空藏棍"，一路开山拳的"童子拜观音"等的出处应是《西游记》。

少林转堂拐的"拐李下山""采和挎篮""国舅敷板""果老骑驴"，少林天罡劈水扇的"洞宾穿剑"等来自"八仙"的神话传说。

"太公钓鱼""子牙斩将"出自"武王伐纣"的故事，"孙膑排兵"等出自历史典故，少林十八罗汉手的"僧敲钟""僧推门"二式来自唐诗人贾岛的诗句。其他"沉香劈山""二郎担山""嫦娥奔月""敬德举鞭""霸王开弓""刘邦招兵""周楚捉龙""大禹定海""伍员托枪""苏秦背剑""寇准脱靴""武松断臂""由基神射""黄飞虎催牛"等招式都来自古代神话或历史典故。

Xiangyaoquan), Kongming Waving the Fan (Kongming hui shan) , Guangong Lifting Up the Gown (Guangong Liao Pao), Zhao Yun Forcing through the Pass (Zhao Yun chuang guan), Zhangfei Hustling a Horse (Zhang Fei pian ma), etc.

The names of some Kungfu movements were inspired by the *Journey to the West*. For instance, Nezha Overturning the Sea (Ne Zha Jiao Hai) in the second routine of Shaolin Five Match Boxing (Shaolin Wuhequan), Monk Pig Turning Rakes (Bajie Fan Pa) and Heavenly King Holding a Pagoda (Tian Wang Tuo Ta) in the first and the second routine of Shaolin Fierce Tiger Boxing (Shaolin Menghuquan), Monkey King Hides his Staff in Shaolin Sickle (Wukong Canggun), Boy Worshiping Kwan-Yin Bodhisattva (Tong Zi Bai Guanyin), etc.

And Some were derived from the fairy tales of the Eight Immortals, as Iron-Crutch Li Going Downhill (Guaili Xia Shan), Lan Caihe Carrying a Flower-basket (Caihe Kua Lan), Cao Guojiu Unfolding Jade-plates (Guojiu Fu Ban), Zhang Guolao Riding a Donkey (Guolao Qi Lu) in Shaolin Zhuantang Crutch (Shaolin zhuan tang guai), and Lv Dongbin Stabbing Sword (Dongbin Chuan Jian) in Shaolin Tiangang Pishui Fan.

There are still some movement names inspired by the Story of Emperor Wuwang (of Zhou dynasty) overthrowing Emperor Zhou (of Shang dynasty), including Jiang Ziya Fishing (Ziya Diao Yu) and Jiang Ziya Executing his General (Ziya Zhan Jiang). Still other names were inspired by poems of Jia Dao in the Tang dynasty as Monk Tolling (Seng Qiao Zhong) and Monk Pushing the Door (Seng Tui Men) in the routine of Shaolin Eighteen Arhats Boxing (Shaolin Shiba Luohanshou), and still others inspired by mythology or historical allusions as Chenxiang Splitting the Mountain (Chenxiang Pi Shan), Erlang Carrying the Mountain (Er lang Dan Shan), the Goddess Chang'er Flying to the Moon (Chang'er Ben Yue), Jingde lifting Steel Mace (Jingde Ju Bian), Bawang Drawing the Bow (Ba Wang Kai Gong), Liubang Recruiting Soldiers (Liu Bang Zhao Bing), Zhou Chu Capturing the Dragon (Zhou Chu Zhuo Long), Dayu Settling the Sea (Da Yu Ding Hai), Wu Yuan Lifting the Spear (Wu Yuan Tuo Qiang), Su Qin Carrying the Sword on his Back (Sun Qin Bei Jian), Kouzhun Taking off his Boots (Kouzhun Tuo Xue), Wu Song losing his Arm (Wu Song Duan Bi), (Archer Yang) Youji Shooting Arrow (You ji Shen She), Huang Feihu Rushing his Ox

图4-19 少林棍术
Shaolin Cudgel

少林功夫是少林最有代表的文化，所以历代文人墨客也留下了大量反映少林功夫的诗歌和小说、杂文等文学作品。"少林十三棍僧救唐王""少林僧兵抗倭"等故事早已流传民间，人们耳熟能详，这些不仅仅是少林功夫宝贵的历史资料，同样也丰富了中国古代文学。

唐开元十六年（728年），玄宗时光禄大夫、吏部尚书、上柱国裴漼撰文并书丹《皇唐嵩岳少林寺碑》，文章洋洋洒洒二千余字描述了少林寺以昙宗为首的十三武僧助唐平定王世充的事迹。

张鷟，字文成，生卒年不详，当于唐武后到玄宗朝前期，以词章知名，下笔神速，今存著述有《朝野佥载》《龙筋凤髓判》和《游仙窟》。《朝野佥载》为作者耳闻目睹的社会札记，内容十分广泛，记述了唐代前期朝野遗事轶闻，尤以武后朝事迹为主。书中记载了当时有关人物事迹、典章制度、社会风尚、传闻逸事，也站在反对派的角度对武后朝的政治黑暗、吏治腐败、酷吏横暴、民生疾苦有所揭露，暴露了"贿货纵横，赃物狼藉"的现实世相。因属时人记时事，所载内容，多

(Huang Fei Hu Cui Niu), etc.

Shaolin Kungfu is the most representative of the Shaolin Culture. Thus, the literati of the past dynasties wrote myriads of poems, novels and essays related to Shaolin Kungfu. For instance, Thirteen Staff Kungfu Monks Rescuing Emperor of Tang and Shaolin Monk Warrors Resisting Wokou have been widespread and become household stories. These documents not only provide valuable historical materials about Shaolin Kungfu, but also enrich ancient Chinese culture.

In the 16th year of the Kaiyuan Emperor's reign (728 CE) in the Tang dynasty during the reign of Emperor Xuanzong, a senior official named Pei Cui wrote the inscription on the *Shaolin Monastery Stele on Mount Song*, which elaborates in over 2000 words on the story of 13 Kungfu monks led by Tanzong helping the Tang dynasty crack down Wang Shichong.

Zhang Zhuo, style name Wencheng, whose birth and death years are unknown, lived between the period of Empress Wu Zetian's reign and the early period of Emperor Xuanzong's reign of the Tang dynasty. He was renowned for his poems and essays as well as his amazing writing speed. His extant works include *Anecdotes in Court and Commonalty*, *Long Jin Feng Sui Pan*, *A Tour in the Fairy Cave (you xian ku)*. *Anecdotes in Court and Commonalty* consists of extensive notes on social events that the author has either experienced or heard of, including the anecdotes of those in the court and the commonality alike in the early Tang dynasty, especially the events during the reign of Empress Wu Zetian. The book records the events of multiple people, rules and regulations, social customs, rumors and anecdotes. It also from the opposition's perspective exposes the political darkness during the reign of Empress Wu Zetian, such as the corruption of bureaucrats, the violence and brutality of government officials, and people's hardship, depicting a scene of "prevalent bribery and thefts". Because most of contents in the book were based on first-hand information, it made a valuable reference. It had been widely quoted in *Collections of Taiping* (tai ping guang ji), *Zi Zhi Tong Jian* (literally: *Comprehensive Mirror in Aid of Governance*) and the later historians' writing on the Tang dynasty. In this book, the author accounts the Shaolin Kungfu monk Sengchou's practice in a mythical way.

Xu Xuemo, style name Quanming, once appointed as the Minister of Rites, wrote books such as *Spring and Autumn Memories* (*Chun Qiu Yi*), *Spring Draft*

为第一手资料,所以颇有参考价值,为《太平广记》《资治通鉴》以及后世治唐史者广为引用。书中作者用带有神话色彩的笔法描述了少林武僧僧稠禅师的习武活动。

徐学谟,字权明,明嘉靖时进士,官至礼部尚书,著有《春秋忆》《春明稿》等。万历初,徐学谟游少林寺,观看了少林武僧习武后,联想到唐代少林武僧昙宗曾被封为大将军僧的碑刻,有感而发,写了首知名的赞武僧诗《少林杂诗》:"名香古殿自氤氲,舞剑挥戈送落曛。怪得僧徒偏好武,昙宗曾拜大将军。"

俞大猷,字志辅,号虚江,明嘉靖时抗倭名将。曾任湖广总兵、福建总兵,大败倭寇,除却边患。明嘉靖四十年(1561年),俞大猷自大

图4-20 徐学谟
Xu Xuemo

同赴沿海抗倭前线,途经少林寺。少林寺住持小山选年轻武僧宗擎、普从随俞大猷到沿海抗倭前线,习武抗倭三年之久。后二武僧回到少林寺传棍。万历五年(1577年),宗擎去北京,俞大猷非常激动,作文写诗赞颂宗擎的功夫。俞大猷文称:他很早就听说了名冠天下的少林寺有神

(*Chun Ming Gao*). He once visited the Shaolin Temple and watched Shaolin monks practicing Kungfu. Afterwards, inspired by the stele recording Shaolin Kungfu monk Tanzong's appointment as a monk general, he wrote a famous poem commending Shaolin Kungfu monks: Ancient temple dense with incense burnt fragrance; aglow with the setting sun swords shining in performance; no wonder monks here much prefer martial art; their master Tanzong once honored as General for his part.

Yu Dayou, style name Zhifu, pseudonym Xujiang, once served as Huguang Garrison Commander and Fujian Garrison Commander. He was also a renowned anti-Wokou general, restoring peace in the border area through bitterly beating Wokou. In the 40th year of the Jiajing Emperor's reign (1561 CE), Yu Dayou went to the coastal anti-Wokou front and passed by the Shaolin Temple on his way to the coastal front. The abbot of the Shaolin Temple named Xiaoshan chose two Kungfu monks, one named Zongqing and the other Pucong to follow Yu to the anti-Wokou front. They stationed there for three years practicing staff fighting methods while taking up resistance against Wokou. Later they returned to the Shaolin Temple to teach the staff techniques. In the 5th year of the Wanli Emperor's reign (1577 CE), Zongqing went to Beijing, and Yu Dayou was so exhilarated to see him that he wrote poems to commend Zongqing's Kungfu. According to Yu Dayou, he had heard that the Shaolin Monastery in Henan possessed a divinely transmitted method of staff fighting. Later, when he went to anti-Wokou coastal front from Shanxi via Henan, he took a special trip to visit the Shaolin Temple. More than a dozen Kungfu monks in the temple, who were skilled in staff fighting, came out to perform. After viewing their performance, he concluded that they have lost the ancient secrets of the art. Upon hearing this, all the monks said that they would like to follow Yu's instruction. Yu Dayou said that one had to dedicate years to master the staff technique. So, the Shaolin Temple chose two young and courageous Kungfu monks, one named Zongqing, and the other Pucong to follow Yu Dayou to the anti-Wokou front. The two monks learned the genuine Shaolin staff method from Yu Dayou while taking up the resistance against the Wokou. After practicing the staff methd for three years under the instruction of Yu Dayou, Zongqing and Pucong mastered the Shaolin staff method for real combats. So, they requested for permission to return

人传授的棍术技法。后来俞自山西大同回沿海抗倭前线路经河南，他取道专程拜访了少林寺。寺僧中精于棍法的十多个武僧，皆出来为之演练棍法。他看后认为，少林流传的技法的真诀已遗失了。在告诉了众僧之后，他们都说：愿听指教。俞大猷说这不是一时就能学会的，需要时间。于是众人推举年轻力壮的两名武僧，一名宗擎，一名普从，随俞大猷赴沿抗倭前线，一边抗倭，一边向俞大猷学习实战少林棍法。在俞大猷三年的谆谆教诲之下，宗擎、普从掌握了实战的少林棍法，于是请求回少林寺传艺。俞大猷同意后，他们离去了。忽然一天有人报说一僧人求见，见面后方知是离别13年的宗擎。宗擎告诉俞大猷说，普从已因病离世，只有自己回到寺院将实践棍法回传于少林寺，众武僧深得其技者近百人，可以永远流传下去了。在听了宗擎的讲述之后，高兴万分的俞大猷遂作诗一首赠宗擎，其诗云："学成伏虎剑，洞悟降龙禅。杯渡游南粤，锡飞入北燕。能行深海底，更陟高山巅。莫讶物难舍，回头是岸边。"

俞大猷所著的《正气堂集》《重建十方禅院碑》中也记述了此事：我早就闻知河南少林寺，那里有神传的棍术。嘉靖四十年（1561年），我在山西大同奉命赴沿海抗倭前线，顺道访问了河南嵩山少林寺。寺僧称精于少林棍法者，都出来为我展示棍术。我告诉少林寺住持（方丈）小山上人说：你们少林寺以棍法名扬天下，但传久而讹，真诀都已经失传了。之后我穿着草鞋扶着竹杖，游览了少林寺周围所属的大小寺庵，还亲历达摩洞观看了面壁石。到少林寺山门时，见寺前边有一山地地形奇特，便又告诉少林寺住持小山上人：此地可建一个小院，用来增加少林的胜景。小山方丈欣然应允并说道：建院的责任，是我的责，我马上平整土地开始动工。但棍术真诀失传了，请你传我们少林真诀，这就有劳俞大猷将军了。我听后对小山方丈说：传真棍术正经，非一朝一夕之事啊！小山听后即选择寺僧中年轻而有勇气的二位僧人，一名宗擎，一名普从。即派二僧随我南征倭寇三年。这三年之间，一边抗倭，一边

to the Shaolin Temple to teach the staff method. With Yu Dayou's approval, they returned to Shaolin Temple. Thirteen years passed swiftly. One day Yu's gatekeeper reported that a monk wished to see him. After seeing each other, Yu found that the visitor was Zongqing. Zongqing told Yu Dayou that Pucong had passed away for illness. Only Zongqing returned to the Temple and taught the Shaolin monks what he had learned. Up to one hundred Kungfu monks had acquired profound knowledge of the staff technique. Thus, it could be transmitted for ever and ever. Upon hearing this, Yu Dayou was so delighted that he wrote a poem for Zongqing, which said: With the art of tiger-taming sword in hand, and insight of subduing dragon in mind; able to travel by cup across the water in south, and fly by staff over the land in north; and stroll around the bottom of sea deep, and ascend to the top of the hill steep. No surprise to find abandoning physical desire hard. Never too late to mend is of life the yard.

It is recorded in the Stele of *On Reconstruction of Chan Courtyard for All Directions*, collected in *Collections of Righteousness* (*Zheng Qi Tang Ji*) by Yu Dayou that "I have heard of the Shaolin Temple for long for its magic skills of staff. In the 40th year of the Jiajing Emperor's reign (1561 CE), I was appointed to serve in the war against Wokou at coastal area and visited Shaolin Temple on my way from Datong city of Shanxi province. The Monks in the temple displayed their skills for me. I told the Abbot, Eminence Xiaoshan, "Shaolin staff technique enjoys reputation for long, but some mistakes were made and its essence got lost in its passing from generation to generation." Then, I visited the temples around Shaolin, and the Bodhidharma Cave (Damo Cave), in my straw sandals and by a bamboo walking stick. I found an unusual hilly area in front of the gate of the Shaolin Temple, so I told Eminence Xiaoshan, "A courtyard could be constructed here to increase the interest of the Shaolin Temple."

Eminence Xiaoshan readily agreed and said, "It is my responsibility and I will launch the construction work soon. But I have to bother Your Excellency to teach us the genuine staff skills to make up the losses." I replied that it couldn't be achieved overnight. He immediately selected two brave monks, one named Zongqing, and the other named Pucong to follow me for the battles against Wokou in the following three years. And in that period, I passed them the authentic skills of staff during the war. Although their skills were not perfect

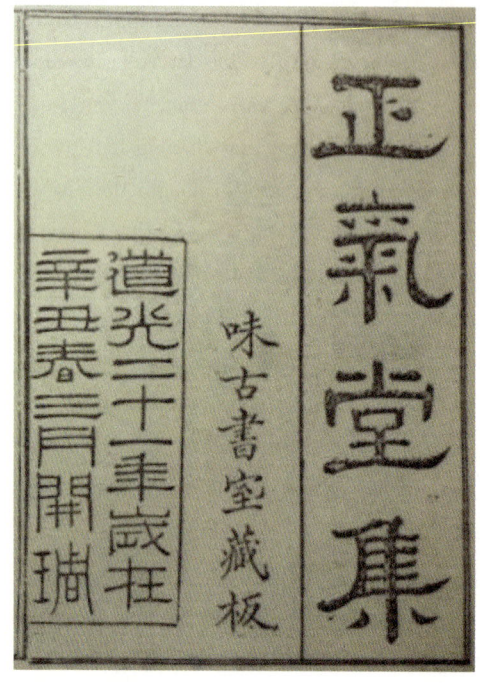

图4-21 俞大猷著《正气堂集》
Collections of Righteousness (Zheng Qi Tang Ji) by Yu Dayou

谆谆教诲少林传流棍术的真谛。二僧虽然并没有练得炉火纯青的地步，但也可以说已达到"十步一人，千里不留行"的地步。于是二僧辞归。过了十四五年，到了明万历五年（1577年）四月间。我恰好在京师神机营训练军队，忽报一僧求见，他进来之后，我发现乃是宗擎。他告诉我说普从已圆寂（去世），只有他将少林棍术真诀广传于寺内，得到少林传流棍术真诀的武僧甚多。我听后非常高兴，又授予宗擎以"剑经"之法，鼓励他认真演习，精益求精。过了一段时间，少林寺又有一个叫普明的僧人来找我说："你提议在寺前建一个小院，方丈小山和尚有志去完成，但未竟而圆寂（去世）。接替小山方丈职务的幻休大师，决心完成小山的遗愿，命寺僧普明主持建小院。普明乃少林寺无空大师的嫡孙，他怕自己身单力薄，不能完成，于是赴京师求助于无空大师的俗徒御马监太监张遐、卢鼎、高才，他们共同出资帮助建设。近日小院终于完工了，这个小院就命名为'十方禅院'。所以派我来请俞大猷将军写一篇修建纪念碑，因为这是俞大猷提议建的。"我答应了，我认为十方

yet, they've developed to ten-step a killing and unstoppable in one-thousand-li marching. Then they went back to the Shaolin Temple. About fourteen or fifteen years later, in April of the 5th year of the Wanli Emperor's reign (1577 CE) in the Ming dynasty, a monk came to see me when I had my soldiers of Firearms Camp drill in the capital. I recognized it was Zongqing, who told me Pucong had passed away. It was himself who passed the genuine staff skills to the monks in the Shaolin Temple and a large number of them had mastered them. I was very happy for it and taught him my sword fencing skill and encouraged him to perfect it through practice. Later, a monk named Puming from the Shaolin Temple found me. He told me that Abbot Xiaoshan had passed away before he finished the construction of the courtyard in front of the Temple as I suggested. Eminent Xiuhuan succeeded him and decided to carry on his last wish. He ordered Puming to be responsible for the courtyard construction. Puming is the grand disciple of eminent Wukong. Unconfident of his inability to fulfill it, he went to the capital to seek help. Wukong's secular disciples Zhang Xian, Lu Ding and Gao Cai, eunuchs of the Imperial Horse Department of the Palace made joint financial aids. Eventually the courtyard had been completed recently, and was named the Courtyard of Chan for All Directions. I was sent here to invite your Excellency to draft a stele inscription because it was your suggestion to build the courtyard." Knowing it was Eminent Puming in charge and supported by the eunuchs, I agreed. So, I expressed my best wishes to the long-living of the emperor, peace and contentment of people, temples for monks with residence, and spreading of the staff skills.

Gong Ding, style name Xiaoyu, is from Mengyin. He was awarded the rank of Jinshi in the 29th year of the Wanli Emperor's reign (1601 CE). He served as the compiler of the National Academy, and finally the Assistant Minister of Rites. He is studious, learned, fair and capable. During the Wanli Emperor's reign, he once visited the Shaolin Temple on the Mid-autumn Festival, and appreciated Kungfu monks' performance. Shocked by the grand scenes and attracted by the monks' superb skills, he composed the poem *Demonstration of Kungfu in the Shaolin Temple*, which gives a vivid description of Kungfu monks' demonstration through both a direct depiction and vivid metaphors.

In this poem, each of the warrior's movements is revealed lively through his

图4-22 少林寺塔林小山塔
The Pagoda in Memory of Master Xiaoshan, in the Shaolin Pagoda Forest

禅院乃普明上人主持建设，两三个宫内人支持而成。因此焚香祝颂：一是祝愿皇上万寿无疆；二是祝愿四海百姓安居乐业；三是四方游僧有栖息之地；四是宗擎所传棍法得以广传。

公鼎，字孝与，蒙阴人。万历二十九年进士，初授编修，后任礼部侍郎。鼎好学博闻，磊落有器识。万历时，公鼎于中秋节游少林寺，在观看了武僧演武之后，为武僧宏大的演武场面，精湛的武技所吸引，于是奋笔写下专门歌颂少林武僧的七言古诗《少林观僧比武歌》。该诗通过写真、形象比喻等手法，真实再现了当年少林武僧演武的场面。

在这首诗里，公鼎通过生动的语言、形象的描述、恰如其分的比喻，把每一个少林武僧演武的姿态刻画得惟妙惟肖。可以说是当时少林武僧演武的一个完美写照，也是一首极为难得的长篇叙事诗。

公鼎的诗，不仅反映出明代少林武僧高超的武技，同时也反映出明代中后期少林寺极为盛行的演武之风。所以明代许多官吏到少林寺，在其所写的游记、诗文中都有记载少林武僧演武的场面。

傅梅，字元鼎，河北邢台人，明万历举人。万历三十五年（1607年）至四十一年（1613年）任登封知县，后任刑部主事，台州知府。傅

vivid words, visual narration and appropriate metaphors. It is a rare long narrative poem, perfectly picturing Shaolin monks' Kungfu demonstration.

The poem not only displayed Shaolin Kungfu monks' superb skills in the Ming dynasty, but also reflected the popularity of Kungfu in the Shaolin Temple in that period. So, a lot of officials in the Ming dynasty visited Shaolin Temple and recorded Shaolin Kungfu monks' demonstration in their travel accounts, poems and essays.

Fu Mei, style name Yuanding, is from Xingtai of Hebei province. He was awarded the rank of Juren in the Wanli Emperor's reign of the Ming dynasty. He served as the Magistrate of Dengfeng county between the 35th year (1607 CE) and 41st year (1613 CE) of the Wanli Emperor's reign, then Master of Penalty Ministry, and finally Magistrate of Taizhou City. When managing in Dengfeng county, he visited the places of interest in Songshan Mountain and compiled the *Book of Songshan Mountain* with thirteen articles, in addition, he also composed 60 poems of the mountain. The poem *Stop by the Shaolin Temple* is one of them. "One path connects steep Mount Shaoshi and Taishi, and the Shaolin Temple locates in the lush of them. The temple becomes extraordinary since the Liang and Wei dynasty, and monks advocated Kungfu from Sui and Tang. Buddhism principles were handed down, and heritages are also left. In recent years, I was inspired by Buddhist doctrine and did feel it till I am in this mountain." The second section of the poem is well-known in that it reveals Shaolin Kungfu.

Zhou Yi, whose birth and death date are unknown, lived in the Ming dynasty. His poem of *Visit to the Shaolin Temple* is a commendation on Shaolin Kungfu monks after appreciating their practice. "Both the Shaolin Temple and the monks enjoy great reputation. They studied Buddhist doctrine and practiced Kungfu as well. Monks displayed their peerless bravery and skillful Kungfu. They responded to authority's conscription with their outstanding performance in the battles." This poem displayed superb Shaolin Kungfu with monk warriors' relentless practice, heroic spirits and lofty sentiments of safeguarding the homeland.

Li Sixiao, living in the Wanli Emperor's reign of the Ming dynasty, once served as Governor of Henan province and Chief-director of Discipline Inspection Ministry. In the 38th year of the Wanli Emperor's reign (1610 CE), he composed a poem titled *The Shaolin Temple* after appreciating the warriors'

梅任登封令，遍查嵩山名胜，著《嵩书》十三篇，并写嵩山诗六十首。《过少林寺》这首诗是傅梅在登任职期间过少林寺而写的："二室巉屼一径通，少林寺在翠微中。地从梁魏标灵异，僧自隋唐好武名。若道传衣终著相，须知遗履亦非空。年来悟得西为旨，才到名山便不同。"其中第二句"地从梁魏标灵异，僧自隋唐好武名"是非常有名的反映少林功夫的名句。

周易，明代人，生卒不详。《入少林寺》一诗为周易游少林寺后在观看了武僧习武后写的一首赞少林武僧的诗篇："梵宇称奇绝，山僧负胜名。谈玄更演武，礼佛爱论兵。勇冠三军气，心雄万夫英。中原飞羽檄，借尔戮长鲸。"其中的"山僧负胜名"指的就是少林寺僧以武功名天下。第二句写武僧不仅谈禅而且演武，不仅礼佛且练习武功。第三句写武僧有勇冠三军的英雄气势。最后一句实际上是写僧兵收到官府檄文后为国参战的豪情。

李思孝，明万历时人，曾任巡抚河南石企都御史。万历三十八年（1610年），李思孝游少林寺，在观看了武僧演武后写了《少林寺》一诗："五峰屏绕少林开，宝树秦封识大槐。佛自千年留影长，僧从百战立功来。卿云缥缈依飞枝，仙药氤氲切上台。欲访无生王事急，偶因登礼一徘徊。"诗中"僧从百战立功来"之句就是写唐代、明代少林僧兵参战立功的史实，从另一个侧面反映出明代官吏对少林僧兵的推崇。

袁宏道，字中郎，号石公，湖北公安人，万历时进士，著名文学家，公安派代表人物，有《瓶花斋杂录》《袁中郎集》等传世。明万历三十七年（1609年），袁宏道赴陕西主考，回来路过嵩山，游览后写《嵩游记》五篇，写游少林寺五言律诗三首，其中《山中逢老衲少时从征有功者》写的是袁宏道在少林寺五乳峰下游览时遇到昔日征战有功的少林僧兵：

"头发遮眉白，归来五乳峰。梦中间虎笑，定起看经慵。戒铁支为

performance. "Surrounded by five mountains, there is the Shaolin Temple, and the aged Chinese Scholar Tree there was offered an official post even in the Qin dynasty. Bodhidharma's reflection has been embedded in the stone-wall of the cave for over one thousand years and monks won numerous military rewards generations after generation. Clouds float in the trees in the woods at the peak, and fairy herbs are there at the cliffs. I intended to consult eminent monks for Buddhism, but I have to leave because of government business. So, I just stay for a short while attending their ceremony by chance." The verse about monk warriors in battles refers to the historical facts that monks attended wars and were rewarded in both the Tang and the Ming dynasty, which also reflected officials' esteem to the monk warriors of the Shaolin Temple in the Ming dynasty.

Yuan Hongdao, style name Zhonglang and pseudonym of Shigong, is from Gong'an of Hubei province. He was awarded the rank of Jinshi in the Wanli Emperor's reign. As a famous litterateur in that period, he was also known as a representative of School of Gong'an Writers and Poets with his works as *Anecdotes of Flower-in-Vase Studio* (*Ping Hua Zhai Za Lu*) and *Collections of Yuan Zhonglang's Works* (*Yuan Zhonglang Ji*), etc. In the 37th year of the Wanli Emperor's reign (1609 CE) in the Ming dynasty, after he finished his job hosting the national examination in Shaanxi province, he passed by the Shaolin Temple and wrote five travel accounts and three poems of Songshan Mountain. The one entitled *Meeting an Old Monk Who Won Military Reward When Young* describes his encounter with an old monk warrior who won a military award when he was young.

"Long hair falls down and covers his white brow; the old monk comes down from the Wuru Mountain. He laughs for the victories of the battles in dreams, and nodded off in reading Buddhist scriptures awake. He takes his iron cane as the pillow and hangs his costume at the branch of pine. He can still walk through the wall and seize fierce dragon when needed."

At the beginning of the poem, he describes an old monk descending from Wuru Mountain, who once won military rewards in his youth but he is so old now that his eyebrows turn white. Then he tells us the monk dreams about fighting in the battles but scarcely studied Buddhist scriptures for years of fighting. The third verse draws a picture that he takes a nap after Kungfu practice resting head

图4-23 袁宏道
Yuan Hongdao

枕,衲衣挂在松。闲时穿洞壁,俗去缚狞龙。"

诗开头写过去征战有功者现在眉毛都白了,他刚从五乳峰上下来。接着写他梦中曾看到征战沙场的敌人,由于只重武功,经书不念了。第三句写他练功后以戒铁为枕,衣服挂在松树上。最后两句是借用崂山道士穿壁的故事来比喻他虽老,仍有穿洞壁的功力,同时还时常想着去征战杀敌。从诗中写的武僧看,这位想立功的老僧年纪相当大,其征战立功应在明嘉靖时期。这是歌咏明代征战立功僧的一首佳作。

顾炎武,字宁人,江苏昆山人,明末清初著名思想家,文学家,著有《日知录》《顾亭林文集》等。清康熙十八年(1679年),顾炎武游少林寺,赋五言古诗一首,同时还撰了《少林僧兵》一文于《日知录》中。《少林寺》一诗为游少林寺名篇。诗中追忆隋唐时惠玚等助唐王平定王世充使少林寺走向鼎盛的经历,盛慨清朝少林寺的衰败,希望精于功夫的少林寺再出现惠玚那样的英勇武僧,期待明皇室出现像秦王李世民那样的伟人,在武僧的帮助下恢复大明王朝。诗文

Chapter IV The Rich Connotation of Shaolin Kungfu

on his cane and hanging his costume in a pine. The last verse tells us that though he is getting old, he still thinks about returning to battlefield to defeat enemies, alluding to a story about the Taoist in Laoshan who could walk through walls. We deduce that the monk who still wants to attend battles is very old and he was rewarded in the Jiajing Emperors' reign of the Ming dynasty. This poem is a masterpiece on Kungfu monks' attending battles and winning rewards of the Shaolin Temple in the Ming dynasty.

Gu Yanwu, style name Ningren, native to Kunshan of Jiangsu province, was a famous ideologist and litterateur at the beginning of the Qing dynasty. His works are known as *Daily Reflection (Ri Zhi Lu)*, *Collections of Gu Tinglin (Gu Tinglin Wen Ji)*, etc. In the 18th year of Kangxi Emperor's reign (1679 CE), he visited the Shaolin Temple and composed a poem, and wrote an article on Shaolin monk warriors which is collected in *Daily Reflection*. The poem named *Shaolin Temple* is a classic one among those about the Temple. In the poem, he recalls the rise of the Shaolin Temple to its prosperity when Huiyang and other monks aided Emperor of the Tang dynasty in suppressing Wang Shichong in the Sui and Tang dynasties and regrets the declining of the temple in the Qing dynasty. He longs for some heroic Kungfu monks like Huiyang who is skilled in Kungfu and great Emperors like Li Shimin appearing, so as to restore the Ming dynasty aided by Kungfu monks. It reflected his proposition of "Oppose Qing and restore Ming." It is also a mirror to the status of both Shaolin Temple and Shaolin Kungfu monks in the early Qing dynasty.

Jing Rizhen, style name Dongyang and pseudonym of Songya, is from Dengfeng. In the 30th year of the Kangxi Emperor's reign (1691 CE) in the Qing dynasty, he was ranked Jinshi. He took the positions of Deputy Chief-Director of the Logistics Department of Penalty Ministry, Assistant Minister of Finance Ministry and Minister of Rites. He was also a scholar in the study of cultural relics, places of interest and geography. He composed a long poem entitled *On Imperial Edict to the Shaolin Temple by Emperor of the Tang dynasty* after visiting the Shaolin Temple.

He first introduced the various inscriptions on the steles in the Shaolin Temple by celebrities in his poem, and then narrated the account that Shaolin Kungfu monks seized Wang Renze (mistaken for Wang Shichong) and were

图4-24 顾炎武
Gu Yanwu

反映了顾炎武的"反清复明"思想。同时,它也是清初少林寺及少林武僧现状的反映。

　　景日昣,字冬旸,号嵩崖,登封人。康熙三十年(1691年)进士,曾任太仆寺少卿、户部侍郎加礼部尚书衔。景日昣对嵩山文物名胜、山川地理研究极精,为一代大家。《观唐王告少林寺主教》为景日昣游少林寺在观看了李世民碑而写的一首长篇七言古诗。

　　该诗前边主要是写少林寺名刻林林总总,多出自名人之笔。后面是写唐代少林僧兵出战并擒王世充(应为王仁则),受到唐王嘉奖、赐田的事,是歌颂少林武僧的佳作。

　　此外,蒲松龄的《聊斋志异》,刘鹗的《老残游记》,《清稗类钞》等均有以少林功夫为写作元素的内容。

granted rewards and lands by the Emperor of the Tang dynasty. It is a masterpiece commending the Shaolin Kungfu monks.

In addition, Shaolin Kungfu is also recorded in *Strange Stories from a Chinese Studio* (*Liao Zhai Zhi Yi*) by Pu Songling, *The Travels of Lao Can* (*Lao Can You Ji*) by Liu E, and *Extracts from Notes and Newspaper Articles of the Qing dynasty* (*Qing Bai Lei Chao*), etc.

附录
Appendix

中国历史年代简表
A Brief Chronology of Chinese History

五帝时代 Period of the Five Legendary Rulers c. 2600 BC-c. 2070 BC	黄帝 Huangdi (Yellow Emperor)	
	颛顼 Zhuanxu	
	帝喾 Diku (Emperor Ku)	
	（唐）尧 Yao	
	（虞）舜 Shun	
夏 Xia Dynasty	c. 2070 BC— c. 1600 BC	
商 Shang Dynasty	c. 1600 BC— c. 1046 BC	
西周 Western Zhou Dynasty	c. 1046 BC— c. 771 BC	
东周 Eastern Zhou Dynasty 770 BC-256 BC	春秋 Spring and Autumn Period	770 BC—476 BC
	战国 Warring States Period	475 BC—221 BC
秦 Qin Dynasty	221 BC—206 BC	
汉 Han Dynasty 206 BC-220 AD	西汉 Western Han	206 BC—25 AD
	东汉 Eastern Han	25—220
三国 Three Kingdoms 220-280	魏 Wei	220—265
	蜀汉 Shu Han	221—263
	吴 Wu	222—280
晋 Jin Dynasty 265-420	西晋 Western Jin	265—317
	东晋 Eastern Jin	317—420

续表 Continued Table

南北朝 Southern and Northern Dynasties 420—589	南朝 Southern Dynasties	宋 Song	420—479
		齐 Qi	479—502
		梁 Liang	502—557
		陈 Chen	557—589
	北朝 Northern Dynasties	北魏 Northern Wei	386—534
		东魏 Eastern Wei	534—550
		北齐 Northern Qi	550—577
		西魏 Western Wei	535—556
		北周 Northern Zhou	557—581
隋 Sui Dynasty			581-618
唐 Tang Dynasty			618- 907
五代十国 Five Dynasties and Ten States	五代 Five Dynasties 907-960	后梁 Later Liang	907—923
		后唐 Later Tang	923—936
		后晋 Later Jin	936—947
		后汉 Later Han	947—950
		后周 Later Zhou	951—960
	十国 Ten States 902-979	北汉 Northern Han	951—979
		吴 Wu	902—937
		吴越 Wuyue	907—978
		闽 Min	909—945
		南汉 Southern Han	917—971
		荆南(又称"南平") Jingnan (Nanping)	924—963
		楚 Chu	927—951
		南唐 Southern Tang	937—975
		前蜀 Former Shu	907—925
		后蜀 Later Shu	934—965

续表 Continued Table

宋 Song Dynasty 960-1279	北宋 Northern Song	960—1127
	南宋 Southern Song	1127—1279
辽 Liao (契丹 Qidan/Khitan)	907—1125	
金 Jin	1115—1234	
西夏 Xixia (Tangut)	1038—1227	
元 Yuan Dynasty	1206—1368	
明 Ming Dynasty	1368—1644	
清 Qing Dynasty	1616—1911	
中华民国 Republic of China	1912—1949	
中华人民共和国 People's Republic of China	1949—	